At Sylvan, we believe reading is one of life's most important and enriching abilities, and we're glad you've chosen our resources to help your child build these critically important skills. We know that the time you spend with your child reinforcing the lessons learned in school will contribute to his love of reading. This love of reading will translate into academic achievement. A successful reader is ready for the world around him, ready to do research, ready to experience the world of literature, and prepared to make the connections necessary to achieve in school and in life.

We use a research-based, step-by-step process in teaching reading at Sylvan that includes thought-provoking reading selections and activities. As students increase their success as readers they become more confident. With increasing confidence, students build even more success. Our Sylvan workbooks are designed to help you to help your child build the skills and confidence that will contribute to your child's success in school.

Included with your purchase of this workbook is a coupon for a discount at a participating Sylvan center. We hope you will use this coupon to further your child's academic journey. Let us partner with you to support the development of a confident, well prepared, independent learner.

The Sylvan Team

2nd Grade
Super Games & Puzzles

Published in the United States by Random House LLC, New York, and in Canada by Random House of Canada Limited, Toronto.

A Penguin Random House Company

www.tutoring.sylvanlearning.com

The material in this book previously appeared as *Second Grade Spelling Games & Activities*, a trade paperback first published by Random House in 2009; *Second Grade Vocabulary Puzzles*, a trade paperback first published by Random House in 2009; and *Second Grade Math Games & Puzzles*, a trade paperback first published by Random House in 2010.

Source material credits:
Created by Smarterville Productions LLC
Producer: TJ Trochlil McGreevy
Producer & Editorial Direction: The Linguistic Edge
Writers: Michael Artin, Margaret Crocker, and Amy Kraft
Cover and Interior Illustrations: Delfin Barral, Shawn Finley, and Duendes del Sur
Layout and Art Direction: SunDried Penguin
Art Manager: Adina Ficano

ISBN: 978-0-8041-2450-8

This book is available at special discounts for bulk purchases for sales promotions or premiums. For more information, write to Special Markets/Premium Sales, 1745 Broadway, MD 6-2, New York, New York 10019, or email specialmarkets@randomhouse.com.

PRINTED IN CHINA

10 9 8 7 6 5 4 3 2 1

Contents

2nd Grade Spelling Games & Activities

Contents

Puzzle Pairs

FILL IN the two different missing vowels in the word pairs to finish the riddles.

1. This beetle was not small.
   He was a **b__g b__g.**
2. When I left my cap on the stove, I had a **h__t h__t.**
3. I did not sleep well last night. I was on a **b__d b__d.**
4. To get pecans out of the tree,
   I used a **n__t n__t.**
5. The rabbit went **h__p h__p** all
   the way up the hill.

Criss Cross

READ the clues. FILL IN the boxes with the right word for each clue.

Across

1. This says "meow."
3. You clean the floor with this.
6. My cat or my dog is my ____.
8. A hole in the ground
10. "You are it!" in the game of ____
11. You sleep here.

Down

2. The highest spot
4. A young dog
5. You ____ a ball with a bat.
7. Wash up in the bath____.
9. One after nine.

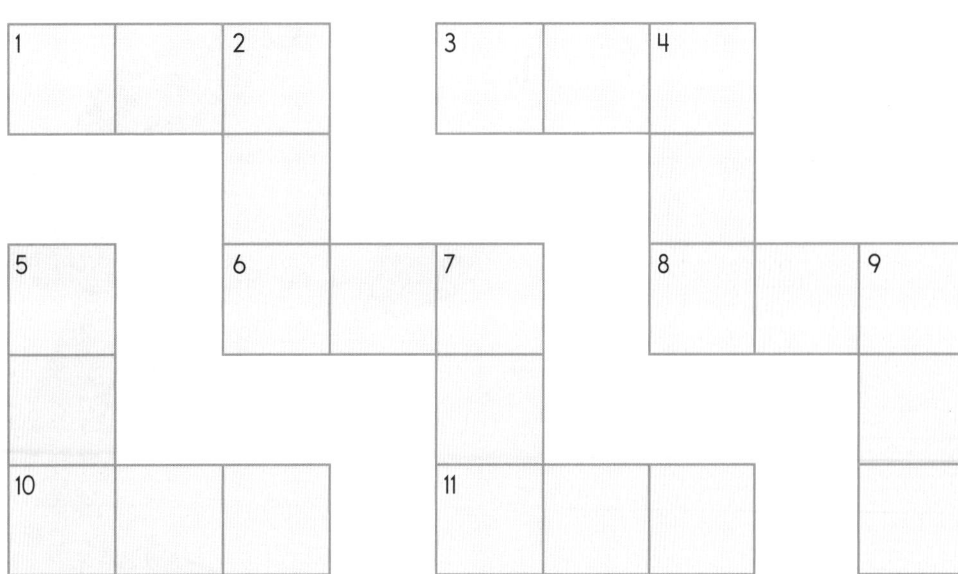

Puzzle Pairs

FILL IN the missing vowels in the word pairs to finish the sentences. Listen for how the final "-e" changes the vowel sound.

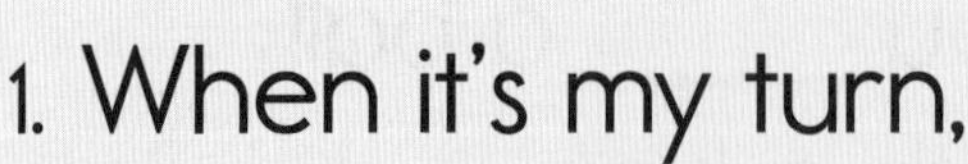

1. When it's my turn,

   I **h__p__** I can **h__p**.

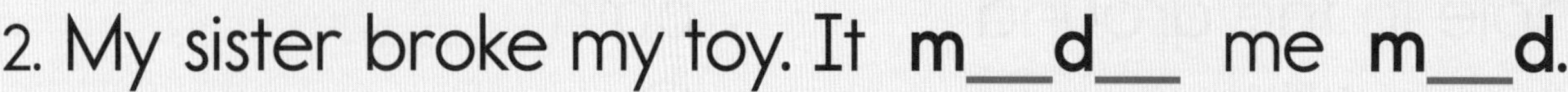

2. My sister broke my toy. It **m__d__** me **m__d**.
3. Pete is my dog. If you want, you can **p__t P__t__**.
4. Maya went to the salon and got a **c__t__ c__t**.

5. The shark was a star.

   He had a **f__n__ f__n**.

Not Quite!

CIRCLE the words that are misspelled in this story.

I saw a very cut kitten. I gav him a pok. That mad him hid from me. I hat when that happens! I hop I see him again some tim.

WRITE the circled words correctly.

1. ______________________ 5. ______________________

2. ______________________ 6. ______________________

3. ______________________ 7. ______________________

4. ______________________ 8. ______________________

Beginning Consonant Combos

Blank Out

FILL IN the missing "ch," "sh," "wh," or "th" in these sentences.

SPELLING LIST

chat
chick
chop
shapes
ship
shop
shut
thick
thin
what
when
white

1. Miguel was _____**ite** as a ghost!
2. I always cry when I _____**op** onions.
3. Yay! Mom gave me a _____**ick** slice of cake!
4. Tom helps his dad _____**op** for food.
5. I want to hear about your day.
   Let's have a little _____**at**.
6. Bella went for a cruise on a _____**ip**.
7. Grandma always feeds me too much.
   She says I look _____**in**.
8. Close the washer door _____**en**
   you wash your clothes.

Match Up

DRAW a line to the correct word ending.

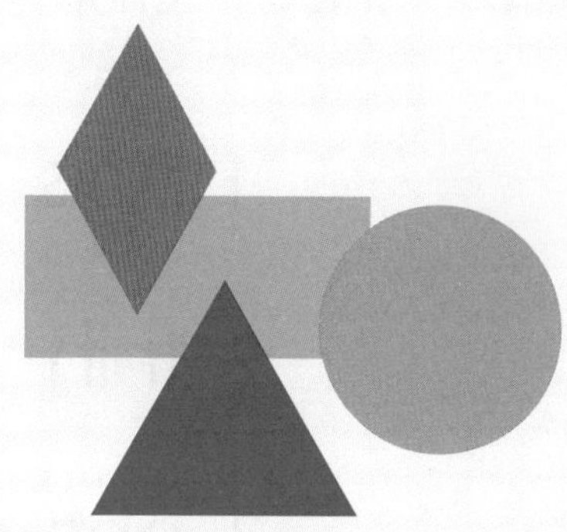

1. **ch**

en ick

2. **wh**

ite ig

3. **sh**

apes ogs

4. **sh**

ig ip

5. **ch**

an op

6. **sh**

op ug

Word Scramble

UNSCRAMBLE each word and write it correctly. LOOK at the word box for help. CROSS OUT each word as you make it.

thin	thick	chop	chick	chat	shop	ship	shapes	what	white

1. hpis ________________
2. tnih ________________
3. ahtw ________________
4. kichc ________________
5. ithew ________________
6. ohpc ________________
7. thac ________________
8. spesah ________________
9. citkh ________________
10. psoh ________________

Riddle Me This!

UNSCRAMBLE the words in the riddles.

1. **Q.** Why did the bookworm start eating the dictionary at T?

   A. He wanted to eat through **chitk** and **inht**.

   ______________________ ______________________

2. **Q.** What do you call talking while eggs hatch?

   A. A **ccikh thca**.

   ______________________ ______________________

3. **Q.** Why did the captain build his house like a boat?

   A. He liked things **isph aphes**.

   ____

   ____

Ending Consonant Combos

Blank Out!

FILL IN the missing "th," "sh," "ch," or "tch" in these sentences.

SPELLING LIST

bath
math
with
dash
fish
rich
which
catch
watch
witch

1. Johnny ate **fi**______ sticks for lunch.
2. Come **wi**______ me to the fair.
3. Tim wondered **whi**______ way to go.
4. My **wa**______ says it's five-thirty.
5. Julie was the winner of the 100-yard **da**______.
6. I like numbers, so **ma**______ is fun for me.
7. Becky put on her **wi**______ costume for the party.
8. Kim didn't think she'd **ca**______ such a big fish!

Word Split

DRAW lines to connect word beginnings with the correct endings.

1.

2.

3.

4.

Word Blocks

FILL IN the word blocks with words of the same shape from the word box. Use the pictures as clues.

rich	fish	bath	math	witch	watch

1.

4.

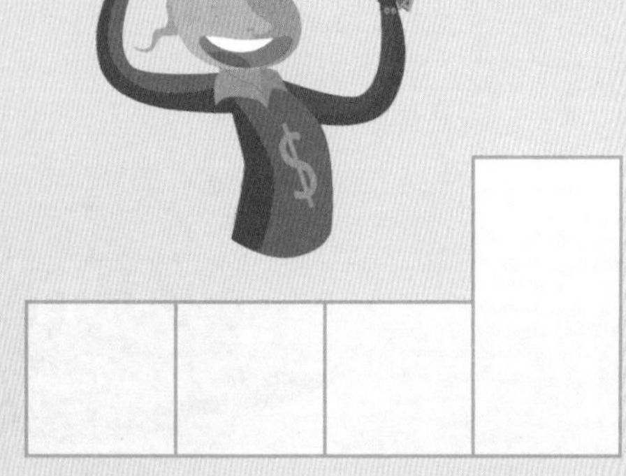

2.

5.

3.

6.

Not Quite!

CIRCLE the words that are misspelled in this story.

Sam caught a fish, whish made him happy.

"I am really a wich," it said. "Throw me back, and I will make you ritsh."

"But I might not catsh another fish," said Sam.

"You can buy another one," said the fich. "Come on! Do the maf!"

Sam ate him wif a datsh of salt.

WRITE the circled words correctly.

1. ______________________
2. ______________________
3. ______________________
4. ______________________
5. ______________________
6. ______________________
7. ______________________
8. ______________________

Word Scramble

UNSCRAMBLE each word and write it correctly. LOOK at the word box for help. CROSS OUT each word in the word box as you make it.

belt coat dress pants shirt shorts skirt shoe

SPELLING LIST

belt
coat
dress
pants
shirt
shoe
shorts
skirt

1. sreds ____________________
2. tisrk ____________________
3. strih ____________________
4. atoc ____________________
5. hoes ____________________
6. elbt ____________________
7. rhtoss ____________________
8. snapt ____________________

Word Hunt

CIRCLE the words from the word box in the grid. Words go down and across, not diagonally or backward.

belt coat dress pants shirt shorts skirt shoe

b	o	r	t	s	p	o	e
e	r	s	s	e	a	k	r
l	c	o	k	c	n	i	a
t	s	h	i	r	t	r	p
s	h	d	r	e	s	s	n
c	o	a	t	s	h	o	i
o	e	s	h	o	r	t	s

WRITE each word that you circled.

Sort and Spell

LISTEN for the **ch** or **sh** sound at the start or end of each word pictured. DRAW a line from the picture to the correct sound box. WRITE the word in the box.

shoe	chick	rich	ship	chop	fish

ch	sh
______	______
______	______
______	______

Around We Go!

CIRCLE the things that have a **ch** sound. Write the words on the lines.

12:30

2+3=5

Criss Cross

READ the clues. FILL IN the boxes with the right word for each clue.

Across

3. _____ way did he go?
5. Something that sails on the sea
7. Opposite of fat
8. The rhino has very _____ skin.
10. To cut a tree with an ax
13. The color of milk
14. You throw the ball, and I will _____ it.
15. Working with numbers

Down

1. A square is a _____, and so is a triangle.
2. You wear this to cover your belly
4. In the summer you wear these so your legs stay cool
6. A swimming animal
9. A baby hen
11. You tuck your shirt into your _____.
12. This helps hold up your pants
14. Two people talking are having a _____.

1 2 3 4 5 6 7 8 9 10 11 12 13 14 15

Beginning Consonant Blends

Knock Out

CROSS OUT the pictures whose words **don't** begin with two consonant sounds together.

SPELLING LIST

clam
crab
frog
slide
slip
spill
steps
stick
stop
trap
trip
truck

WRITE the words for the pictures you didn't cross out.

Blank Out

FILL IN the missing letters for each word.

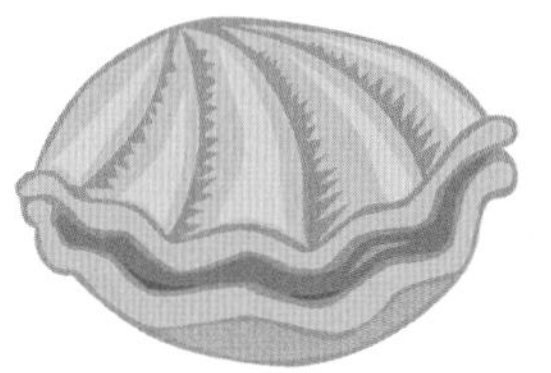

1. ___ ___ am

4. ___ ___ og

2. ___ ___ ill

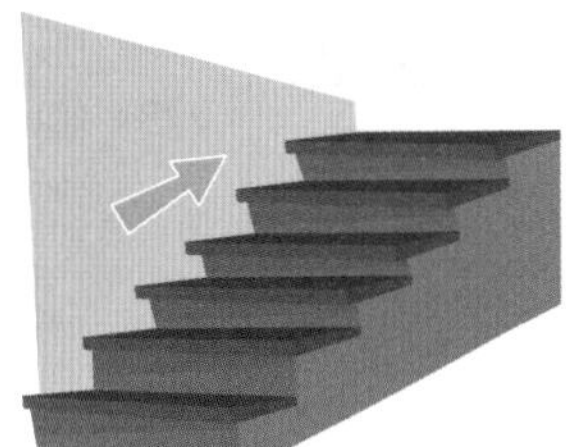

5. ___ ___ eps

3. ___ ___ ap

6. ___ ___ ab

Beginning Consonant Blends

Puzzle Pairs

FILL IN the missing letters in the word pairs to finish these sentences.

1. The firefighters **tuck** their shirts in before they get on the **t__uck**.
2. The **fog** was so thick at the pond I couldn't even see a **f__og** jump.
3. I felt **sick** about breaking grandpa's walking **s__ick**.
4. **Tap** him on the shoulder and warn him. This is a **t__ap**.
5. Take a **sip** from the stream, but don't **s__ip** and fall in!
6. I took a **cab** to the beach, where I saw a **c__ab**.
7. Chang peeked over the **side** before he went down the **s__ide**.
8. Here's a **tip**: Be careful not to **t__ip**.

Word Scramble

UNSCRAMBLE the words. LOOK at the word box for help. CROSS OUT each word in the word box as you make it.

clam	frog	slide	stick	steps	trip
crab	slip	spill	stop	truck	trap

1. ipsl ________________
2. rtpa ________________
3. pesst ________________
4. amlc ________________
5. skict ________________
6. barc ________________
7. ospt ________________
8. lispl ________________
9. ilsed ________________
10. prit ________________
11. orgf ________________
12. urckt ________________

Blank Out

FILL IN the missing pair of letters at the end of each word.

SPELLING LIST

gift
lamp
camp
jump
desk
mask
band
hand
ant
tent
cast
nest

1. ha __ __

4. gi __ __

2. de __ __

5. ne __ __

3. la __ __

6. ma __ __

7. ju __ __

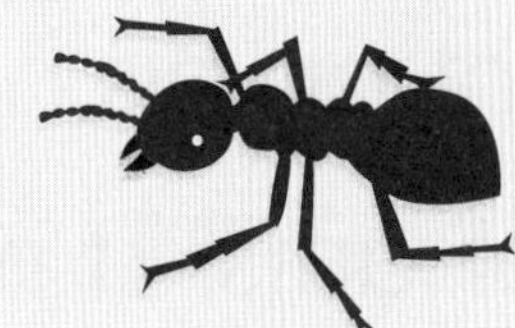

10. a __ __

8. te __ __

11. ca __ __

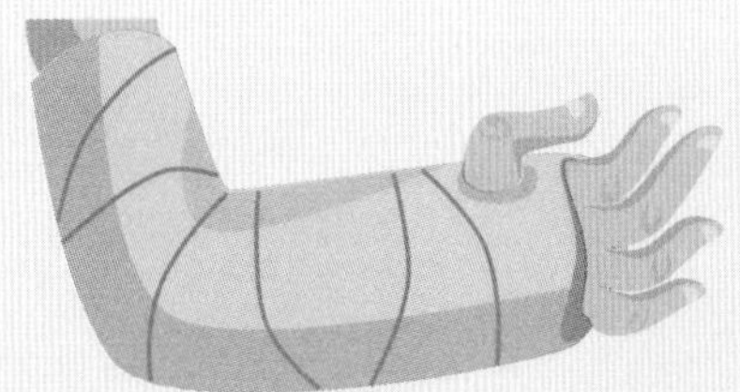

9. ca __ __

12. ba __ __

Not Quite!

CIRCLE the words that are misspelled in this story.

Hank made a capm. He sat by his tenk and ate a sandwich. An ankt was crawling on it. Yuck! Then he saw an ant on his hamd. He was sitting on a whole ness of ants! It made him jum! He fell and broke his arm. Now he has a casp.

WRITE the circled words correctly.

1. ____________________
2. ____________________
3. ____________________
4. ____________________
5. ____________________
6. ____________________
7. ____________________

Knock Out

CROSS OUT the pictures whose words **don't** end with two consonant sounds together.

WRITE the words for the pictures you didn't cross out.

Word Scramble

UNSCRAMBLE each word and write it correctly. LOOK at the word box for help. CROSS OUT each word in the word box as you make it.

apple bread banana carrot cookie milk pizza steak

SPELLING LIST

apple
banana
bread
carrot
cookie
milk
pizza
steak

1. zapiz ____________________
2. kiml ____________________
3. racort ____________________
4. nnaaab ____________________
5. dearb ____________________
6. ioeock ____________________
7. sekat ____________________
8. pleap ____________________

Word Hunt

CIRCLE the words from the word box in the grid. Words go down and across, not diagonally or backward.

apple	bread	banana	carrot	cookie	milk	pizza	steak

b	r	e	a	d	a	n	s
i	b	c	a	r	r	o	t
z	a	o	p	p	a	z	e
z	n	o	p	i	z	z	a
a	a	k	l	m	i	l	k
b	n	i	e	p	p	i	d
b	a	e	i	l	k	p	p

WRITE each word that you circled.

________________ ________________

________________ ________________

________________ ________________

________________ ________________

Sort and Spell

LISTEN for two consonant sounds together at either the **start** or the **end** of each word pictured. DRAW a line from the picture to the correct sound box. WRITE the word in the box.

Start	End
__________	__________
__________	__________
__________	__________

Circle It

CIRCLE the pictures with words that have a long vowel sound.

WRITE the words that have a long vowel sound.

____

____

____

WRITE the words that have a short vowel sound.

____

____

____

Criss Cross

READ the clues. FILL IN the boxes with the right word for each clue.

Across

1. Covers up a broken arm
3. Hop into the air
6. Male ruler of a country
7. Where birds lay eggs
9. A piece of meat you eat for dinner
11. Red juicy fruit
13. I'm going on a _____ to another state.
15. Yellow fruit with thick skin

Down

1. Sweet, round snack
2. Firefighters drive a fire _____.
4. A belt helps you hold these up
5. The outside part of a sandwich
8. Careful you don't _____ on the wet stairs.
10. Where you sleep when you're camping
12. Round crusty food covered with cheese
14. Help me out. Give me a _____.

1 2

3 4

5

6

7 8

9 10

11 12

13

14

15

Puzzle Pairs

ADD an "r" to the vowel in each word pair to finish the sentance.

SPELLING LIST
card
chart
hard
part
her
chirp
first
skirt
bird
worm
hurt
turn

1. Don't **pat** Carlos on the head. It will mess up the __________ in his hair.
2. That baby bird is a **chip** off the old block. He can __________ like a champ.
3. In the **skit**, Jayla had to wear an ugly __________.
4. I bumped my head going into the **hut**. Boy, did it __________!
5. How do you punch? Making a **fist** is the __________ step.
6. Brit **bid** on an old painting with a __________ in a nest.
7. Dion had a **chat** with the mapmaker, who showed him his best __________.

Herd a Word

WRITE each word from the Spelling List next to the word with the same vowel sound.

girl ______________________

____

____

____

____

____

____

____

car ______________________

____

____

____

Word Scramble

UNSCRAMBLE the words. LOOK at the word box for help. CROSS OUT each word in the word box as you make it.

card hard chart part her first chirp bird skirt worm hurt turn

1. drac ____________
2. rathc ____________
3. adhr ____________
4. ridb ____________
5. romw ____________
6. trifs ____________
7. urnt ____________
8. thru ____________
9. kitrs ____________
10. aprt ____________
11. criph ____________
12. rhe ____________

Not Quite!

CIRCLE the words that are misspelled in this story.

It's not hord to play musical chairs. Ferst, you walk around while the music plays. When the music stops, grab a seat! If someone beats you to the seat, let heer have it. Be a good sport. That's port of the game. And don't feel hert. You'll get another torn. It's just like with a berd. The early one gets the werm.

WRITE the circled words correctly.

1. ____________________
2. ____________________
3. ____________________
4. ____________________
5. ____________________
6. ____________________
7. ____________________
8. ____________________

More Vowels with "R"

Word Split

DRAW lines to connect word beginnings with the correct endings.

SPELLING LIST

- more
- store
- deer
- cheer
- steer
- dear
- gear
- near
- care
- dare
- share
- chair
- hair
- pair

1.

2.

3.

4.

Which Is Which?

FILL IN the missing letters in this e-mail.

D__ __**r** Mom,

I saw three **d**__ __**r** in the yard today.

—Levon

Blank Out

FILL IN the missing "ee" or "ea" in these sentences.

1. Peggy had too much **g**__ __**r** when she went camping.
2. I gave her some ice cream to **ch**__ __**r** her up
3. It's hard to **st**__ __**r** in this driving game.
4. Martha's grandmother was very **d**__ __**r** to her.
5. Don't go too **n**__ __**r** that barking dog.

More Vowels with "R"

Blank Out

FILL IN the missing "air," "are," or "ore" in each word.

1. Thad must learn to **sh**__ __ __ his food.
2. Do you **c**__ __ __ if I skip the game?
3. Zach went to the **st**__ __ __ to buy milk.
4. I got a new **p**__ __ __ of shoes today.
5. Kate climbed the tree on a **d**__ __ __.
6. Please stay in your **ch**__ __ __ during dinner.
7. Oliver asked for **m**__ __ __ food.
8. Tanya likes to admire her **h**__ __ __.

Word Scramble

UNSCRAMBLE each word and write it correctly. LOOK at the word box for help. CROSS OUT each word in the word box as you make it.

more	store	cheer	steer	gear	near	dare	share	chair	pair

1. apir ______________
2. ehrec ______________
3. reag ______________
4. eanr ______________
5. hraic ______________
6. tesre ______________
7. remo ______________
8. eard ______________
9. hreas ______________
10. orste ______________

Word Hunt

CIRCLE the words from the Spelling List in the grid. Words go across and down, not diagonally or backward.

SPELLING LIST

- cloud
- cold
- rain
- shower
- snow
- warm
- weather
- wind

w	e	a	t	c	w	e	r
a	o	u	d	r	a	i	n
r	a	w	e	i	r	s	c
s	h	o	c	n	m	h	l
n	c	l	o	u	d	o	o
o	n	d	l	i	n	w	u
w	i	n	d	d	w	e	r
w	e	a	t	h	e	r	m

WRITE each word that you circled.

________________ ________________

________________ ________________

________________ ________________

________________ ________________

Word Scramble

UNSCRAMBLE each word and write it correctly. LOOK at the Spelling List for help.

1. ianr ____________________
2. wamr ____________________
3. ocdl ____________________
4. dniw ____________________
5. rwheeat ____________________
6. ludco ____________________
7. shwoer ____________________
8. nswo ____________________

Circle It

LISTEN for the words with the same vowel sound. WRITE the word in the correct box.

HINT: One sound can be spelled different ways.

Sounds like *far*	Sounds like *fur*
______	______
______	______
______	______

Word Scramble

UNSCRAMBLE each word and write it correctly. LOOK at the word box for help. Then CIRCLE all the words that have the same vowel sound as *fur*.

hard	chart	first	chirp	her	hurt	turn	warm	cold	skirt

1. hicrp ____________
2. rwam ____________
3. ruht ____________
4. iksrt ____________
5. tcrah ____________
6. rhe ____________
7. tsrfi ____________
8. ardh ____________
9. dloc ____________
10. nrtu ____________

Criss Cross

READ the clues. FILL IN the boxes with the right word for each clue.

Across

1. White and puffy in the sky
3. The sun shone and made it _____.
4. To turn the wheel of a car
6. Something to sit on
9. A sudden burst of rain
10. Cold and white, falling from the sky
11. To change your direction
15. Water falling from the sky
16. An animal who lives in the woods

Down

2. A word at the beginning of a letter
3. You choose your outfit based on the _____ outside that day.
4. To give some to someone else
5. Before anything else.
7. She liked to brush _____ hair.
8. When I finish this bowl, I would like some _____.
12. Close by
13. It helps make kites fly when it blows.
14. You switch to a new _____ on your bike when you go uphill.

1				2

3, 4, 5, 6, 7, 8, 9, 10, 11, 12, 13, 14, 15, 16

The Long "A" Way

Sort and Spell

LISTEN for the long **a** sound in each word pictured. DRAW a line from the picture to the box that shows how long **a** is spelled. WRITE the word correctly in the box.

SPELLING LIST

gray
play
say
tray
braid
mail
paint
snail
train
weigh
weight
neighbor

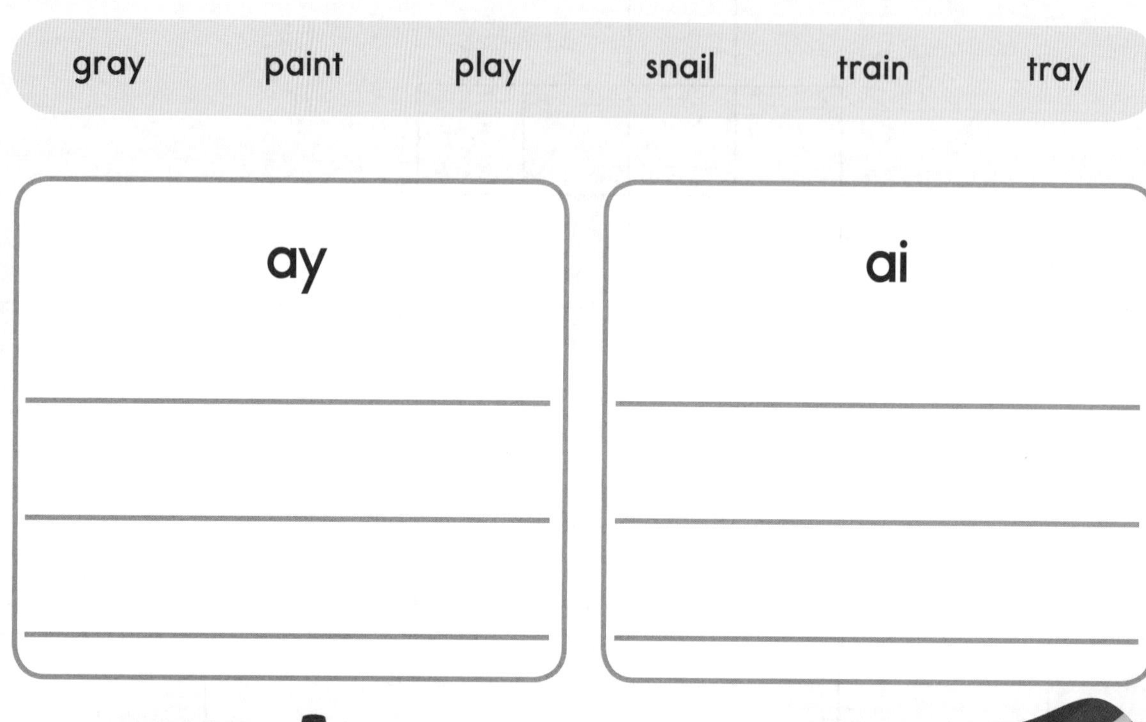

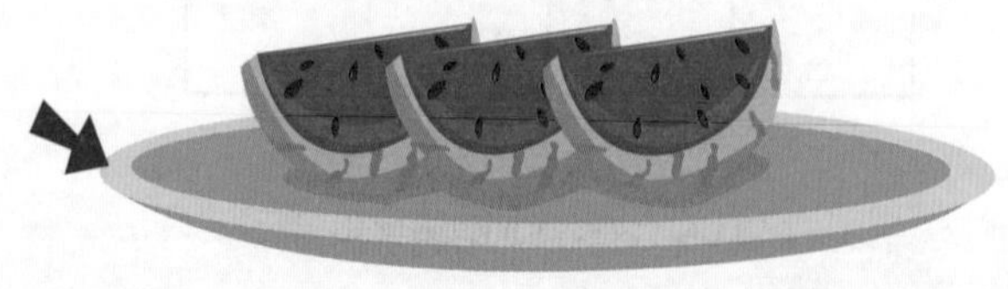

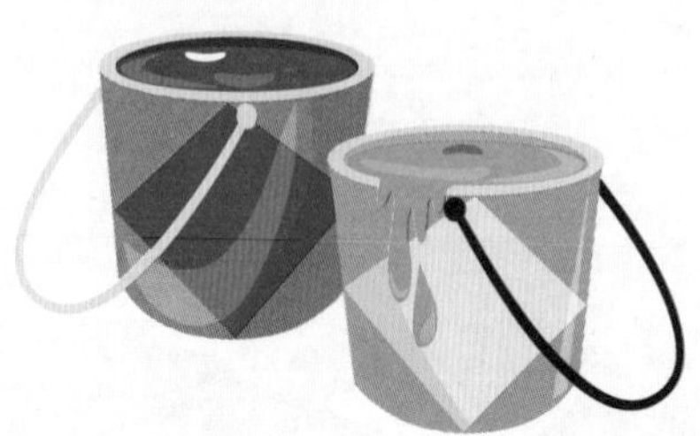

Knock Out

CROSS OUT the pictures that show words **without** the long **a** sound.

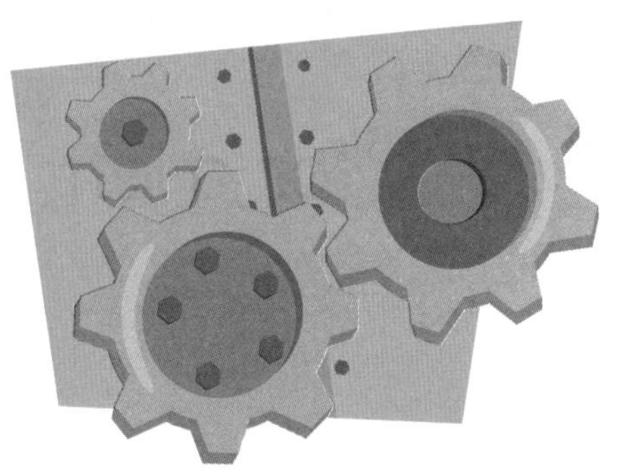

WRITE the words for the pictures you didn't cross out.

______________________ ______________________

______________________ ______________________

Blank Out

FILL IN the missing words in these sentences. LOOK at the word box for help.

say	play	gray	train	mail	paint	weigh	neighbor

1. Shen checked the __________ every day for a letter from his friend.
2. I get on the scale to see how much I __________.
3. Stella's dad takes the __________ to work.
4. Penn wants to __________ his room blue so it feels like the ocean.
5. Sometimes I don't know what to __________ when I meet someone new.
6. Janice likes to __________ on the monkey bars.
7. Tad went next door to meet the new __________.
8. The elephant has tough, __________ skin.

Not Quite!

CIRCLE the words that are misspelled in this story.

I went out to plai. My nayber was checking her mayl. She's kind of old, with gra hair—a lot of hair! She has the biggest brade I ever saw. It must wey a ton. She said, "If I roll up this braid, my head will look like a giant snale!" What do you sae to that?

WRITE the circled words correctly.

1. ____________________ 5. ____________________

2. ____________________ 6. ____________________

3. ____________________ 7. ____________________

4. ____________________ 8. ____________________

Sort and Spell

LISTEN for the long **e** sound in each word pictured. DRAW a line from the picture to the box that shows how long **e** is spelled. WRITE the word in the box.

SPELLING LIST

- green
- teeth
- tree
- wheel
- beach
- leaf
- seal
- speak
- key
- monkey
- candy
- puppy

beach green leaf seal teeth wheel

ea	ee
______	______
______	______
______	______

Riddle Me This!

UNSCRAMBLE the words in the riddles. LOOK at the Spelling List for help.

1. **Q.** What did the dentist say when the **acnyd**-loving **pppyu** showed him her **eteth**?

   ______________________ ______________________

   ____

   A. Your bite is worse than your bark.

2. **Q.** A **nmeyok** saw a Spanish sparrow and a French hen in a **rete**. What language did he **eapks**?

   ______________________ ______________________

   ____

   A. None. Monkeys can't talk.

Knock Out

CROSS OUT the pictures whose words **don't** have a long **e** sound.

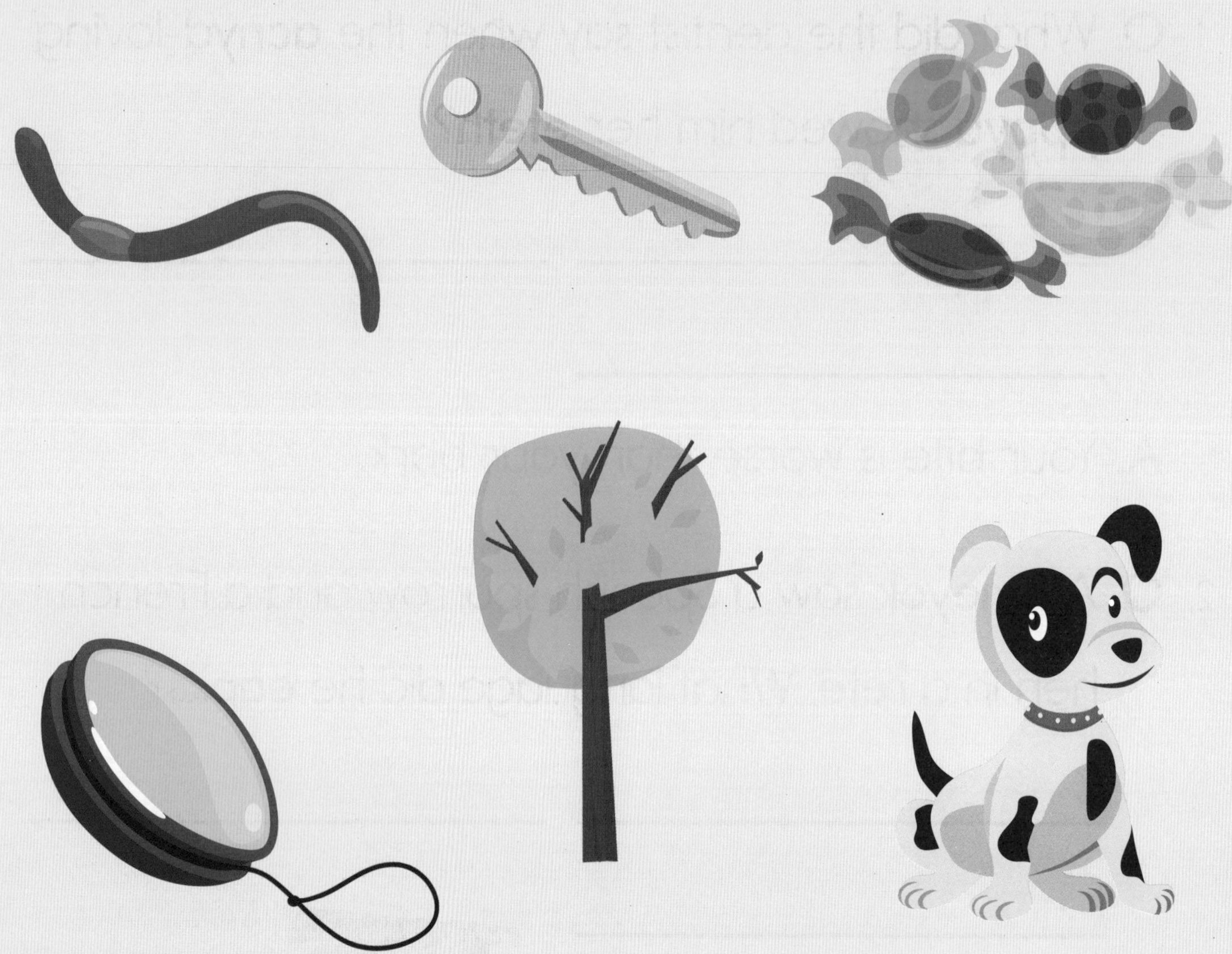

WRITE the words for the pictures you didn't cross out.

Word Scramble

UNSCRAMBLE each word and write it correctly. LOOK at the word box for help. CROSS OUT each word in the word box as you make it.

green teeth wheel beach leaf seal speak key monkey puppy

1. eelhw ________________
2. abche ________________
3. slae ________________
4. tthee ________________
5. mekoyn ________________
6. ngree ________________
7. kye ________________
8. pupyp ________________
9. elfa ________________
10. ksepa ________________

Blank Out

FILL IN the missing "i," "igh," or "y" in these sentences.

SPELLING LIST

blind
find
kind
mind
fly
spy
try
bright
high
light
right
sigh

1. What **k__nd** of sandwich do you want?
2. Joel was singing "Three **bl__nd** mice."
3. I know I hate eggplant, so I don't need to **tr__** it.
4. Sierra's bad mood made her mother **s______**.
5. The cookies are too **h______** up for me to reach.
6. Taye hid so well they couldn't **f__nd** him.
7. Jay was so **l______t** I could lift him easily.
8. The sun is too **br______t** for me to keep sleeping.

Riddle Me This!

UNSCRAMBLE the words in the riddles. LOOK at the Spelling List for help.

1. **Q.** What do you call a desk lamp that gets straight As?

   A. A **bhgitr htigl.**

   ______________________ ______________________

2. **Q.** Why did the crazy guy keep turning left?

   A. He wasn't in his **girth nimd.**

   ______________________ ______________________

3. **Q.** What has six legs, wings, and buzzes in code?

   A. A **lfy yps.**

   ____________ ____________

Word Hunt

CIRCLE the words from the word box in the grid. Words go down and across, not diagonally or backward.

blind	bright	fly	high	kind	light	mind	try

s	f	l	y	i	t	e
b	r	i	g	h	t	n
h	i	g	i	n	r	d
i	f	h	y	k	y	g
g	t	t	g	i	h	s
h	b	l	i	n	d	p
s	m	i	n	d	i	o

WRITE each word that you circled.

Word Scramble

UNSCRAMBLE each word and write it correctly. LOOK at the word box for help. CROSS OUT each word in the word box as you make it.

blind	find	kind	mind	spy	bright	high	light	right	sigh

1. dkin ________________
2. fidn ________________
3. mnid ________________
4. ihhg ________________
5. inbdl ________________
6. rthibg ________________
7. pys ________________
8. igrht ________________
9. ithlg ________________
10. gshi ________________

Sort and Spell

LISTEN for the long **o** sound in each word pictured. DRAW a line from the picture to the correct sound box. WRITE the word in the box.

SPELLING LIST

- bow
- bowl
- crow
- own
- show
- slow
- boat
- coach
- goal
- goat
- road
- soap

coach bow goat crow boat bowl

oa	ow

Blank Out

FILL IN the missing "oa" or "ow" in these sentences.

1. Let me **sh**___ ___ you how to do that.
2. Greg was going too **sl**___ ___, so I gave him a push.
3. Ayla poured cereal into her **b**___ ___**l**.
4. TJ scored the winning **g**___ ___**l** at the soccer game.
5. Mike doesn't ___ ___**n** any fancy clothes.
6. The **c**___ ___**ch** showed me a better way to kick the ball.
7. I hold my father's hand when I cross the **r**___ ___**d**.
8. I couldn't find any **s**___ ___**p** for my bath.

Knock Out

CROSS OUT the pictures that show words that **don't** have a long **o** sound.

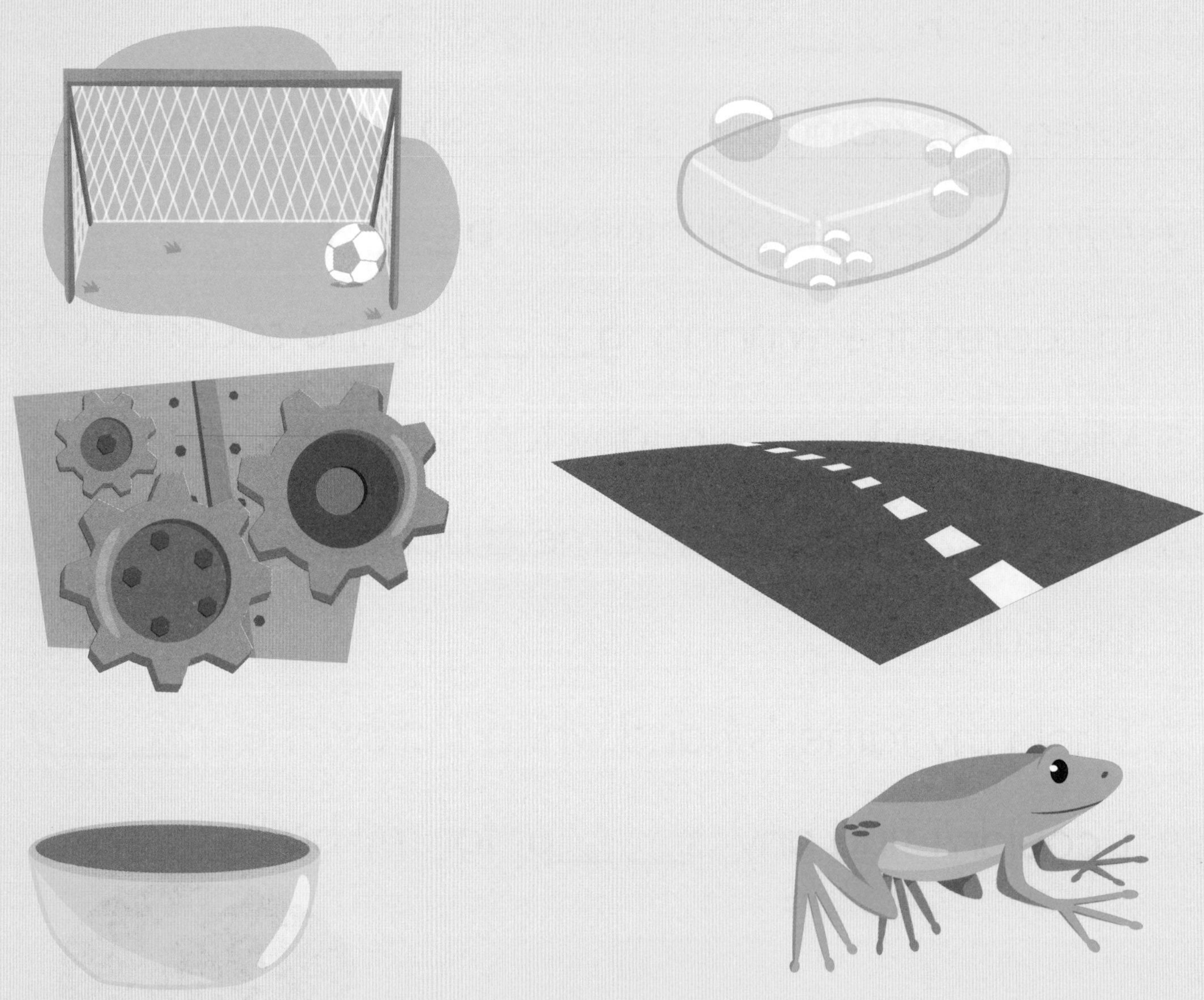

WRITE the words for the pictures you didn't cross out.

Word Scramble

UNSCRAMBLE each word and write it correctly. LOOK at the word box for help. CROSS OUT each word in the word box as you make it.

bow	crow	own	show	slow	boat	coach	goal	goat	road

1. atob ____________
2. rdoa ____________
3. wob ____________
4. wrco ____________
5. algo ____________
6. accoh ____________
7. onw ____________
8. oatg ____________
9. oslw ____________
10. swho ____________

Blank Out

FILL IN the missing "ue," "ui," "oo," or "ew" in these sentences.

SPELLING LIST

blue
glue
true
fruit
few
flew
chew
threw
boot
broom
moon
tooth

1. Grab a **br____m** and sweep up.
2. I still have a **f____** things to do before we go.
3. Mom always tells me to **ch____** my food before I swallow.
4. None of the things Billy told me about Mars were **tr____**.
5. Tony **thr____** the ball to Jamal.
6. I like to have **fr____t** in my cereal.
7. The sun shone down on the **bl____** sea.
8. Andrea plans to be the first woman on the **m____n**.

Knock Out

CROSS OUT the pictures that show words that **don't** have a long **u** sound.

WRITE the words for the pictures you didn't cross out.

Word Blocks

FILL IN the word blocks with words of the same shape from the word box. Use the pictures as clues.

blue glue boot broom tooth fruit

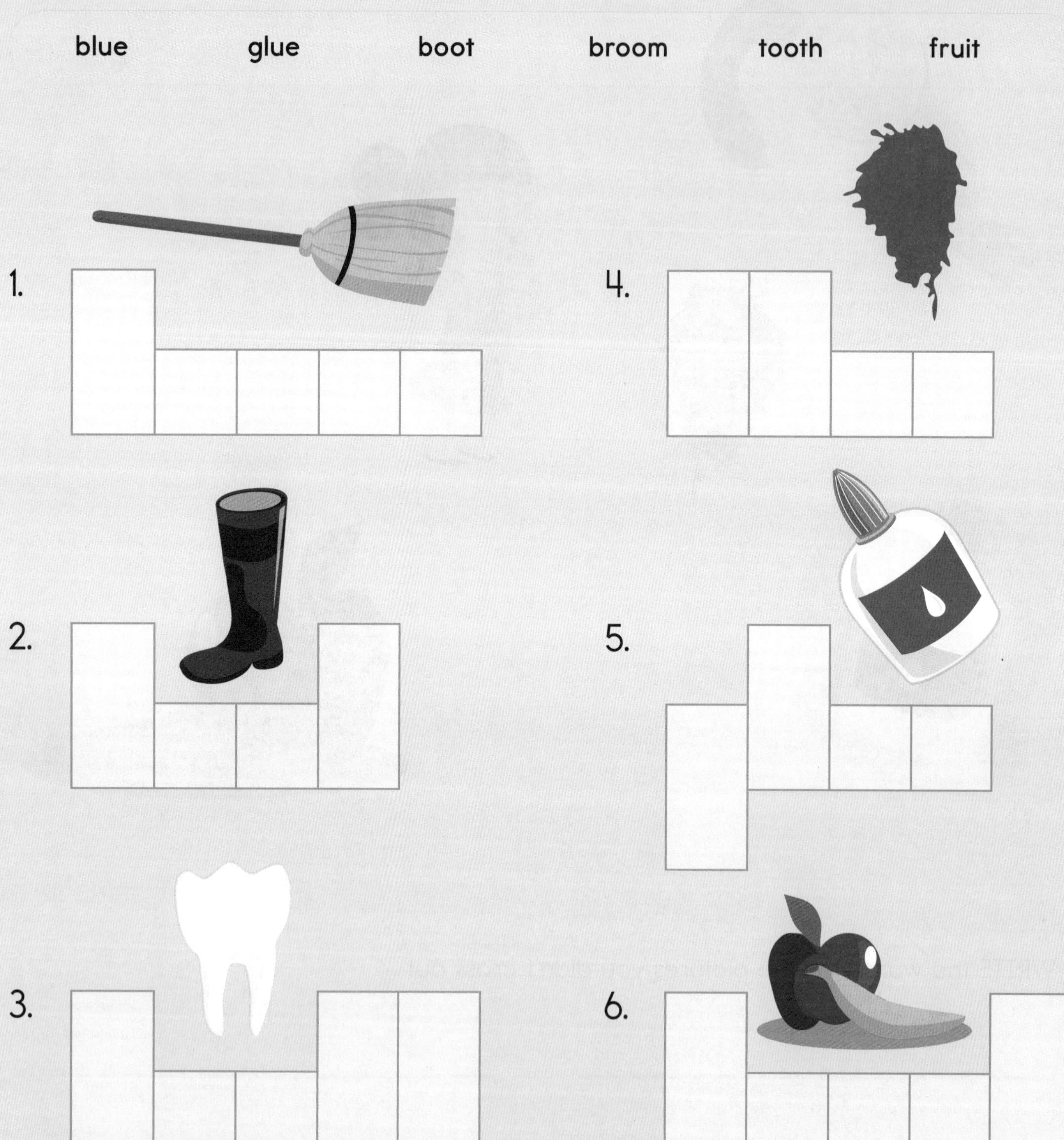

Word Scramble

UNSCRAMBLE each word and write it correctly. LOOK at the word box for help. CROSS OUT each word in the word box as you make it.

glue	true	few	chew	threw	flew	boot	broom	moon	tooth

1. rewht ____________
2. efw ____________
3. hcwe ____________
4. welf ____________
5. noom ____________
6. rteu ____________
7. elgu ____________
8. ottho ____________
9. rmboo ____________
10. oobt ____________

Sort and Spell

LISTEN for the long **a** sound or the long **e** sound in each word pictured. DRAW a line from the picture to the correct sound box. WRITE the word in the box.

Long **a**	Long **e**
____________	____________
____________	____________
____________	____________

Circle It

CIRCLE the pictures that show words that have a long **o** sound.

WRITE the words that have a long **o** sound.

____

____

____

____

The words you didn't circle have what vowel sound?

____

WRITE those words.

____

____

Criss Cross

READ the clues. FILL IN the boxes with the right word for each clue.

Across

1. Do this again if you don't succeed the first time.
2. A young dog
4. The person who lives next door
6. _____ me what's in your hand
8. A very heavy thing
11. What you bring to the post office
12. Bigger and thicker than a shoe
14. An animal that hangs from its tail

Down

1. Your mouth is filled with them
2. To color your walls
3. What gets rid of darkness
5. When it's very light, it's _____.
7. Your bicycle has one in front and one in back.
9. Sweet and yummy treat
10. _____ what's on your mind.
13. To have something for yourself

1 2 3 4 5 6 7 8 9 10 11 12 13 14

You Old Soft "C"!

Sort and Spell

The letter "c" can make a hard **k** sound, as in *cook*, or soft **s** sound, as in *twice*. LISTEN for the soft or hard **c** in each word pictured. DRAW a line from the picture to the correct sound box. WRITE the word in the box.

SPELLING LIST

face
race
place
space
trace
ice
mice
nice
price
slice
twice
city
cake
clock

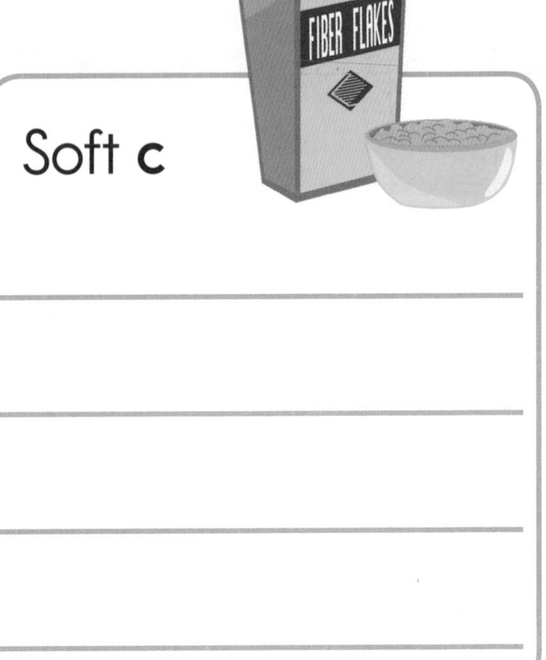

Soft **c**

Hard **c**

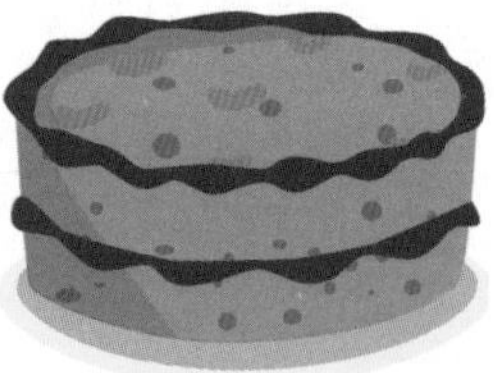

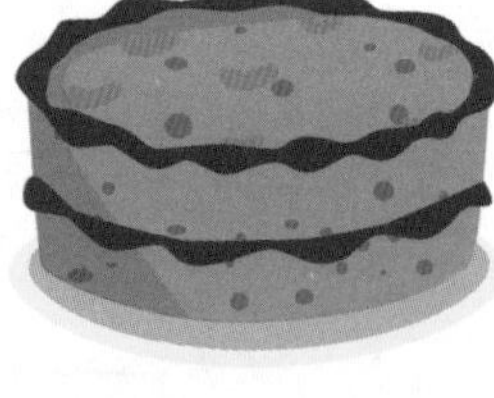

Blank Out

FILL IN the missing "ace" or "ice" to complete words with the soft **c** sound.

1. One way to learn how to draw is to **tr**_______ other pictures.
2. Wipe that smile off your **f**_______, Mister!
3. It was Cale's party, so he had a second **sl**_______ of cake.
4. It was very **n**_______ of you to give me your seat.
5. Someday Bess is going to fly a rocket into **sp**_______.
6. I won't buy this. The **pr**_______ is too high.
7. Fido couldn't find a good **pl**_______ to bury his bone.
8. The cheese goes so fast in our house, Mom says we must have **m**_______.
9. I'll **r**_______ you home!
10. That movie was so good, we watched it **tw**_______.

Match Up

The letter "g" can make both a hard **g** sound, as in *gum*, or a soft **j** sound, as in *age*. WRITE the word from the word box that matches each picture. CIRCLE the pictures that show words that make the **j** sound.

SPELLING LIST

cage
charge
gem
giant
huge
large
page
stage
girl
goat
leg

cage gem stage girl leg goat

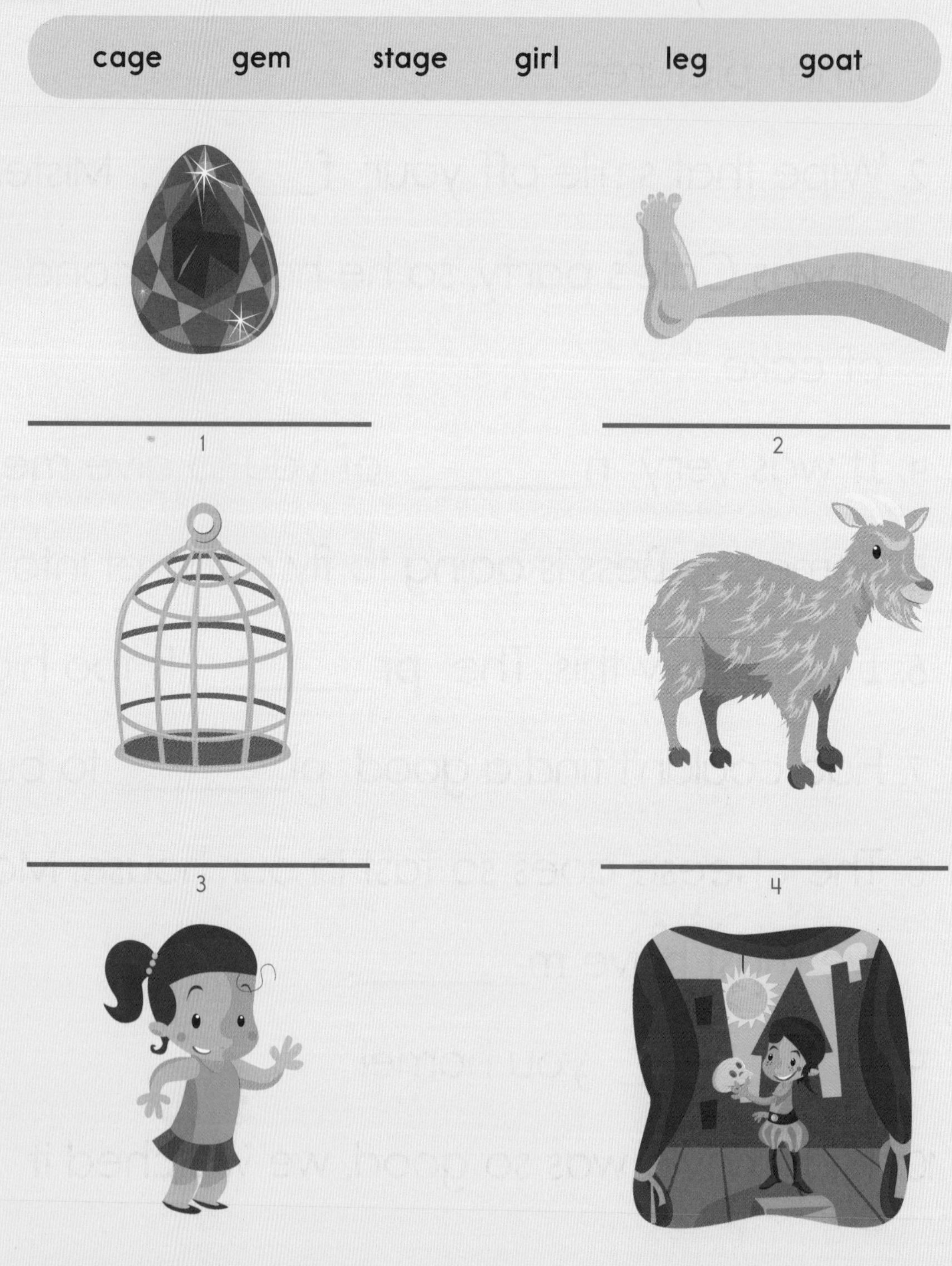

1 ____________

2 ____________

3 ____________

4 ____________

5 ____________

6 ____________

Word Scramble

UNSCRAMBLE each word and write it correctly. LOOK at the word box for help. CROSS OUT each word in the word box as you make it.

cage	charge	gem	giant	huge	large	page	stage

1. meg ________________
2. aglre ________________
3. ghue ________________
4. hregac ________________
5. gesat ________________
6. intga ________________
7. geap ________________
8. geca ________________

UNSCRAMBLE the words to complete the riddle.

Q. Why did the monster buy a **igtan** battery?

____

A. He needed a **lrgae hgaerc**.

________________ ________________

Blank Out

FILL IN the missing word to complete the sentence.

SPELLING LIST

could
might
should
would

1. I **sh**__________ keep looking at these words if I want to learn them.
2. Kayla said she **w**__________ try the spinach.
3. **W**__________ you keep an eye on Scamp?
4. I **m**__________ make it home if the bus ever comes.
5. Jamal **c**__________ do even the hardest math.
6. You **sh**__________ never be afraid to ask.
7. I **c**__________ sure use a hot fudge sundae right now.

Word Hunt

CIRCLE the words from the word box in the grid. Words go across and down, not diagonally or backward. Each word appears twice!

might	could	should	would

s	h	o	u	l	d	i	o
r	i	c	o	u	l	d	u
m	w	u	d	c	s	h	l
i	o	m	i	g	h	t	d
g	u	o	u	c	o	u	l
h	l	l	c	o	u	l	d
t	d	w	o	u	l	d	a
l	i	g	h	t	d	o	u

WRITE each word that you circled.

_______________ _______________

_______________ _______________

Sort and Spell

LISTEN for the soft **c** or soft **g** sound in each word pictured. DRAW a line from the picture to the correct sound box. WRITE the word in the box.

city	face	giant	gem	mice	stage

Soft **c**	Soft **g**
__________	__________
__________	__________
__________	__________

Word Scramble

UNSCRAMBLE each word and write it correctly. LOOK at the word box for help. CROSS OUT each word in the word box as you make it.

charge	place	stage	could	would
giant	price	twice	should	might

1. wietc ________________
2. angti ________________
3. hgcrea ________________
4. ulwdo ________________
5. ceapl ________________
6. getsa ________________
7. ldouhs ________________
8. rpiec ________________
9. hgtmi ________________
10. lcodu ________________

Criss Cross

FILL IN the grid by answering the clues.

Across

1. He _____ come if he has time.
4. Don't forget to _____ your cell phone so the battery doesn't die.
5. Where you perform a play
6. Two times
8. Small, medium, _____
10. Serving size of cake
13. Was able to
14. A great, big, _____ whale

Down

1. More than one mouse
2. Very big person
3. Rockets go to outer _____.
5. You _____ say "please" when you ask for something.
7. _____ you like some popcorn?
9. To run to see who's fastest
11. Place to keep wild animals
12. This looks like a good _____ to eat.

1 2
3
4
5
6 7
8 9 10 11
12
13
14

Blank Out

FILL IN the missing "j" or "dge" to complete the sentence.

SPELLING LIST

bridge
dodge
edge
fudge
hedge
judge
lodge
ridge
jelly
juice
joke

1. Maya loves to eat ______**elly** beans.
2. Deshi is really good at **do**______ ball.
3. I think a troll lives under this **bri**______.
4. Lin has a glass of ______**uice** every morning.
5. The scouts had a meeting at the **lo**______.
6. Mom makes the best **fu**______ in the world!
7. Max really knows how to tell a ______**oke.**
8. I get scared when I stand too close to the **e**______.

Write and Rhyme

FILL IN the word from the Spelling List that best fits the picture. Then WRITE another word from the list that rhymes with it.

1

____

____

2

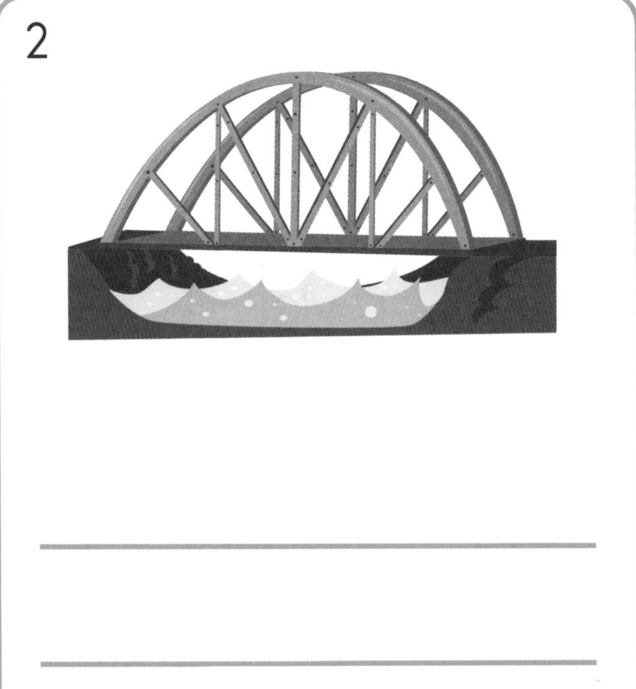

____

____

3

____

____

4

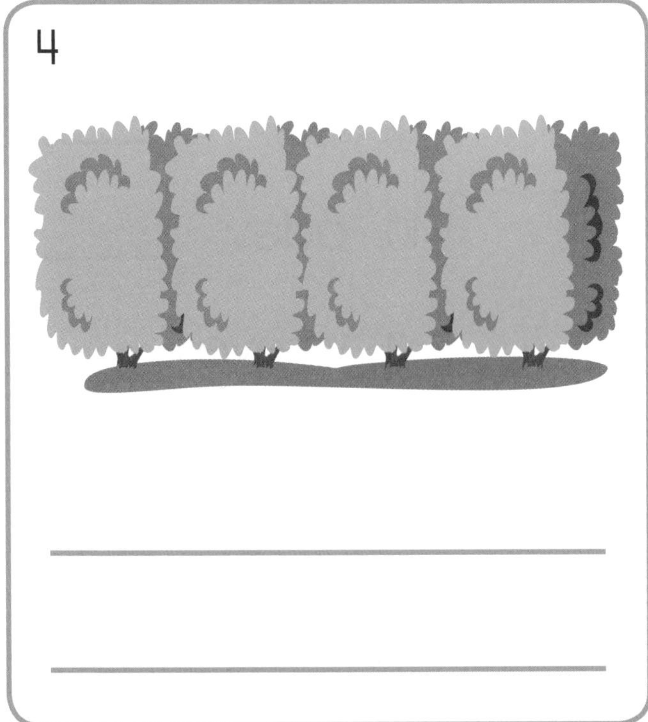

____

____

Word Scramble

UNSCRAMBLE each word and write it correctly. Look at the Spelling List for help.

SPELLING LIST

curve
serve
swerve
have
move
prove
dove
glove
love
shove
give
live

1. vepro ______________
2. emvo ______________
3. lvoeg ______________
4. vlei ______________
5. ovseh ______________
6. aevh ______________
7. elov ______________
8. eivg ______________
9. rseve ______________
10. odev ______________
11. wreves ______________
12. cruve ______________

Blank Out!

FILL IN the word from the Spelling List that best fits the sentence.

1. Tasha has a mean __________ at Ping-Pong!

2. Please don't __________! We'll all make it onto the bus.

3. This is the house where I __________.

4. During the quake, Dan could feel the earth __________.

5. The car had to __________ so it wouldn't hit the deer.

6. Would you __________ me a hand with this?

7. The sign warned us of a __________ in the road.

8. I think I'll __________ a triple-fudge sundae for dessert.

9. __________, __________, and __________ all rhyme with shove, and I can __________ it!

Who's Hiding?

LOOK at the word box. CIRCLE the silent letter or letters in each word. WRITE each word in the box labeled with the silent letter.

caught	daughter	thumb	knife	lamb	walk
talk	knee	wrong	comb	sign	write

SPELLING LIST

caught
daughter
thumb
comb
lamb
walk
talk
knee
knife
wrong
write
sign

b

g

k

l

w

Not Quite!

CIRCLE the words that are misspelled in this story.

The king said to his dotter, "Your hair is a mess. You need to cowm it."

"Rong!" she said. "Tock to the hand!" But she cot her thum in her hair. "This is a bad sayn," she said. She tried to pull free, but soon her hands and her feet were stuck in her hair. She couldn't even wok.

"That's it," said the king. He got a nife and cut her hair short. Now she doesn't need a comb!

WRITE the circled words correctly.

There Their!

There is about a place, and *their* is about people. For example, *Their key was there.* WRITE the right form of *there* or *their* to complete each sentence.

SPELLING LIST
again
because
favorite
friend
people
said
they
there
their
were

________ (1) were once three little pigs. ________ (2) mother sent them out into the world. "Hold on!" said one pig. "________ (3) are wolves out here!" So they put ________ (4) heads together, and decided to get a house. "________ (5) is a nice house," said one pig, pointing to a straw house. "You're kidding, right?" said the others. That was ________ (6) first fight. In the middle of ________ (7) argument, a wolf came by. "________ (8) is nothing like brick to keep wolves out," he said. He sold them a nice brick house.

"Wait," said the pigs. "Why didn't you eat us?"

"________ (9) is more money in real estate," said the wolf.

He bought a nice steak dinner.

Word Hunt

CIRCLE the words from the word box in the grid. Words go across and down, not diagonally or backward.

because	they	people	favorite	friend	were	said	again

t	b	r	a	g	a	i	n
h	e	n	d	a	f	r	t
e	c	a	w	e	r	e	h
f	a	v	o	r	i	t	e
s	u	d	r	a	e	p	y
a	s	a	i	n	n	d	a
i	e	o	p	l	d	g	h
d	a	p	e	o	p	l	e

WRITE each word that you circled.

Blank Out

WRITE the word from the word box that best fits the sentence.

because	they	people	favorite	friend	were	said	again

1. Carlos likes to skate with his ____________ Kiki.
2. Some ____________ are born lucky.
3. My stomach hurt ____________ I ate too much.
4. I didn't hear you. Could you tell me that ____________?
5. Eddie and Ming bought everything ____________ saw.
6. Jake's mother ____________ he was late.
7. ____________ you able to answer that last question?
8. No one believes that snails are my ____________ food.

Word Scramble

UNSCRAMBLE each word and write it correctly. LOOK at the word box for help. CROSS OUT each word in the word box as you make it.

because	they	people	favorite	their
there	friend	were	said	again

1. aagni ____________
2. htire ____________
3. iafeotrv ____________
4. aesebcu ____________
5. nriefd ____________
6. erew ____________
7. aisd ____________
8. eleopp ____________
9. yeth ____________
10. rheet ____________

Circle It

CIRCLE the pictures that show words that have silent letters.

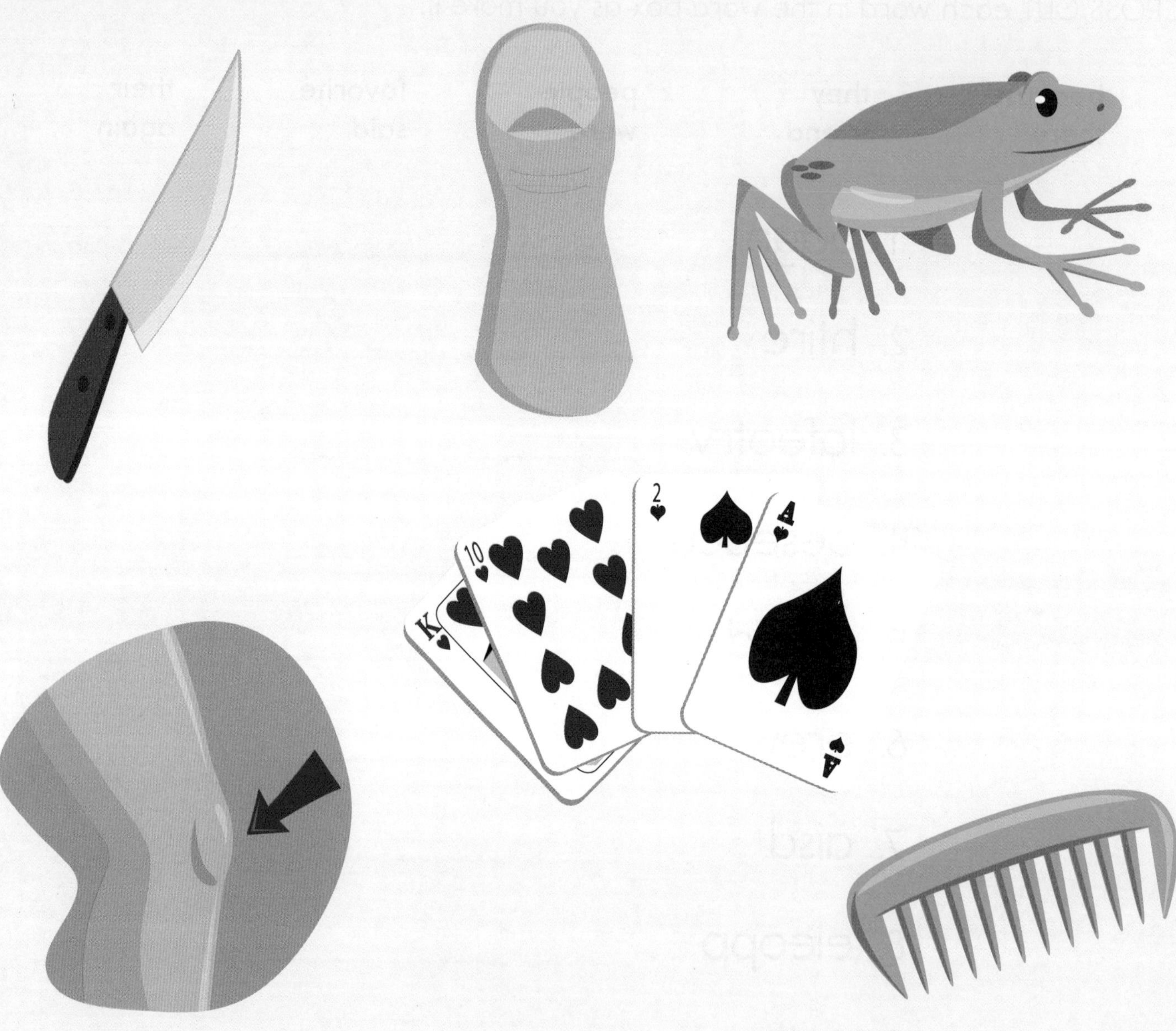

WRITE the words that have a long vowel sound.

________________________ ________________________

____

Sort and Spell

DRAW a line from the picture to the box that shows the correct word ending.
WRITE the word in the box.

bridge dove glove hedge judge love

-ve	-dge
____________	____________
____________	____________
____________	____________

Criss Cross

READ the clues. FILL IN the boxes with the right word for each clue.

Across

4. Where the page ends
5. To present something to someone
6. A metal tool you use to cut things
8. Chocolate treat
10. The answer to "why?"
12. Get out of the way
13. He is standing over _____.
14. A bend in the road

Down

1. Where the name of a store is written
2. One more time
3. More than one person
7. The one I like best
8. A person you like
9. A son's sister
10. A way to get across a river
11. I wish you _____ here.

1 2 3 4 5 6 7 8 9 10 11 12 13 14

Double or Nothing!

To make a verb past tense, you usually add "-ed." When the verb has a short vowel and ends with one consonant, you usually double the consonant first. WRITE the past tense of each verb in the correct box.

Make Room!

Usually when a verb ends in "e," you remove the final "e" before adding "ed" to the word. WRITE the past tense of each verb in the correct box.

Sort and Spell

READ each word and listen to how it sounds. In some words, the "d" at the end makes a **d** sound. In others, it makes a **t** sound.

MARK each word with a T or a D. Then WRITE the word in the correct word box.

○ hugged ○ seemed

○ kicked ○ tripped

○ served ○ climbed ○ baked

○ jumped ○ piled ○ camped

d	t
________	________
________	________
________	________
________	________
________	________

Extra Baggage

CIRCLE the words in which the "-ed" adds an extra syllable to the word.
WRITE the words in the correct boxes.

shouted

joked

marked

grinned

tasted

chewed

sipped

darted

rested

nodded

No Extra Baggage

____

____

____

____

____

Extra Baggage

____

____

____

____

____

Samurai Speller!

CROSS OUT the final "e" in the words below. WRITE the correct form of the word with "-ing" at the end.

div~~e~~ + ing = diving

1. bake + ing = ______________
2. pile + ing = ______________
3. joke + ing = ______________
4. serve + ing = ______________
5. live + ing = ______________
6. poke + ing = ______________
7. dine + ing = ______________
8. taste + ing = ______________
9. prove + ing = ______________
10. rake + ing = ______________

Double Up

ADD a second consonant to the end of each word. WRITE the correct form of the word with "-ing" on the end.

nod + d + ing = nodding

1. rub + ___ + ing = ____________________
2. dip + ___ + ing = ____________________
3. drop + ___ + ing = ____________________
4. plan + ___ + ing = ____________________
5. hum + ___ + ing = ____________________
6. shop + ___ + ing = ____________________
7. trip + ___ + ing = ____________________
8. grin + ___ + ing = ____________________
9. plan + ___ + ing = ____________________
10. chat + ___ + ing = ____________________

This Way Please!

WRITE the "-ing" form of each word in the correct box. CROSS OUT each word as you write it.

bake

joke

sip

plan

gulp

kick

Double Final Consonant

Drop Final **e**

Leave Alone

Two's Company

WRITE the plural form of each word by adding "-s" to the end.

1. pig + ____ = ____________________
2. cape + ____ = ____________________
3. path + ____ = ____________________
4. belt + ____ = ____________________
5. stick + ____ = ____________________
6. truck + ____ = ____________________
7. king + ____ = ____________________
8. lamp + ____ = ____________________
9. nest + ____ = ____________________
10. carrot + ____ = ____________________

To "E" or Not to "E"

ADD an "-es" to these words to make them plural.

1. glass + ____ = ____________
2. witch + ____ = ____________
3. dish + ____ = ____________
4. fox + ____ = ____________
5. lash + ____ = ____________
6. wish + ____ = ____________
7. guess + ____ = ____________
8. bus + ____ = ____________
9. miss + ____ = ____________
10. box + ____ = ____________
11. watch + ____ = ____________
12. itch + ____ = ____________

Sort and Spell

LISTEN for the sound the “s” makes at the end of each word. DRAW a line from the picture to the correct sound box. WRITE the word in the box.

bananas books chairs girls sticks trucks

s	z
__________	__________
__________	__________
__________	__________

Extra Baggage

CIRCLE the words where the "s" or "es" adds an extra syllable to the word.
WRITE the words in the correct boxes.

glasses showers

witches

itches

boots

carrots

cards

buses

baths

matches

No Extra Baggage

____

____

____

____

____

Extra Baggage

____

____

____

____

____

Word Scramble

Some words form plurals in unusual ways:

End in EN	OO → EE	OUSE → ICE	No Change
man → men woman → women child → children	foot → feet tooth → teeth	mouse → mice	sheep deer fish

UNSCRAMBLE each word and write it correctly. LOOK at the word box for help.

1. ftee ______________
2. meonw ______________
3. tehet ______________
4. cmie ______________
5. delicrnh ______________

Word Hunt

CIRCLE the plural words from the word box in the grid. Words go across and down, not diagonally or backward.

men **women** **children** **feet** **teeth** **mice** **deer** **sheep** **fish**

f	i	m	w	o	m	e	n
m	o	u	n	e	g	t	w
i	c	f	e	e	t	e	o
c	h	i	l	d	r	e	n
e	o	s	f	e	w	t	d
e	s	h	e	e	p	h	r
m	e	n	e	r	e	n	e

WRITE each word that you circled.

Blank Out

FILL IN the missing "-er" or "-est" in these sentences.

1. Chip is pretty tall, but Jason is **tall**_____.

2. King Midas must have been the **rich**_____ person in the world!

3. I wish this knife were **sharp**_____. I can't cut anything with it.

4. This is the **soft**_____ pillow I've ever had.

5. Mom was proud of me for winning the game, but even **proud**_____ for being a good sport.

6. If this hill gets any **steep**_____, I won't be able to get to the top.

7. Lola thought she had the **kind**_____ grandmother ever!

So Lonesome...

When a word has a short vowel sound and ends with one consonant, double that consonant before adding "-er" or "-est."

DOUBLE the last consonant. WRITE the correct form of each word.

1. big + ____ + er = ______________
2. fat + ____ + est = ______________
3. sad + ____ + est = ______________
4. dim + ____ + er = ______________
5. red + ____ + er = ______________
6. fit + ____ + est = ______________
7. tan + ____ + est = ______________
8. wet + ____ + er = ______________
9. hot + ____ + est = ______________
10. fat + ____ + er = ______________
11. big + ____ + est = ______________
12. sad + ____ + er = ______________

Samurai Speller!

CROSS OUT the final "e" in the words. WRITE the correct form of the word with "-er" or "-est" at the end.

1. nice + er = __________
2. fine + est = __________
3. safe + er = __________
4. stale + est = __________
5. brave + er = __________
6. white + er = __________
7. wise + est = __________
8. rude + er = __________
9. late + est = __________
10. ripe + est = __________

Not Quite!

CIRCLE the words that are misspelled in this story.

The bigest mistake I made was staying latter than I should have. The sky was getting darkker. The wind was blowing the wilddest I had ever seen. Mom, who's oldder and wisser than I am, said I should hurry home. "I'm not scared," I said. "I'm braveer than that."

Brave, maybe, but not the smarttest.

It rained hardder than ever. When I got home, I was weter than I'd ever been.

WRITE the circled words correctly.

1. ____________________
2. ____________________
3. ____________________
4. ____________________
5. ____________________
6. ____________________
7. ____________________
8. ____________________
9. ____________________
10. ____________________

Quick Change

CROSS OUT the final "y" in each word and change it to an "i." Then WRITE the correct form of the word with "-er" or "-est."

1. dry + ____ + er = ____________________
2. lovely + ____ + est = ____________________
3. pretty + ____ + est = ____________________
4. skinny + ____ + er = ____________________
5. noisy + ____ + er = ____________________
6. funny + ____ + est = ____________________
7. ugly + ____ + est = ____________________
8. heavy + ____ + er = ____________________
9. lucky + ____ + est = ____________________
10. early + ____ + er = ____________________
11. sandy + ____ + est = ____________________
12. friendly + ____ + er = ____________________

Word Hunt

CIRCLE the words from the word box in the grid. Words go across and down, not diagonally or backward.

driest earlier funniest goofiest heaviest meatier prettier tastier

e	r	o	g	o	o	f	i	e	s	t
a	e	s	t	p	r	e	d	i	e	a
r	o	o	f	y	d	o	r	b	d	s
l	e	a	f	u	n	n	i	e	s	t
i	p	r	e	t	t	i	e	r	s	i
e	h	e	a	v	i	e	s	t	i	e
r	f	u	n	m	e	a	t	i	e	r

WRITE each word that you circled.

This Way Please!

WRITE the "-er" form of each word in the correct box. CROSS OUT each word as you write it.

funny

fine

fat

hot

Drop Final **e**

______

______

______

______

______

Double Final Consonant

______

______

______

______

______

Change **y** to **i**

______

______

______

______

______

Word Scramble

UNSCRAMBLE each word and write it correctly. LOOK at the word box for help. CROSS OUT each word in the word box as you make it.

bravest	older	loveliest	strangest	smaller	richest
skinniest	clearest	cleaner	bigger	stronger	wiser

1. agrstenst ________________
2. bgeigr ________________
3. grersnot ________________
4. arnlece ________________
5. slelrma ________________
6. eeilvtlso ________________
7. aeseltcr ________________
8. elrdo ________________
9. sitskneni ________________
10. streich ________________
11. avsebtr ________________
12. sweri ________________

Answers

Page 2
1. big bug
2. hot hat
3. bad bed
4. nut net
5. hip hop

Page 3

ACROSS	DOWN
1. cat	2. top
3. mop	4. pup
6. pet	5. hit
8. pit	7. tub
10. tag	9. ten
11. bed	

Page 4
1. hope, hop
2. made, mad
3. pet, Pete
4. cute, cut
5. fine, fin

Page 5
1. cut → cute
2. gav → gave
3. pok → poke
4. mad → made
5. hid → hide
6. hat → hate
7. hop → hope
8. tim → time

Page 6
1. white
2. chop
3. thick
4. shop
5. chat
6. ship
7. thin
8. when

Page 7
1. chick
2. white
3. shapes
4. ship
5. chop
6. shop

Page 8
1. ship
2. thin
3. what
4. chick
5. white
6. chop
7. chat
8. shapes
9. thick
10. shop

Page 9
1. thick, thin
2. chick chat
3. ship shape

Page 10
1. fish
2. with
3. which
4. watch
5. dash
6. math
7. witch
8. catch

Page 11
1. bath
2. rich
3. catch
4. dash

Page 12
1. math
2. rich
3. watch
4. bath
5. fish
6. witch

Page 13
1. whish → which
2. wich → witch
3. ritsh → rich
4. catsh → catch
5. fich → fish
6. maf → math
7. wif → with
8. datsh → dash

Page 14
1. dress
2. skirt
3. shirt
4. coat
5. shoe
6. belt
7. shorts
8. pants

Page 15

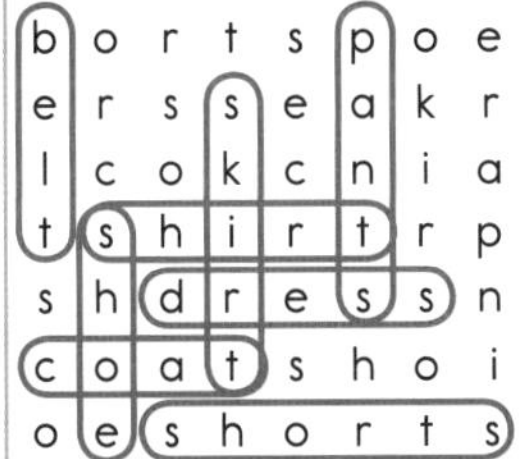

Page 16
ch: chop, chick, rich
sh: fish, shoe, ship

Page 17
watch, witch, catch

Pages 18–19

ACROSS	DOWN
3. which	1. shape
5. ship	2. shirt
7. thin	4. shorts
8. thick	6. fish
10. chop	9. chick
13. white	11. pants
14. catch	12. belt
15. math	14. chat

Page 20
Cross out: duck, kite
Write: truck, frog, stick, slide

Page 21
1. clam
2. spill
3. trap
4. frog
5. steps
6. crab

Page 22
1. truck
2. frog
3. stick
4. trap
5. slip
6. crab
7. slide
8. trip

Page 23
1. slip
2. trap
3. steps
4. clam
5. stick
6. crab
7. stop
8. spill
9. slide
10. trip
11. frog
12. truck

Pages 24–25
1. hand
2. desk
3. lamp
4. gift
5. nest
6. mask
7. jump
8. tent
9. cast
10. ant
11. camp
12. band

Page 26
1. capm → camp
2. tenk → tent
3. ankt → ant
4. hamd → hand
5. ness → nest
6. jum → jump
7. casp → cast

Page 27
Cross out: fan, clam, key
Write: desk, lamp, gift, mask

Page 28
1. pizza
2. milk
3. carrot
4. banana
5. bread
6. cookie
7. steak
8. apple

Page 29

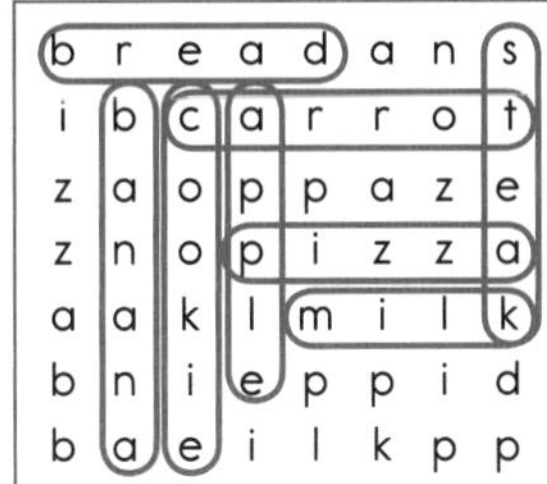

Page 30
Start: trap, slide, frog
End: mask, tent, lamp

Page 31
Long vowel: shapes, white, slide
Short vowel: truck, desk, spill

Pages 32–33

ACROSS	DOWN
1. cast	1. cookie
3. jump	2. truck
6. king	4. pants
7. nest	5. bread
9. steak	8. slip
11. apple	10. tent
13. trip	12. pizza
15. banana	14. hand

Page 34
1. part
2. chirp
3. skirt
4. hurt
5. first
6. bird
7. chart

Page 35
girl: her, chirp, first, hurt, turn, bird, skirt, worm
car: card, chart, hard, part

Page 36
1. card
2. chart
3. hard
4. bird
5. worm
6. first
7. turn
8. hurt
9. skirt
10. part
11. chirp
12. her

Page 37
1. hord → hard
2. ferst → first
3. heer → her
4. port → part
5. hert → hurt
6. torn → turn
7. berd → bird
8. werm → worm

Answers

Page 38
1. deer
2. store
3. gear
4. chair

Page 39
Dear, deer

1. gear
2. cheer
3. steer
4. dear
5. near

Page 40
1. share
2. care
3. store
4. pair
5. dare
6. chair
7. more
8. hair

Page 41
1. pair
2. cheer
3. gear
4. near
5. chair
6. steer
7. more
8. dare
9. share
10. store

Page 42

Page 43
1. rain
2. warm
3. cold
4. wind
5. weather
6. cloud
7. shower
8. snow

Page 44
far: car, cards, yarn
fur: bird, skirt, worm

Page 45
1. chirp
2. warm
3. hurt
4. skirt
5. chart
6. her
7. first
8. hard
9. cold
10. turn

Circle: chirp, hurt, her, first, turn

Pages 46–47

ACROSS	DOWN
1. cloud	2. dear
3. warm	3. weather
4. steer	4. share
6. chair	5. first
9. shower	7. her
10. snow	8. more
11. turn	12. near
15. rain	13. wind
16. deer	14. gear

Page 48
ay: gray, play, tray
ai: paint, train, snail

Page 49
Cross out: car, gear
Write: weight, mail, braid, snail

Page 50
1. mail
2. weigh
3. train
4. paint
5. say
6. play
7. neighbor
8. gray

Page 51
1. plai → play
2. nayber → neighbor
3. mayl → mail
4. gra → gray
5. brade → braid
6. wey → weigh
7. snale → snail
8. sae → say

Page 52
ea: beach, leaf, seal
ee: green, teeth, wheel

Page 53
1. candy, puppy, teeth
2. monkey, tree, speak

Page 54
Cross out: worm, yo-yo
Write: key, candy, tree, puppy

Page 55
1. wheel
2. beach
3. seal
4. teeth
5. monkey
6. green
7. key
8. puppy
9. leaf
10. speak

Page 56
1. kind
2. blind
3. try
4. sigh
5. high
6. find
7. light
8. bright

Page 57
1. bright light
2. right mind
3. fly spy

Page 58

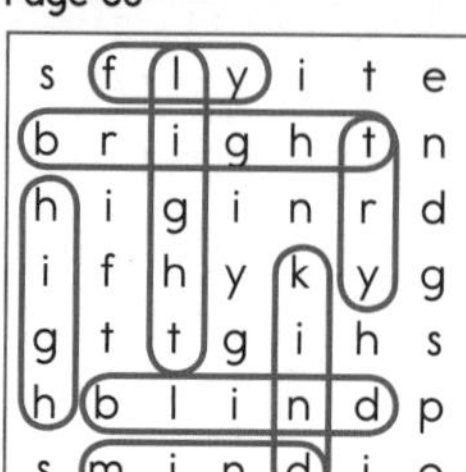

Page 59
1. kind
2. find
3. mind
4. high
5. blind
6. bright
7. spy
8. right
9. light
10. sigh

Page 60
oa: boat, coach, goat
ow: bow, bowl, crow

Page 61
1. show
2. slow
3. bowl
4. goal
5. own
6. coach
7. road
8. soap

Page 62
Cross out: gear, fork
Write: goal, soap, road, bowl

Page 63
1. boat
2. road
3. bow
4. crow
5. goal
6. coach
7. own
8. goat
9. slow
10. show

Page 64
1. broom
2. few
3. chew
4. true
5. threw
6. fruit
7. blue
8. moon

Page 65
Cross out: watch, girl
Write: blue, moon, glue, fruit

Page 66
1. broom
2. boot
3. tooth
4. blue
5. glue
6. fruit

Page 67
1. threw
2. few
3. chew
4. flew
5. moon
6. true
7. glue
8. tooth
9. broom
10. boot

Page 68
Long a: braid, mail, weight
Long e: beach, gear, leaf

Page 69
Long o: soap, bowl, coach, boat
Long u: moon, broom

Pages 70–71

ACROSS	DOWN
1. try	1. teeth
2. puppy	2. paint
4. neighbor	3. light
6. show	5. bright
8. weight	7. wheel
11. mail	9. candy
12. boot	10. say
14. monkey	13. own

Page 72
Soft c: face, ice, city, mice
Hard c: clock, cake

Page 73
1. trace
2. face
3. slice
4. nice
5. space
6. price
7. place
8. mice
9. race
10. twice

Page 74
1. gem
2. leg
3. cage
4. goat
5. girl
6. stage

Circle: gem, cage, stage

Page 75
1. gem
2. large
3. huge
4. charge
5. stage
6. giant
7. page
8. cage

Riddle: giant, large charge

Page 76
1. should
2. would
3. Would
4. might
5. could
6. should
7. could

Page 77

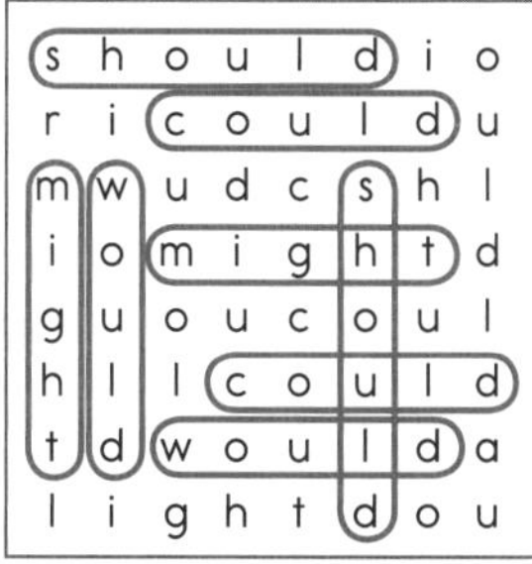

Page 78
Soft c: mice, face, city
Soft g: giant, gem, stage

Page 79
1. twice
2. giant
3. charge
4. would
5. place
6. stage
7. should
8. price
9. might
10. could

Pages 80–81

ACROSS	DOWN
1. might	1. mice
4. charge	2. giant
5. stage	3. space
6. twice	5. should
8. large	7. would
10. slice	9. race
13. could	11. cage
14. huge	12. place

Page 82
1. jelly
2. dodge
3. bridge
4. juice
5. lodge
6. fudge
7. joke
8. edge

Page 83
1. judge, fudge
2. bridge, ridge
3. lodge, dodge
4. hedge, edge

Page 84
1. prove
2. move
3. glove
4. live
5. shove
6. have
7. love
8. give
9. serve
10. dove
11. swerve
12. curve

Page 85
1. serve
2. shove
3. live
4. move
5. swerve
6. give
7. curve
8. have
9. Dove, glove, love, prove

Page 86
b: comb, thumb, lamb
g: caught, daughter, sign
k: knee, knife
l: walk, talk
w: wrong, write

Page 87
1. dotter → daughter
2. cowm → comb
3. rong → wrong
4. tock → talk
5. cot → caught
6. thum → thumb
7. sayn → sign
8. wok → walk
9. nife → knife

Page 88
1. There
2. Their
3. There
4. their
5. There
6. their
7. their
8. There
9. There

Page 89

t	b	r	a	g	a	i	n
h	e	n	d	a	f	r	t
e	c	a	w	e	r	e	h
f	a	v	o	r	i	t	e
s	u	d	r	a	e	p	y
a	s	a	i	n	n	d	a
i	e	o	p	l	d	g	h
d	a	p	e	o	p	l	e

Page 90
1. friend
2. people
3. because
4. again
5. they
6. said
7. Were
8. favorite

Page 91
1. again
2. their
3. favorite
4. because
5. friend
6. were
7. said
8. people
9. they
10. there

Page 92
Circle: thumb, knee, comb, knife
Write: knee, comb, knife

Page 93
-ve: dove, glove, love
-dge: bridge, hedge, judge

Pages 94–95

ACROSS	DOWN
4. edge	1 sign
5. give	2. again
6. knife	3. people
8. fudge	7. favorite
10. because	8. friend
12. dodge	9. daughter
13. there	10. bridge
14. curve	11. were

Page 96
Add a Letter: shopped, hugged, hummed, tripped, dropped
Ready to Go: camped, worked, jumped, kicked, spelled

Page 97
Remove the e: poked, dined, baked, raked, joked
Ready to Go: marked, looked, learned, chewed, glowed

Page 98
d: served, piled, seemed, climbed, hugged
t: kicked, jumped, tripped, camped, baked

Page 99
No extra baggage: joked, chewed, sipped, grinned, marked
Extra baggage (circled): shouted, darted, rested, tasted, nodded

Page 100
1. baking
2. piling
3. joking
4. serving
5. living
6. poking
7. dining
8. tasting
9. proving
10. raking

Page 101
1. b, rubbing
2. p, dipping
3. p, dropping
4. n, planning
5. m, humming
6. p, shopping
7. p, tripping
8. n, grinning
9. n, planning
10. t, chatting

Pages 102–103
Drop Final e: diving, tasting, serving, joking, baking
Double Final Consonant: shopping, hugging, sipping, dropping, planning
Leave Alone: gulping, locking, camping, marking, kicking

Page 104
1. s, pigs
2. s, capes
3. s, paths
4. s, belts
5. s, sticks
6. s, trucks
7. s, kings
8. s, lamps
9. s, nests
10. s, carrots

Answers

Page 105
1. es, glasses
2. es, witches
3. es, dishes
4. es, foxes
5. es, lashes
6. es, wishes
7. es, guesses
8. es, buses
9. es, misses
10. es, boxes
11. es, watches
12. es, itches

Page 106
s: books, sticks, trucks
z: bananas, girls, chairs

Page 107
Extra baggage (circled): glasses, witches, itches, matches, buses
No extra baggage: cards, showers, boots, baths, carrots

Page 108
1. feet
2. women
3. teeth
4. mice
5. children

Page 109

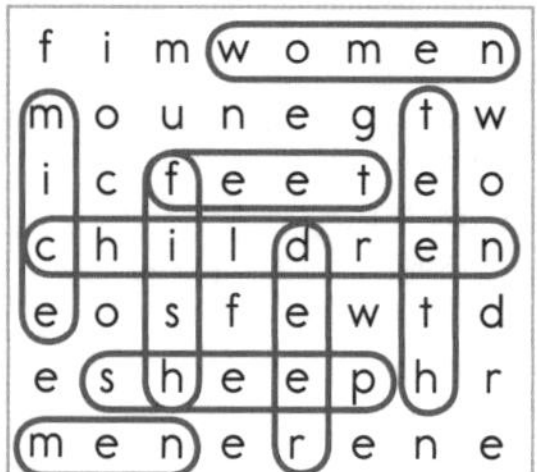

Page 110
1. taller
2. richest
3. sharper
4. softest
5. prouder
6. steeper
7. kindest

Page 111
1. g, bigger
2. t, fattest
3. d, saddest
4. m, dimmer
5. d, redder
6. t, fittest
7. n, tannest
8. t, wetter
9. t, hottest
10. t, fatter
11. g, biggest
12. d, sadder

Page 112
1. nicer
2. finest
3. safer
4. stalest
5. braver
6. whiter
7. wisest
8. ruder
9. latest
10. ripest

Page 113
1. bigest → biggest
2. latter → later
3. darkker → darker
4. wilddest → wildest
5. oldder → older
6. wisser → wiser
7. braveer → braver
8. smarttest → smartest
9. hardder → harder
10. weter → wetter

Page 114
1. i, drier
2. i, loveliest
3. i, prettiest
4. i, skinnier
5. i, noisier
6. i, funniest
7. i, ugliest
8. i, heavier
9. i, luckiest
10. i, earlier
11. i, sandiest
12. i, friendlier

Page 115

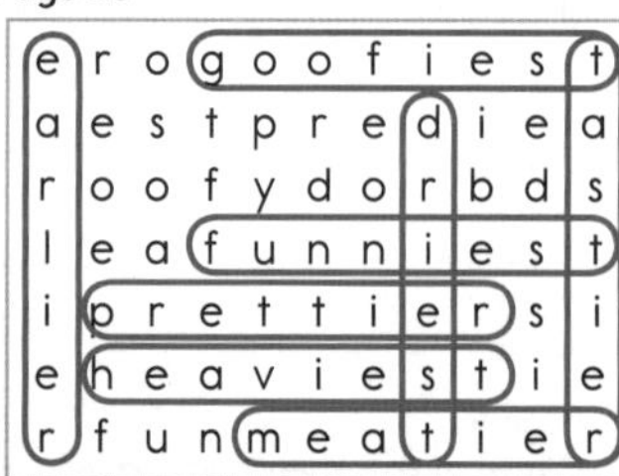

Pages 116–117
Drop Final e: finer, wiser, braver, riper, nicer
Double Final Consonant: fatter, wetter, hotter, sadder, bigger
Change y to i: skinnier, funnier, heavier, drier, noisier

Page 118
1. strangest
2. bigger
3. stronger
4. cleaner
5. smaller
6. loveliest
7. clearest
8. older
9. skinniest
10. richest
11. bravest
12. wiser

2nd Grade Vocabulary Puzzles

Contents

Word List

READ the words and their meanings.

ad·jec·tive—AJ-ihk-tihv *noun* a word that describes something, like *pretty* or *blue*

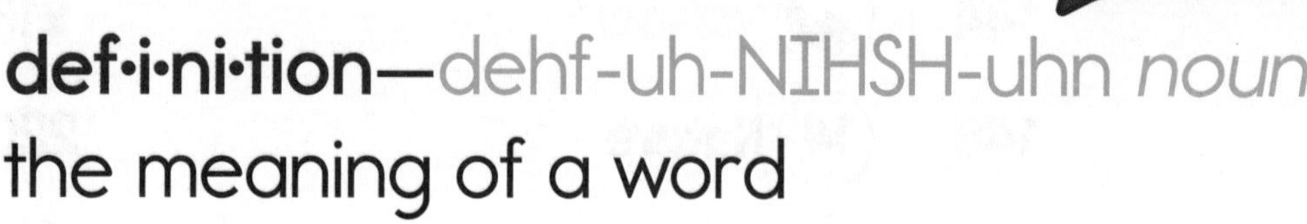

def·i·ni·tion—dehf-uh-NIHSH-uhn *noun* the meaning of a word

de·scribe—dih-SKRIB *verb* to make a picture with words, like "a pretty girl in a blue dress"

dic·tion·ar·y—DIHK-shuh-nehr-ee *noun* a book filled with definitions of words

mean·ing—MEE-nihng *noun* the idea of a word, what it means

noun—nown *noun* a word that stands for a person, place, or thing

verb—verb *noun* a word that stands for an action, like *run*

Match the Meaning

WRITE the words next to their definitions. LOOK at the word box for help.

adjective	definition	dictionary	meaning
noun	~~describe~~	verb	

1. describe to make a word picture
2. ______ the idea of a word
3. ______ an action word
4. ______ a word for a person, place, or thing
5. ______ a word that describes something
6. ______ a book filled with definitions
7. ______ the meaning of a word

ABC-123

Words in a dictionary go in **alphabetical order**. That means words that start with "A" go before words that start with "B."

READ the words in the word box. Then WRITE them in alphabetical order.

machine	octopus	jelly	whisper
balloon	trouble	~~angry~~	learn

1. angry
2. ______
3. ______
4. ______
5. ______
6. ______
7. ______
8. ______

ABCDEFGHIJKLMNOPQRSTUVWXYZ

Pick the One

A **dictionary** tells you whether a word is a *noun*, *adjective*, or *verb*. Those are **parts of speech**.

CIRCLE the correct part of speech for each word.

HINT: If you're not sure, look up the words in a dictionary.

1. **eat**	noun	adjective	(verb)
2. **purple**	noun	adjective	verb
3. **draw**	noun	adjective	verb
4. **animal**	noun	adjective	verb
5. **young**	noun	adjective	verb
6. **wash**	noun	adjective	verb
7. **tooth**	noun	adjective	verb
8. **stove**	noun	adjective	verb

Dictionary Dare

Guide words are the first and last words on a page in a dictionary. They help you figure out if the word you're looking for is on that page.

READ the guide words. CIRCLE the word in each row that comes between them.

HINT: The words are in alphabetical order. Use the second letter of each word to figure out which word should come in between.

1. **folk → football**	food	frost	find
2. **preschool → president**	peace	puppy	present
3. **trade → train**	tuck	taxi	traffic
4. **robot → roller coaster**	recess	rock	rumble
5. **babble → balloon**	bagpipes	beaver	blob
6. **mold → money**	missile	monarch	mucus
7. **uniform → unlucky**	umpire	useless	unique
8. **haunt → hazy**	hawk	hero	hungry

480 folk • football

folk \'fōk\ *n. pl* **folk** or **folks** **1** *archaic*: a group of kindr : PEOPLE **2** : the great p determines the g characteristic f

Blank Out

A dictionary also tells you how many syllables a word has. A **syllable** is each part of a word that takes one beat to say. So *mean* has one syllable and *meaning* has two syllables. A dot shows the break for each syllable: *mean•ing.*

READ each word out loud. Then WRITE the number of syllables.

1. ad•jec•tive ____3____
2. def•i•ni•tion ________
3. de•scribe ________
4. dic•tion•ar•y ________
5. mean•ing ________
6. noun ________
7. syl•la•ble ________
8. verb ________

Word List

READ the words and their meanings.

ar•rive—uh-RIV *verb* to come to a place

at•tempt—uh-TEHMPT *verb* to try to do something

beau•ti•ful—BYOO-tuh-fuhl *adjective* very pretty

en•e•my—EHN-uh-mee *noun* someone who is working against you, a foe

fail—fayl *verb* to lose, to not get what you tried for

gi•ant—JI-uhnt 1. *noun* a huge person or other creature out of a fairy tale 2. *adjective* very big

pred•a•tor—PREHD-uh-ter *noun* an animal or insect that hunts others for its food

suc•ceed—suhk-SEED *verb* to win, to get what you wanted

Match the Meaning

WRITE the words next to their definitions. LOOK at the word box for help.

arrive	attempt	beautiful	enemy
fail	giant	predator	succeed

1. ________________ really large
2. ________________ to lose
3. ________________ to win
4. ________________ a hunter
5. ________________ to come
6. ________________ really pretty
7. ________________ to try
8. ________________ someone who's out to get you

Pick the One

Some words mean the same thing, like *start* and *begin*. Others are **opposites**, like *night* and *day*.

READ each word pair. CIRCLE "same" if they have the same meaning and "opposite" if the words are opposites.

1. arrive	leave	same	opposite
2. giant	huge	same	opposite
3. fail	succeed	same	opposite
4. beautiful	ugly	same	opposite
5. attempt	try	same	opposite
6. predator	hunter	same	opposite
7. enemy	friend	same	opposite
8. arrive	come	same	opposite

Find the Friend

READ the clues. Then WRITE the friend's name under each picture.

Darla is tall and thin.

Joe has curly black hair.

Kira wears the same shirt as Darla.

Talia is facing the opposite direction.

Larry is the opposite of Darla.

Who am I?

1 ______ 2 ______ 3 ______ 4 ______ 5 ______

Criss Cross

READ the clues. FILL IN the boxes with the right word for each clue.

Across

2. Same as *come*
4. Opposite of *tiny*
5. Opposite of *succeed*

Down

1. Same as *pretty*
3. Opposite of *buddy*

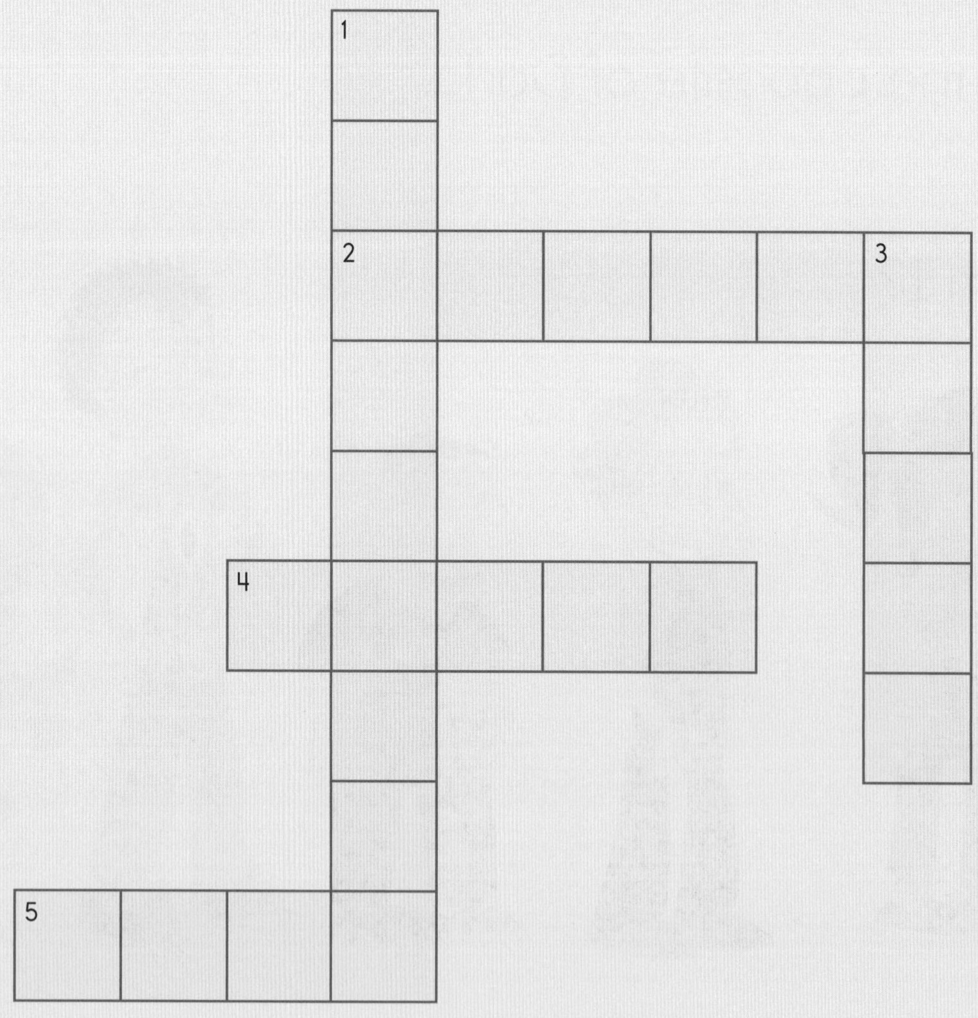

Dictionary Dare

Did you see that the word *giant* had two definitions in the Word List? Some words have more than one meaning. A dictionary gives all the meanings of a word.

READ the definition. Then ANSWER the questions.

skate—skayt 1. *noun* a shoe with a sharp blade that helps you slide on ice 2. *noun* a shoe with wheels that help you roll on the sidewalk 3. *verb* to use skates to move along the ground or on ice

1. How many meanings does *skate* have? ________
2. Is *skate* ever an adjective? Circle one: YES NO
3. Use *skate* in a sentence as a verb. ____________

____

____

____

____________________.

Word List

READ the words and their meanings.

base•ball—BAYS-bahl 1. *noun* a game played with a bat, a ball, and four bases 2. *noun* a ball used for playing baseball

bath•room—BATH-room *noun* a room for bathing and using the toilet

eve•ry•where—EHV-ree-wehr *adverb* in all places

light•house—LIT-hows *noun* a tall building with a big light that helps boats see the shore

side•walk—SID-wawk *noun* a smooth, hard walkway

stop•light—STAHP-lit *noun* a light that helps move traffic safely where two roads cross

sun•rise—SUHN-riz *noun* the time of day when the sun comes up

tooth•paste—TOOTH-payst *noun* a cream used to clean teeth

Match the Meaning

WRITE the words next to their definitions. LOOK at the word box for help.

baseball	bathroom	everywhere	sunrise
lighthouse	sidewalk	stoplight	toothpaste

1. ____________________ all over the world
2. ____________________ the very beginning of the day
3. ____________________ a game played with a bat
4. ____________________ a walkway
5. ____________________ a guide for ships at sea
6. ____________________ what you use to brush your teeth
7. ____________________ where you find a toilet
8. ____________________ a traffic light at a corner

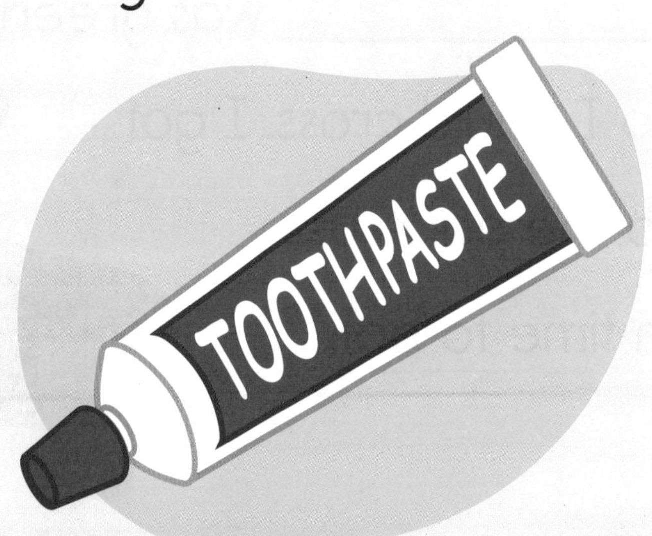

Finish the Story

READ the story. FILL IN the blanks with words from the word box.

bathroom	baseball	sidewalk	stoplight	sunrise	toothpaste

Just in Time

I got up at ________________ to play ________________
1 2
with my pals. As I raced to get ready, I dripped
________________ from my brush onto the floor in
3
the ________________. Mom wasn't up yet, so I didn't
4
clean it. I grabbed my bat and ran down the
________________ to the corner. Luckily the
5
________________ was green,
6
so I could cross. I got to the park just in time to bat!

Add It Up

Compound words are made by putting two words together.

ADD UP the smaller words to make compound words that match the definitions.

Example: *light + house = lighthouse*
a light that helps keep ships safe

1. **grand** + ___________ = ______________________

your mother's father

2. ___________ + **board** = ______________________

a board with wheels used to roll down the sidewalk

3. ___________ + **ground** = ______________________

a place with slides and swings

4. ________ + __________ = ______________________

a paper filled with the news of the day

5. **green** + ___________ = ______________________

a building to keep plants warm

Night and Day

DRAW a line to match each word under the moon to its opposite under the sun.

HINT: Don't forget to use a dictionary.

sunrise	nothing
troublemaker	playtime
somebody	sunset
downstairs	daytime
nighttime	sidewalk
everything	upstairs
bedtime	peacemaker
highway	nobody

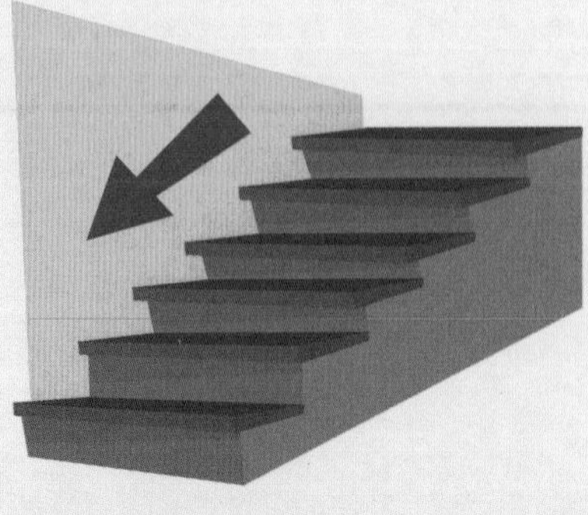

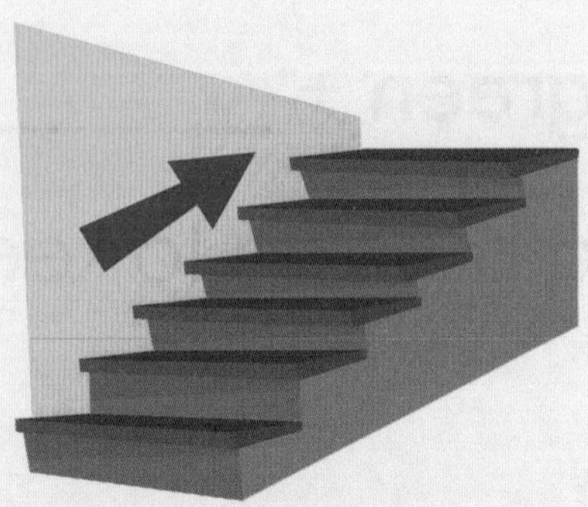

Cross Out

CROSS OUT the words that are NOT compound words.

1. starfish	football	adjective	predator
2. enemy	playground	everybody	arrive
3. lighthouse	beautiful	dictionary	blueberry
4. stoplight	unhappy	nothing	syllable

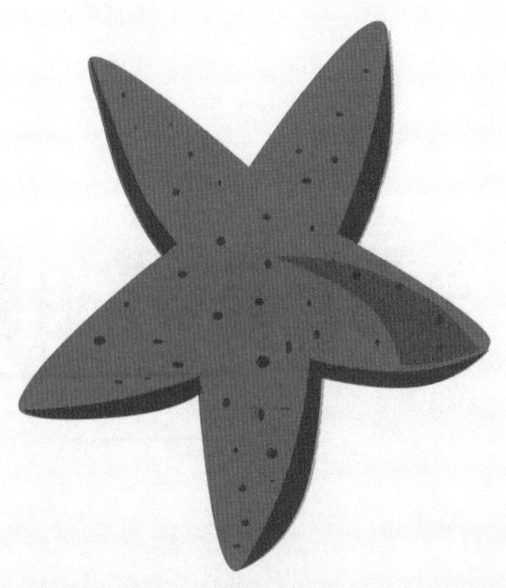

ABC-123

READ the words in the word box. Then WRITE them in alphabetical order.

dictionary	stoplight	arrive	sidewalk
definition	adjective	attempt	describe

1. ____________________
2. ____________________
3. ____________________
4. ____________________
5. ____________________
6. ____________________
7. ____________________
8. ____________________

ABCDEFGHIJKLMNOPQRSTUVWXYZ

Pick the One

CIRCLE the correct part of speech for each word.

1. **beautiful**	adjective	noun	verb
2. **enemy**	adjective	noun	verb
3. **succeed**	adjective	noun	verb
4. **syllable**	adjective	noun	verb
5. **describe**	adjective	noun	verb
6. **tiny**	adjective	noun	verb
7. **arrive**	adjective	noun	verb
8. **bathroom**	adjective	noun	verb

Same or Opposite?

READ each word pair. CIRCLE if they are the same or opposites.

1. giant	tiny	same	opposite
2. fail	lose	same	opposite
3. beautiful	pretty	same	opposite
4. attempt	quit	same	opposite
5. nap	sleep	same	opposite
6. arrive	come	same	opposite
7. sunrise	sunset	same	opposite
8. everything	nothing	same	opposite

Criss Cross

WRITE the word for each clue in the grid.

adjective describe succeed syllable verb

Across

3. To win
4. An action word

Down

1. To make a word picture
2. A word that describes something
3. One beat of a word

1 2 3 4

Word List

READ the words and their meanings.

braid—brayd 1. *noun* hair in a rope-like style 2. *verb* to put hair in a rope-like style

cheek—cheek *noun* the side of your face between your nose and your ear. You have two cheeks.

eye·brow—I-brow *noun* the strip of hair above your eye

freck·les—FREHK-lz *noun* spots on skin from the sun

frown—frown 1. *noun* a sad or mad face, the opposite of a smile 2. *verb* to make a sad or mad face

mouth—mowth 1. *noun* the hole in your face where you put your food 2. *verb* to talk with your lips without making a sound

stom·ach—STUHM-uhk *noun* your tummy, or belly, that tells you when you're hungry or full

throat—throht 1. *noun* the front part of your neck 2. *noun* the tube inside your neck that goes to your stomach and your lungs

Match the Meaning

WRITE the words next to their definitions. LOOK at the word box for help.

braid	eyebrow	frown	stomach
cheek	freckles	mouth	throat

1. ____________________ the opposite of *smile*
2. ____________________ the front of your neck
3. ____________________ where your lips and teeth are
4. ____________________ a rope-like ponytail
5. ____________________ spots on your skin
6. ____________________ the strip of hair above your eye
7. ____________________ the place where food goes after you put it in your mouth
8. ____________________ the side of your face below your eye

Criss Cross

READ the clues. FILL IN the boxes with the right word for each clue.

Across

3. The front of your neck
5. The side of your face

Down

1. The opposite of a smile
2. Your tummy
4. Spots on skin

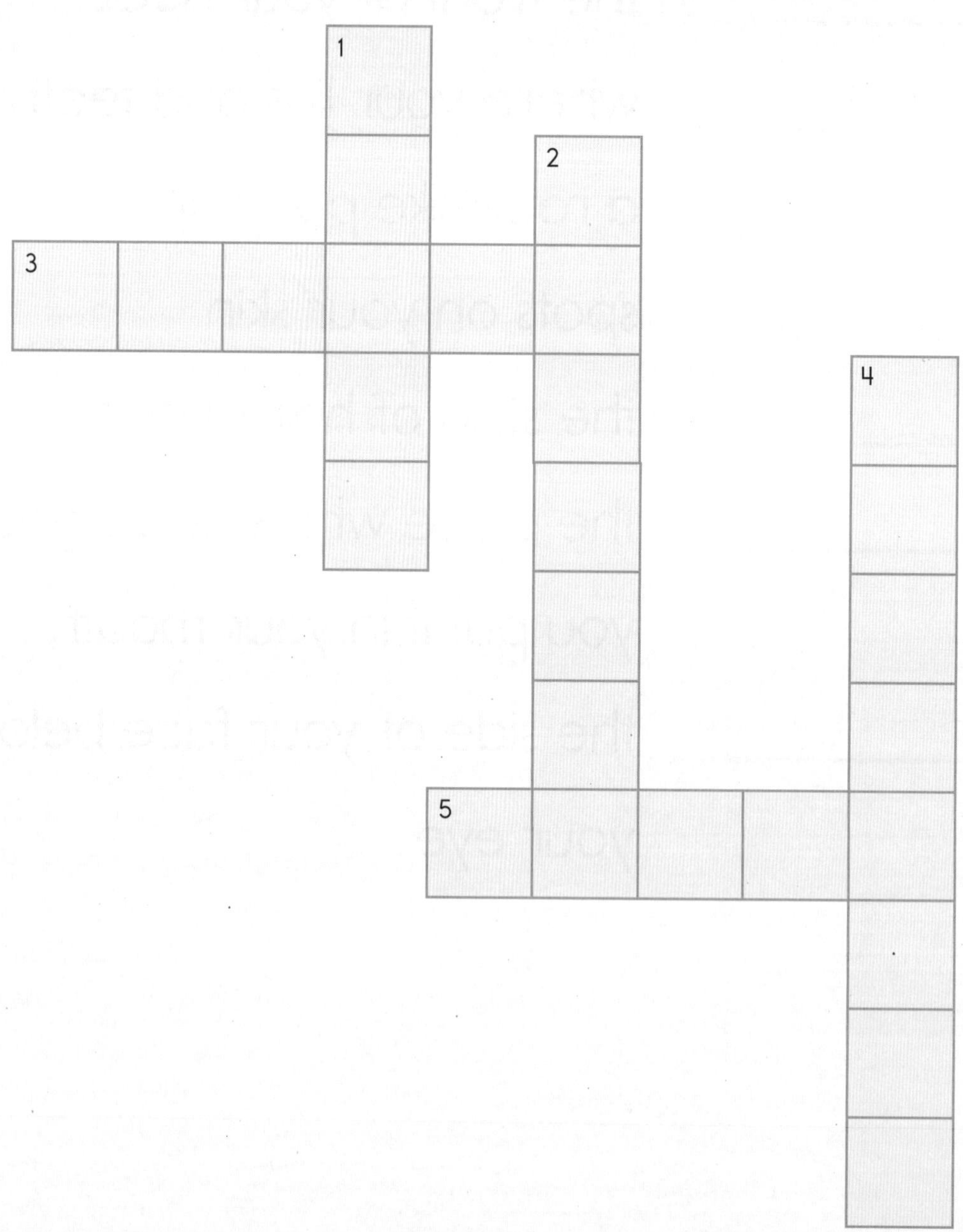

Cross Out

CROSS OUT the words that are **not** parts of the body.

1. finger	throat	verb	definition
2. sunrise	fail	freckles	mouth
3. arm	sidewalk	stomach	attempt
4. syllable	eyebrow	giant	cheek

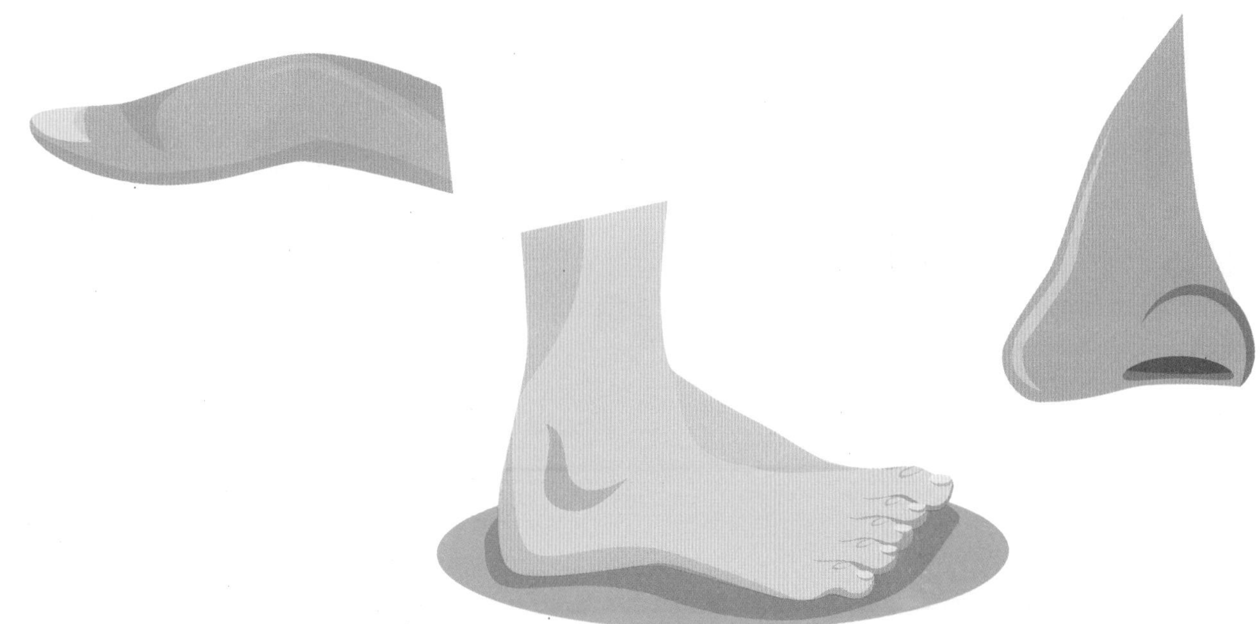

Find the Friend

READ the clues. Then WRITE the friend's name under each picture.

Doug has freckles on his cheeks.

Carly has two braids.

Tyara is frowning.

Jordan has the biggest eyebrows.

Connor has his mouth open.

Who am I?

1 ______ 2 ______ 3 ______ 4 ______ 5 ______

Blank Out

FILL IN the blanks with the correct words for each part of the picture.

1. ______________________

2. ______________________

3. ______________________

4. ______________________

5. ______________________

6. ______________________

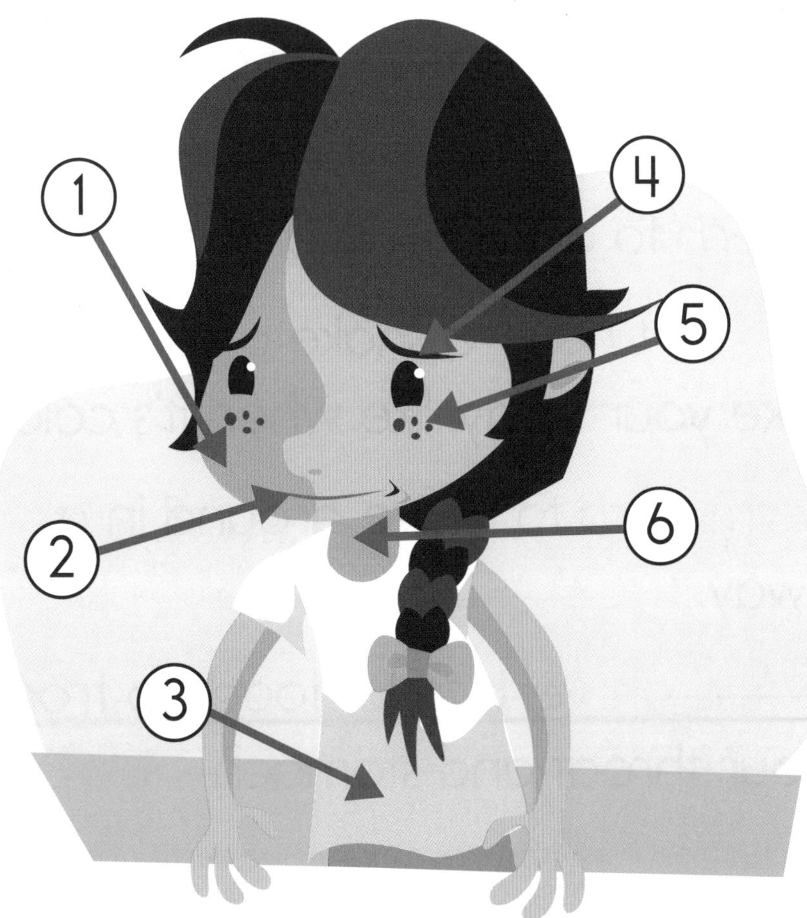

Word List

READ the words and their meanings.

breathe—breeth *verb* to take in air through your mouth or nose

chew—choo *verb* to use your teeth to bite food in your mouth

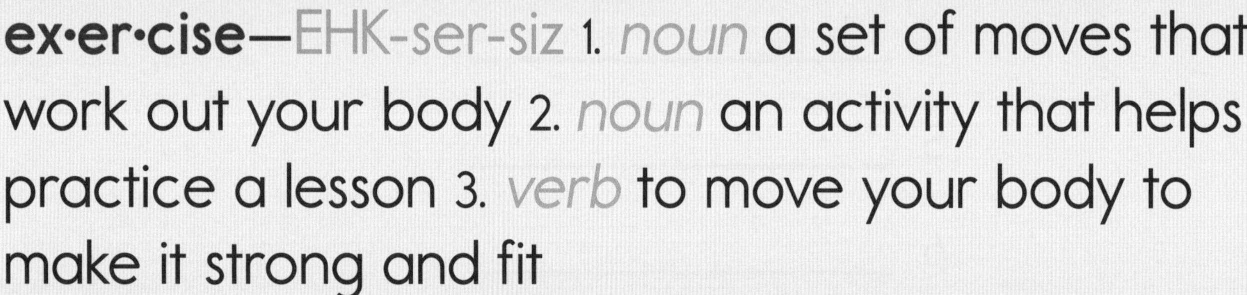

ex·er·cise—EHK-ser-siz 1. *noun* a set of moves that work out your body 2. *noun* an activity that helps practice a lesson 3. *verb* to move your body to make it strong and fit

kneel—neel *verb* to get down on your knees

reach—reech 1. *verb* to put out your hand to get something 2. *verb* to arrive at a place

shiv·er—SHIHV-er 1. *noun* a shake of the body 2. *verb* to shake your body, like when it's cold

squirm—skwerm *verb* to move around in a twisty-turny way

swal·low—SWAHL-oh *verb* to let food go from your mouth into your throat and stomach

Match the Meaning

WRITE the words next to their definitions. LOOK at the word box for help.

breathe	exercise	reach	squirm
chew	kneel	shiver	swallow

1. ____________________ to twist and turn
2. ____________________ to get down on your knees
3. ____________________ to shake
4. ____________________ to bite something in your mouth
5. ____________________ to put food down your throat
6. ____________________ to put out your hand
7. ____________________ to suck in air
8. ____________________ to help your body stay in shape

Right or Wrong?

UNDERLINE the sentence that matches the picture.

1.

Maddy is chewing gum.

Maddy is choosing gum.

2.

Mr. Santos is exiting.

Mr. Santos is exercising.

3.

Ty kicks on the ground.

Ty kneels on the ground.

4.

The baby reaches for her bottle.

The baby reads for her bottle.

Blank Out

FINISH each sentence with a word from the word box.

breathe	exercise	reach	squirming
chew	kneel	shiver	swallow

1. It was so cold out, I started to ______________.
2. Mom goes to the gym to ______________.
3. Ivan is too short to______________ the sink.
4. Aunt Didi always tells me to stop ______________ and sit still.
5. My throat was so sore, it hurt to ______________.
6. I have to ______________ down to look under my bed.
7. If you don't have teeth, how do you ______________?
8. When I get nervous, my mom always tell me, "Just ______________."

Dictionary Dare

LOOK UP the words in a dictionary. Then WRITE the word from the word box that means something similar.

beautiful	chew	reach	squirm
breathe	enemy	shiver	swallow

1. wriggle ____________________
2. inhale ____________________
3. gorgeous ____________________
4. stretch ____________________
5. quake ____________________
6. gulp ____________________
7. gnaw ____________________
8. foe ____________________

DICTIONARY

Word Pictures

COLOR the spaces that show **verbs.**

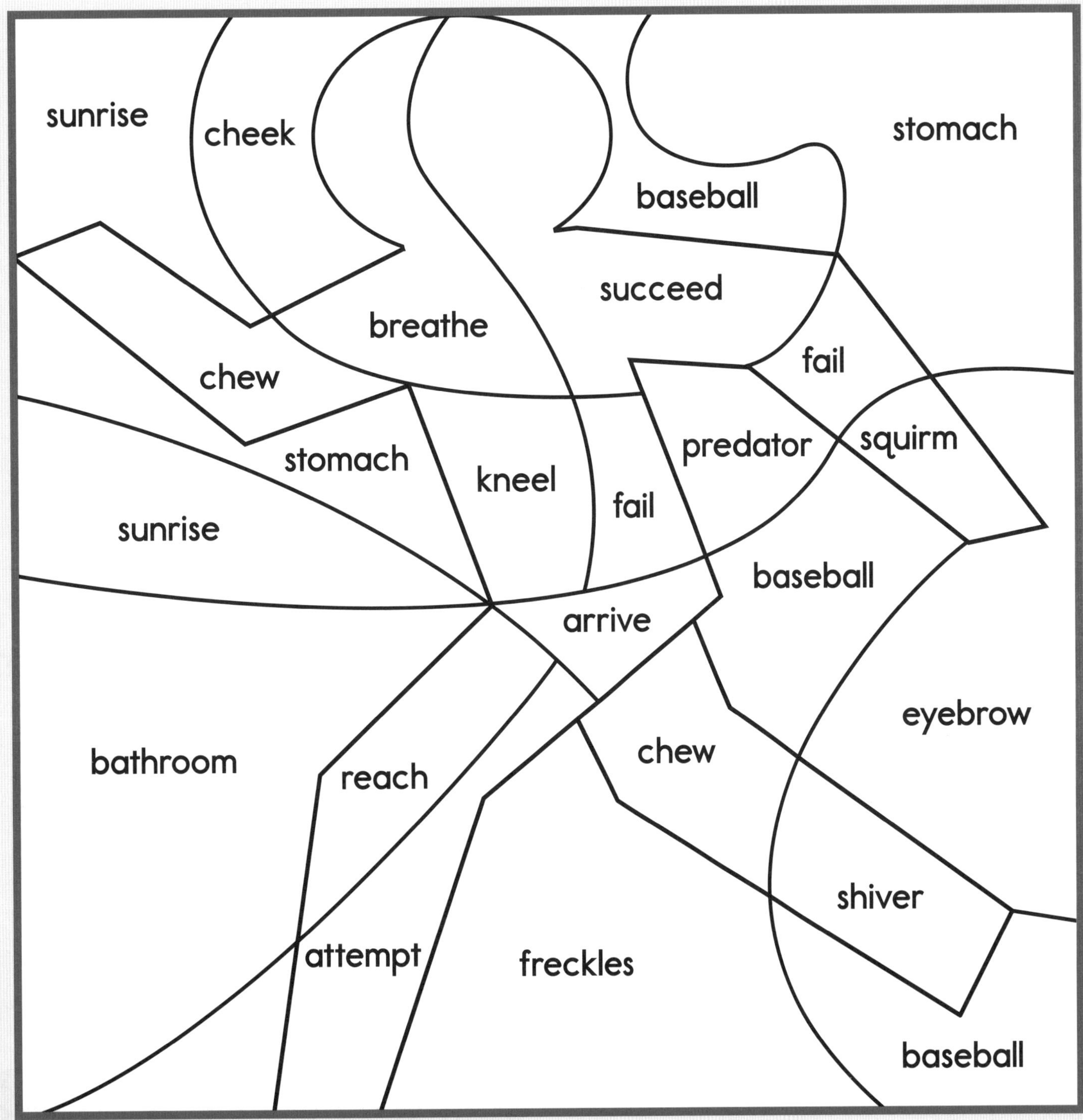

Word List

READ the words and their meanings.

ac·tor—AK-ter *noun* a person who acts on stage or screen

a·dult—uh-DUHLT 1. *noun* a person who is grown up 2. *adjective* fully grown

bar·ber—BAHR-ber *noun* a person who cuts hair

cap·tain—KAP-tihn 1. *noun* the leader of a sports team 2. *noun* the leader of a ship or airplane 3. *noun* the leader of firefighters, police, or the military

crowd—krowd *noun* a lot of people all together

may·or—MAY-er *noun* the leader of a town or city

neigh·bor—NAY-ber *noun* a person who lives next door to or near you

teen—teen *noun* a person who is older than a child but younger than an adult

Match the Meaning

WRITE the words next to their definitions. LOOK at the word box for help.

actor	barber	crowd	neighbor
adult	captain	mayor	teen

1. ____________________ older than a child, but younger than an adult
2. ____________________ someone who is all grown up
3. ____________________ a large group of people
4. ____________________ the star of a movie
5. ____________________ someone who cuts your hair
6. ____________________ the leader of the city
7. ____________________ the head of the team
8. ____________________ a person in the next house

Finish the Story

READ the story. FILL IN the blanks with words from the box.

HINT: Read the whole story before you fill in the blanks.

actor	barber	captain	crowd	mayor	neighbor

Big Game? Big Deal!

Yesterday, I saw a ________ (1) of about one hundred people in front of City Hall. One of them was Mr. Tilcio, the ________ (2) of Folksburg. He gave a big medal to Sara Wells. Sara is the ________ (3) of our soccer team. Mr. Tilcio also gave a medal to Rick Randall, the ________ (4) who stars in Folksburg Follies. But he gave the biggest medal to Mr. Sateen, the ________ (5) who cuts my dad's hair! I couldn't believe it. But my next-door ________ (6) told me that Mr. Sateen saved a baby from a fire. Wow!

Criss Cross

READ the clues. FILL IN the boxes with the right word for each clue.

Across

2. A 15-year-old
4. A grown up
5. A haircutter

Down

1. Someone who lives next door
3. Leader of a town or city

1
2
3
4
5

Find the Friend

READ the clues. Then WRITE the friend's name under each picture.

Cyrus is a barber.

Leena is a teen.

Bart is an actor.

Serena is captain of her team.

Hunter is in a crowd.

Who am I?

________ 1 ________ 2 ________ 3 ________ 4 ________ 5

Maze Crazy!

DRAW a line through the words for **people** to help the boy get to the crowd.

Start at the green arrow.

Word List

READ the words and their meanings.

a·gree—uh-GREE 1. *verb* to think the same way as someone else 2. *verb* to say yes to something

bor·row—BAHR-oh *verb* when someone allows you to take something for a short time, then give it back

ex·plain—ihk-SPLAYN *verb* to tell or teach someone about something

for·give—fer-GIHV *verb* to stop being mad and make up after a fight with someone

fright·en—FRIT-uhn *verb* to scare somebody

re·spect—rih-SPEHKT 1. *noun* a feeling that you honor someone 2. *verb* to honor and show consideration for someone

share—shehr 1. *noun* one person's part of something that can be split 2. *verb* to let other people use your things or eat your food 3. *verb* to use something with other people

sug·gest—suhg-JEHST 1. *verb* to hint at something 2. *verb* to give an idea or plan as an option

Match the Meaning

WRITE the words next to their definitions. LOOK at the word box for help.

agree	explain	frighten	share
borrow	forgive	respect	suggest

1. ____________________ to honor someone
2. ____________________ to let someone use your toys
3. ____________________ to check out a book from the library
4. ____________________ to make someone understand
5. ____________________ to offer an idea
6. ____________________ to say yes
7. ____________________ to scare someone
8. ____________________ to make up and forget a fight

Right or Wrong?

UNDERLINE the sentence that matches the picture.

1.

Tom respects Donna.

Tom does not respect Donna.

2.

Jean shares her pizza with Mike.

Jean won't share her pizza with Mike.

3.

Sondra frightens Neal.

Sondra forgets Neal.

4.

Neal forgives Sondra.

Neal suggests Sondra.

Dictionary Dare

LOOK UP the words in a dictionary. Then WRITE the word from the word box that means the **opposite.**

explain	**enemy**	**agree**	**respect**
beautiful	**share**	**borrow**	**neighbor**

1. loan ____________________
2. confuse ____________________
3. disrespect ____________________
4. hideous ____________________
5. hoard ____________________
6. foreigner ____________________
7. ally ____________________
8. disagree ____________________

Blank Out

FINISH each sentence with a word from the word box.

agree	explain	frighten	shares
borrow	forgive	respect	suggests

1. Miles didn't understand the rules, so I tried to ____________.
2. I will never ____________ Sylvia for calling me a geek!
3. It's important to ____________ the police.
4. Donna ____________ that we play in the tree house today.
5. Mom thinks I should go to bed, but I don't ____________.
6. Taffy never ____________ her popcorn at the movies.
7. Bill tried to ____________ me with his mask, but I wasn't scared.
8. Can I ____________ your video game for a few days?

Cross Out

CROSS OUT the words that are NOT verbs.

1. enemy	beautiful	forgive	attempt
2. frighten	scary	exercise	definition
3. verb	share	throat	borrow
4. respect	sidewalk	suggest	idea

Dictionary Dare

READ the guide words. CIRCLE the word in each row that comes between them.

1. **giggle → girl**	giddy	give	ginger
2. **outline → ovation**	outsmart	outlaw	outcry
3. **spike → spirit**	spindle	spice	spite
4. **attract → author**	auxiliary	aunt	autumn
5. **count → court**	counsel	courtship	country
6. **noon → not**	noise	north	notch
7. **weak → weave**	we	wear	wealth
8. **incline → increase**	incomplete	incense	incite

417 giggle • girl

giggle \'gig-əl\ *vb* giggled; gigg
laugh with repeated short c
vt: to utter with a gigg

Match the Meaning

DRAW a line to match the words that mean the same thing.

1. scare	predator
2. succeed	stomach
3. hunter	arrive
4. try	win
5. meaning	frighten
6. come	shiver
7. tummy	definition
8. shake	attempt

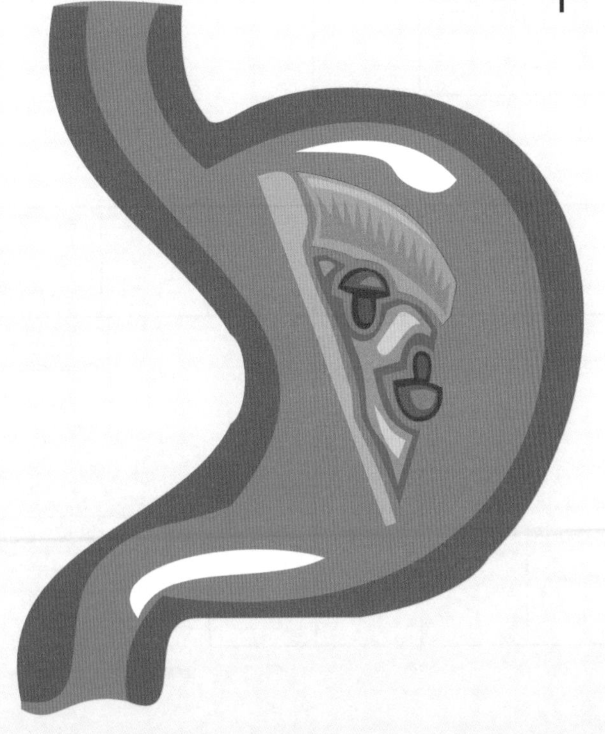

Criss Cross

READ the clues. FILL IN the boxes with the right word for each clue.

chew crowd explain squirm suggest swallow

Across

1. Offer an idea
3. Bite on something
4. Teach or tell something
5. Lots of people

Down

1. Put something down your throat
2. Twist and turn

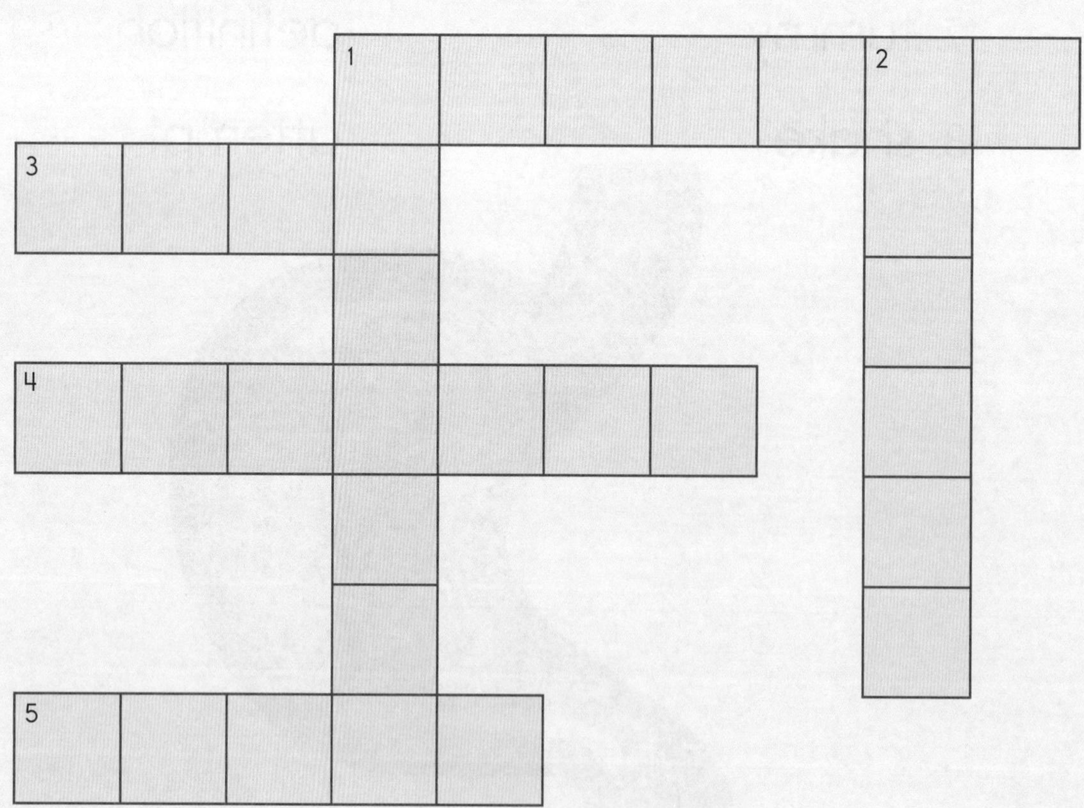

Word Pictures

COLOR the spaces that show words for **parts of the body**.

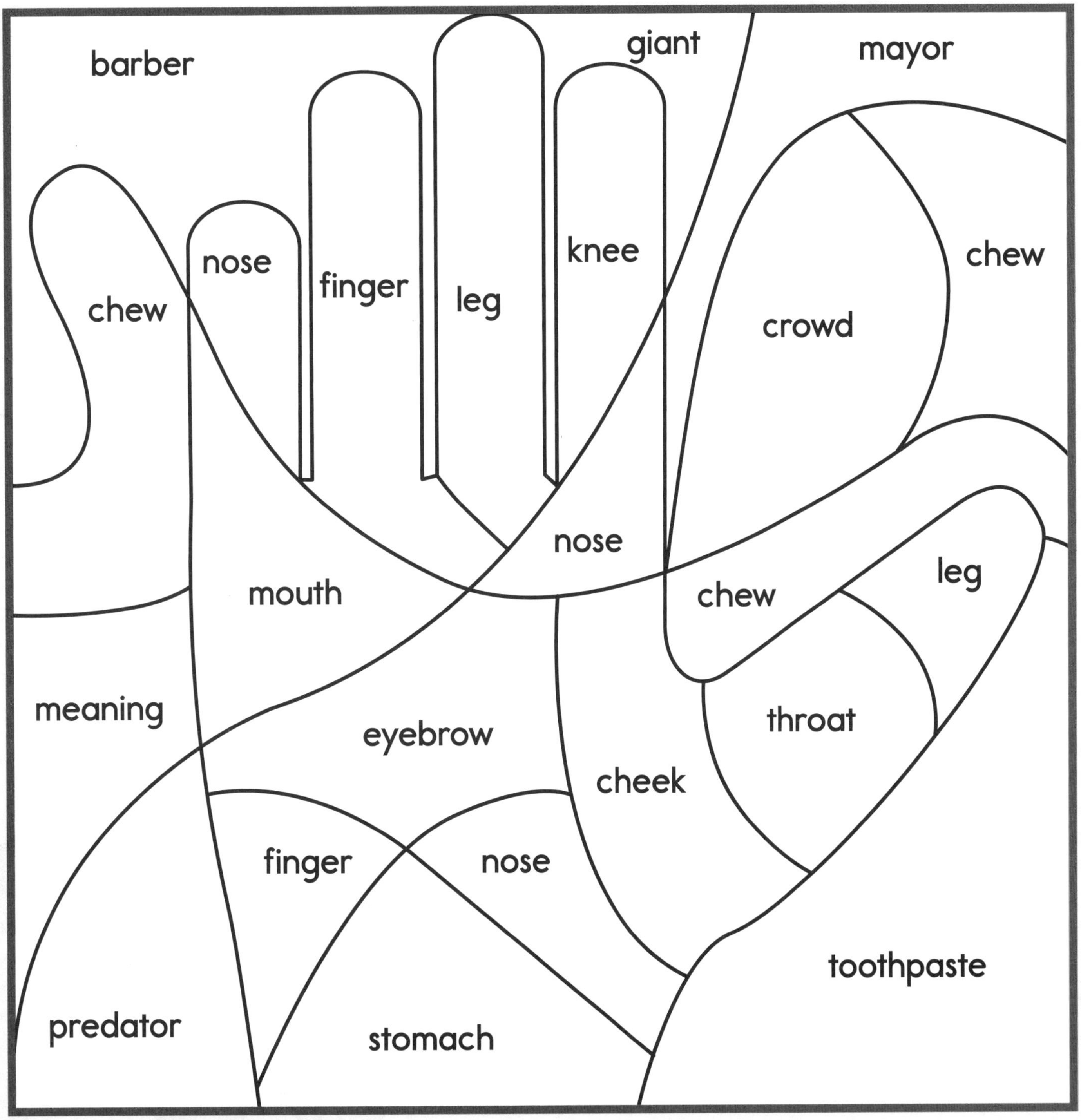

Family

Word List

READ the words and their meanings.

aunt—ant 1. *noun* the sister of your mother or father 2. *noun* the wife of your uncle

broth·er—BRUH*TH*-er *noun* a boy whose mother and father have another child

grand·fa·ther—GRAND-fah-*ther* 1. *noun* the father of your father or mother 2. *noun* your grandmother's husband

grand·moth·er—GRAND-muh*th*-er 1. *noun* the mother of your father or mother 2. *noun* your grandfather's wife

hus·band—HUHZ-buhnd *noun* a man who is married

sis·ter—SIHS-ter *noun* a girl whose mother and father have another child

un·cle—UHNG-kuhl 1. *noun* the brother of your mother or father 2. *noun* the husband of your aunt

wife—wif *noun* a woman who is married

Match the Meaning

WRITE the words next to their definitions. LOOK at the word box for help.

aunt	husband	brother	sister
grandfather	uncle	grandmother	wife

1. ____________________ a man who is married
2. ____________________ your grandmother's husband
3. ____________________ another child (girl) of your parents
4. ____________________ your aunt's husband
5. ____________________ a woman who is married
6. ____________________ another child (boy) of your parents
7. ____________________ your uncle's wife
8. ____________________ your grandfather's wife

Criss Cross

READ the clues. FILL IN the boxes with the right word for each clue.

HINT: You might have to look up some words in the clues.

Across

2. Your parent's father
3. A male spouse

Down

1. A male sibling

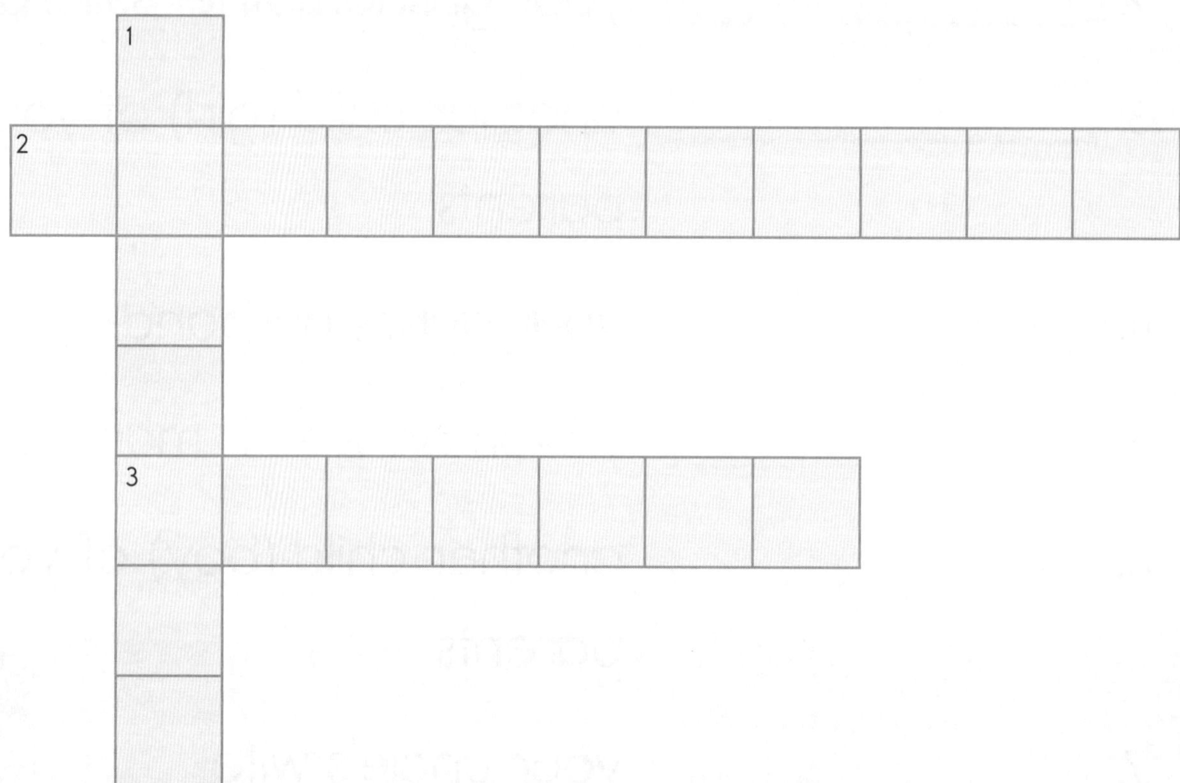

What do these words mean?

parent ____________________

sibling ____________________

spouse ____________________

Blank Out

FILL IN the blanks for each part of the family tree with the words in the word box. Use each word just once.

aunt	brother	grandfather	husband
uncle	sister	grandmother	wife

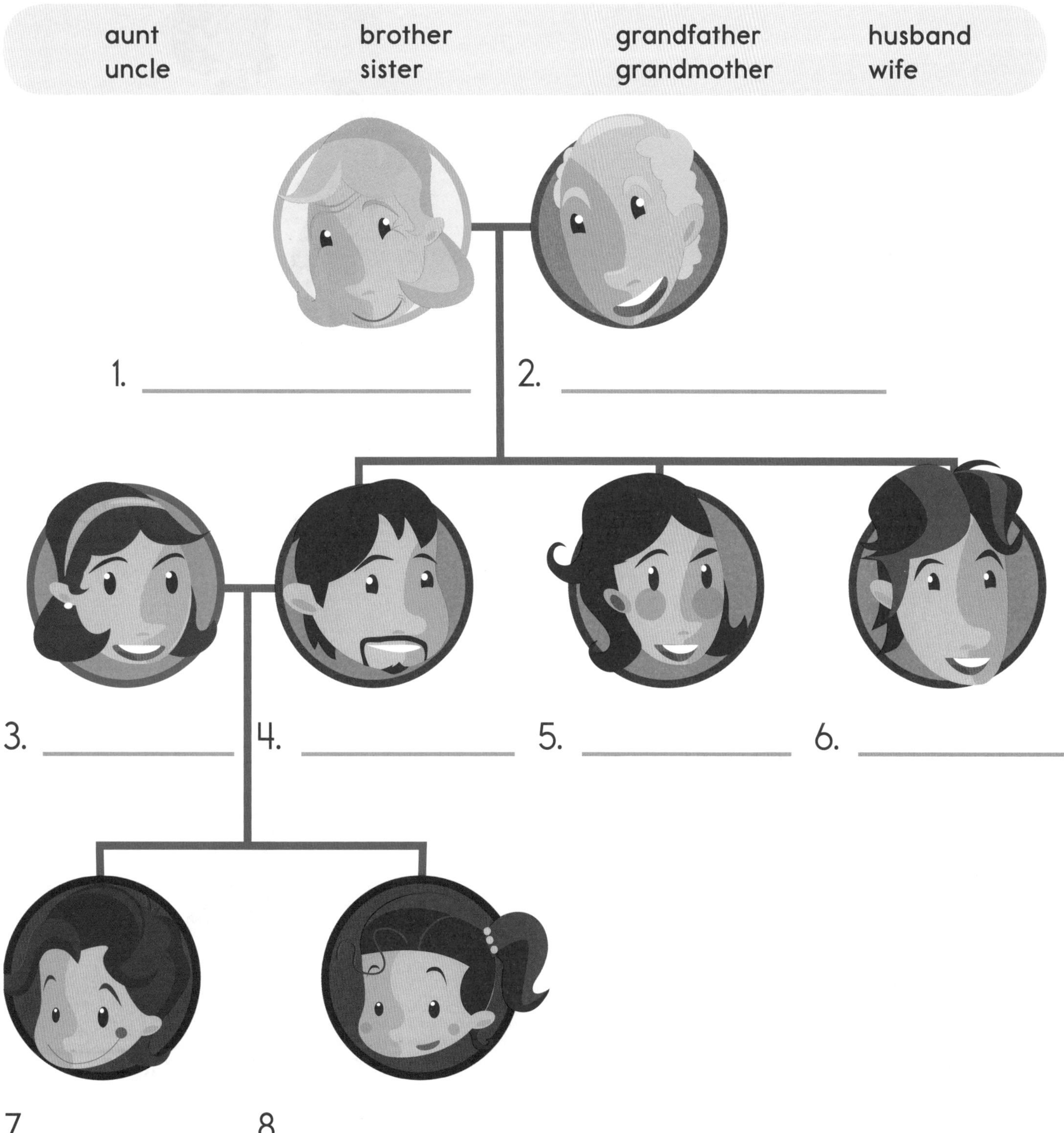

Right or Wrong?

UNDERLINE the sentence that matches the picture.

1.

Jen is Peter's brother.

Jen is Peter's sister.

2.

Stan is Sheila's husband.

Stan is Sheila's wife.

3.

Greg is Karl's grandfather.

Karl is Greg's grandfather.

4.

This is my uncle.

This is my aunt.

Cross Out

CROSS OUT the words that do **not** name family members.

1. grandfather	daughter	frighten	frown
2. son	bathroom	suggest	sister
3. predator	agree	mother	aunt
4. respect	uncle	brother	elephant

Word List

READ the words and their meanings.

base•ment—BAS-muhnt *noun* a room or rooms under a house or building

clos•et—CLAHZ-iht *noun* a very small room to keep clothes and shoes

com•fort•a•ble—KUHM-fer-tuh-buhl 1. *adjective* very soft or easy 2. *adjective* with no pain or fear

emp•ty—EHMP-tee *adjective* having nothing inside

fa•vor•ite—FA-ver-iht *adjective* the one that is liked the most

lawn—lawn *noun* the grass around a house

paint—peynt 1. *noun* color that can be put on walls or objects 2. *verb* to put color on something using paint

re•frig•er•a•tor—rih-FRIHJ-uh-ray-ter *noun* a metal box that keeps food and drinks cold

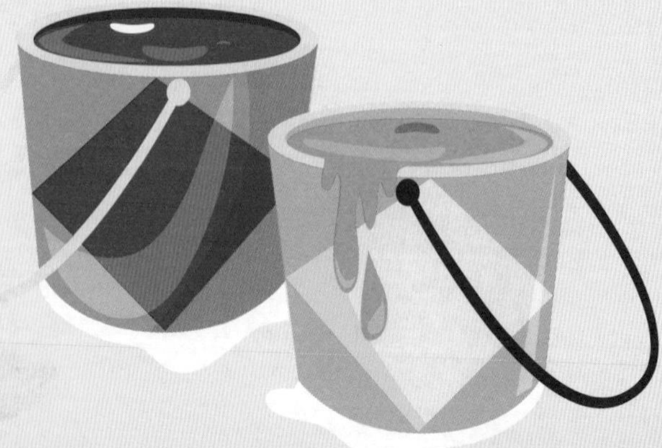

Match the Meaning

WRITE the words next to their definitions. LOOK at the word box for help.

basement	comfortable	favorite	paint
closet	empty	lawn	refrigerator

1. ______________ the opposite of *full*
2. ______________ a room just for coats and shoes
3. ______________ the place under the house
4. ______________ the one you like the best
5. ______________ where you put food to keep it cold
6. ______________ what makes the color on the walls
7. ______________ nice and warm and soft
8. ______________ a yard full of grass

Finish the Story

READ the story. FILL IN the blanks with words from the word box.

comfortable   empty   favorite   lawn   refrigerator

Bad Day

What a bad day! When I was hungry, the

________________ (1) was ________________ (2).

There was nothing to eat! When I turned on the

TV, my ________________ (3) show was over.

So I went to take a nap. Just when I got

________________ (4) on my bed, my brother started

to mow the ________________ (5).

It was too loud to sleep!

I hope tomorrow is better.

Criss Cross

READ the clues. FILL IN the boxes with the right word for each clue.

Across

3. A room for clothes
4. Nothing inside
5. A grassy place

Down

1. Put color on walls
2. The lowest room

1
2
3
4
5

Right or Wrong?

UNDERLINE the sentence that matches the picture.

1.

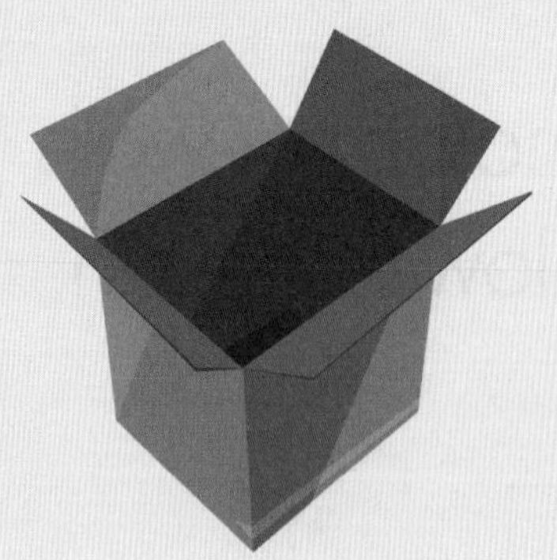

The box is empty.

The box is easy.

2.

The lawn is green.

The lane is green.

3.

That chair looks compatible.

That chair looks comfortable.

4.

That's Dipti's favorite doll.

That's Dipti's flavored doll.

Maze Crazy!

DRAW a line through the **adjectives** to get to the smiley face.
Start at the yellow arrow.

Word List

READ the words and their meanings.

ba•nan•a—buh-NAN-uh *noun* a long, curved fruit with a yellow peel

bread—brehd *noun* a baked food made with flour that's used for toast and sandwiches

car•rot—KEHR-uht *noun* a skinny orange vegetable that grows underground

fruit—froot 1. *noun* a food that can be juicy and sweet, like an apple 2. *noun* the part of a plant that holds the seeds

spread—sprehd 1. *verb* to put something all over, like jam on bread 2. *verb* to open wide

stuffed—stuhft *adjective* filled with something, like a pillow is filled with fluff, or a belly is filled with food

taste—tayst 1. *noun* the way a food is salty, sweet, or icky 2. *verb* to put a bit of food in your mouth to see if you like it

veg•e•ta•ble—VEHJ-tuh-buhl *noun* a food that comes from a plant's leaves or roots

Match the Meaning

WRITE the words next to their definitions. LOOK at the word box for help.

banana	carrot	spread	taste
bread	fruit	stuffed	vegetable

1. ____________ to try a bite of food
2. ____________ an orange vegetable
3. ____________ a fruit with a yellow peel
4. ____________ the leaves or roots of a plant that you can eat
5. ____________ very full of something
6. ____________ part of the plant that has seeds
7. ____________ to put something all over
8. ____________ food that turns into toast

Find the Friend

READ the clues. Then WRITE the friend's name under each picture.

Shama is eating a fruit.

Mai has bananas on her shirt.

Crispin is eating vegetables.

Val has carrots on her shirt.

Lyle is eating bread.

Who am I?

1 ________ 2 ________ 3 ________ 4 ________ 5 ________

Dictionary Dare

LOOK UP these foods in a dictionary. Then CIRCLE if it's a fruit or a vegetable.

1. potato fruit vegetable
2. spinach fruit vegetable
3. cherry fruit vegetable
4. pear fruit vegetable
5. lettuce fruit vegetable
6. broccoli fruit vegetable
7. peach fruit vegetable
8. onion fruit vegetable

Blank Out

FINISH each sentence with a word from the word box.

banana	carrots	spread	taste
bread	fruit	stuffed	vegetables

1. Cartoon rabbits are always chomping on ____________.
2. I love fish sticks, but Amy hates the way they ____________.
3. Nadine helped Mom ____________ frosting on the cake.
4. Isaac ate nothing but ____________ and butter all day.
5. A tomato is really a ____________ because it has seeds.
6. We were all ____________ after Thanksgiving dinner.
7. Chloe peeled the ____________ for the monkey to eat.
8. Saul eats his meat, but no leafy ____________.

Word Pictures

COLOR the spaces that show words for **food** and **eating.**

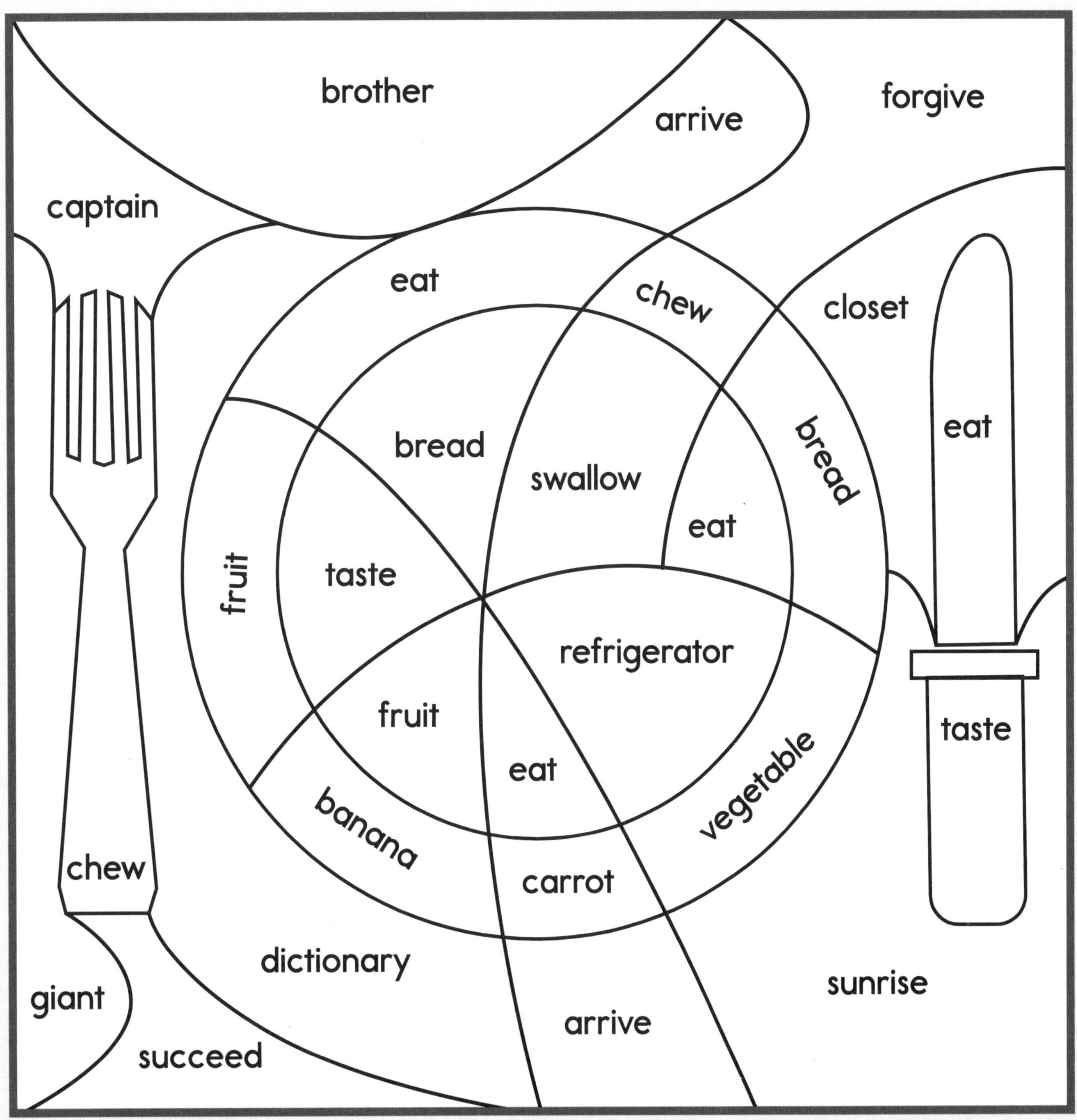

Pick the One

CIRCLE the correct part of speech for each word.

1. **freckles**	adjective	noun	verb
2. **sidewalk**	adjective	noun	verb
3. **favorite**	adjective	noun	verb
4. **agree**	adjective	noun	verb
5. **carrot**	adjective	noun	verb
6. **suggest**	adjective	noun	verb
7. **comfortable**	adjective	noun	verb
8. **fail**	adjective	noun	verb

Criss Cross

READ the clues. FILL IN the boxes with the right word for each clue.

enemy freckles frown spread teen uncle

Across

3. Spots on your skin
6. Not an adult or a child

Down

1. Your mother's brother
2. The opposite of *smile*
4. Put jam on bread
5. The opposite of *friend*

Cross Out

CROSS OUT the words that have more than two syllables.

1. beautiful	empty	braid	comfortable
2. predator	enemy	bathroom	toothpaste
3. meaning	adjective	freckles	everywhere
4. grandmother	throat	definition	lighthouse

Dictionary Dare

LOOK UP the words in a dictionary. Then WRITE the word from the word box that means the same thing.

actor	explain	frighten	taste
comfortable	forgive	frown	teen

1. pardon ____________
2. flavor ____________
3. grimace ____________
4. terrify ____________
5. adolescent ____________
6. thespian ____________
7. clarify ____________
8. snug ____________

Did you know that you can also use a book called a *thesaurus* to see a list of words that mean the same thing?

Word List

READ the words and their meanings.

beast—beest *noun* an animal or other creature that is not human and doesn't act human

crea·ture—KREE-cher *noun* a living animal or human

feath·er—FEH*TH*-er *noun* one of the soft pieces that cover a bird's body and wings

flight—flit 1. *noun* a trip through the air, like on a plane 2. *noun* a fast getaway, escape

flock—flahk 1. *noun* a group of birds 2. *verb* to make a group, like a flock of birds

herd—herd 1. *noun* a group of land animals like cows 2. *verb* to make a group of animals go somewhere

tame—taym 1. *adjective* quiet, safe, and nice 2. *verb* to make a wild animal be nice to humans

wild—wild 1. *adjective* not tame, not safe, not able to live with humans 2. *noun* a place where people don't live, like the jungle

Match the Meaning

WRITE the words next to their definitions. LOOK at the word box for help.

beast	feather	flock	tame
creature	flight	herd	wild

1. ____________________ a group of birds
2. ____________________ unsafe, not tame
3. ____________________ a creature that isn't human
4. ____________________ an air trip
5. ____________________ a human or an animal
6. ____________________ not a danger
7. ____________________ what you pluck from a bird
8. ____________________ a bunch of cows

Finish the Story

READ the story. FILL IN the blanks with words from the word box.

beasts	feathers	flocks	herds	tame	wild

A Trip to Africa

Africa is home to many ______________, like lions.
1

They're cats, but not like the ______________ kitties
2

we have in our homes. Lions are ______________
3

predators that may kill humans. In the skies above Africa, you can see ______________ of beautiful
4

birds with colorful ______________. You might also
5

find giant ______________
6

of elephants walking for miles to find water.

Criss Cross

READ the clues. FILL IN the boxes with the right word for each clue.

Across

1. Birds that fly together
3. A crowd of cows
4. A sky trip

Down

2. A living being
4. It's on a bird's wing

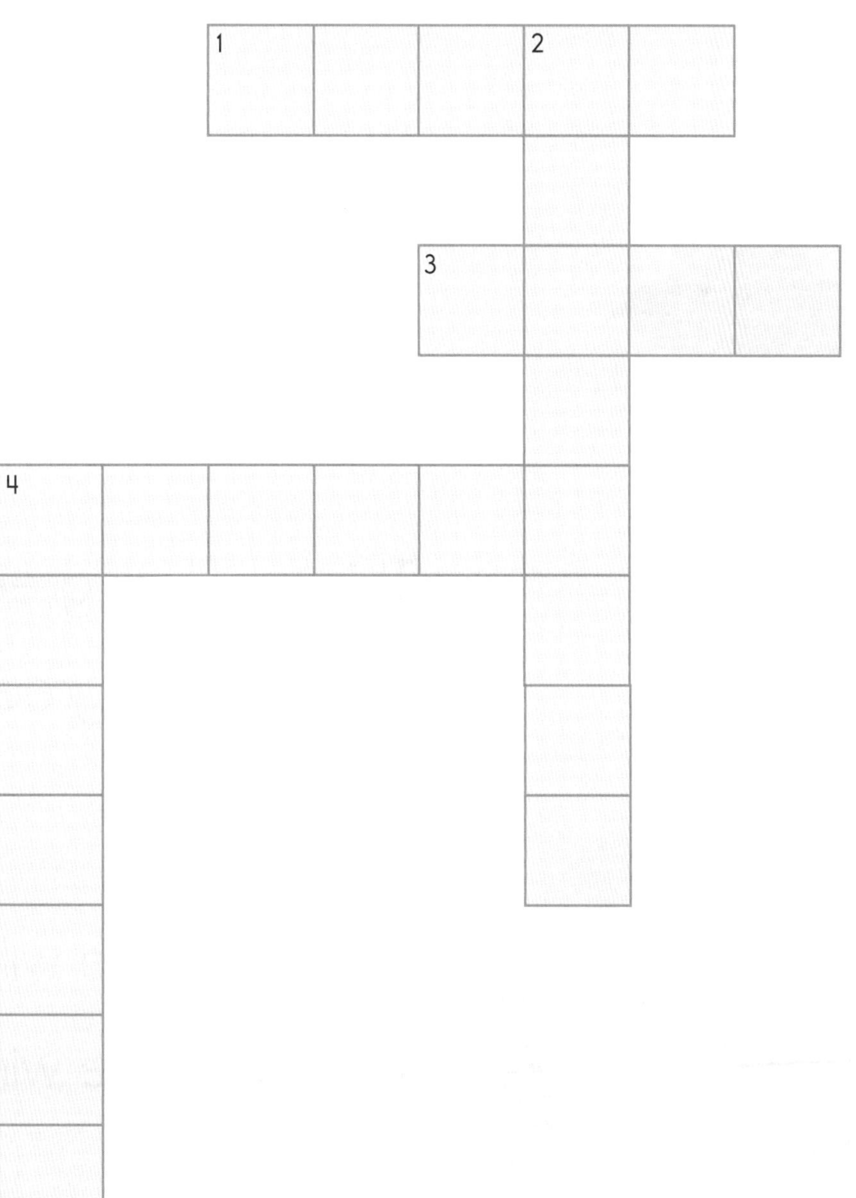

Right or Wrong?

UNDERLINE the sentence that matches the picture.

1.

A herd of geese flew by.

A flock of geese flew by.

2.

Mr. Tibbles is tame.

Mr. Tibbles is wild.

3.

This bird has green fathers.

This bird has green feathers.

4.

We are in the wild.

We are in the wind.

Word Pictures

COLOR the spaces that show words for **parts of animals.**

HINT: Don't forget to look up any words you don't know.

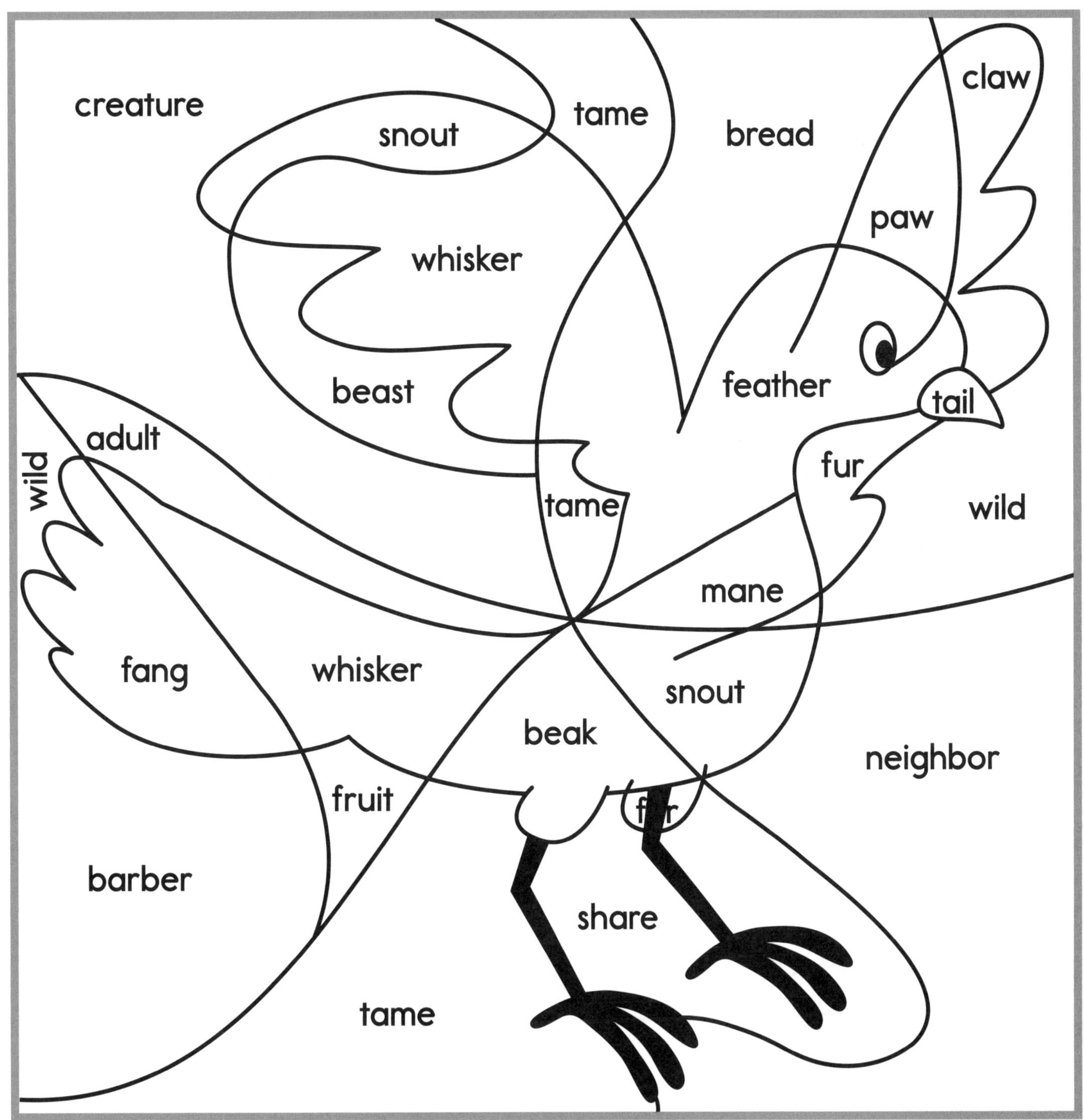

Word List

READ the words and their meanings.

an•ten•nae—an-TEHN-ee *noun* two thin feelers that help a bug sense the world

but•ter•fly—BUHT-er-fli *noun* an insect with large wings that are sometimes very colorful

cat•er•pil•lar—KAT-er-pihl-er *noun* an insect like a worm that turns into a butterfly or a moth

co•coon—kuh-KOON *noun* a silk wrap or bag made by an insect to keep its body or eggs safe. A caterpillar goes into a cocoon while turning into a moth.

hive—hiv *noun* a nest of bees, where they make honey

in•sect—IHN-sehkt *noun* a small creature with no backbone (a bug)

lar•va—LAHR-vuh *noun* a baby insect that looks like a worm. A caterpillar is the larva of a butterfly.

sting—stihng 1. *noun* the feeling of a bug bite or pin prick 2. *verb* to use a stinger or other sharp object to break someone's skin

Match the Meaning

WRITE the words in the box next to their definitions.

antennae	caterpillar	hive	larva
butterfly	cocoon	insect	sting

1. ____________________ a safe, silky wrap
2. ____________________ a bug
3. ____________________ feelers
4. ____________________ the larva of a moth or butterfly
5. ____________________ a sharp pain
6. ____________________ an insect with big wings
7. ____________________ a baby bug
8. ____________________ where bees live

Find the Friend

READ the clues. Then WRITE the friend's name under each picture.

Binky is in a cocoon.

Slinky is a caterpillar.

Tinky lives in a hive.

Pinky is a butterfly.

Dinky has purple antennae.

Who am I?

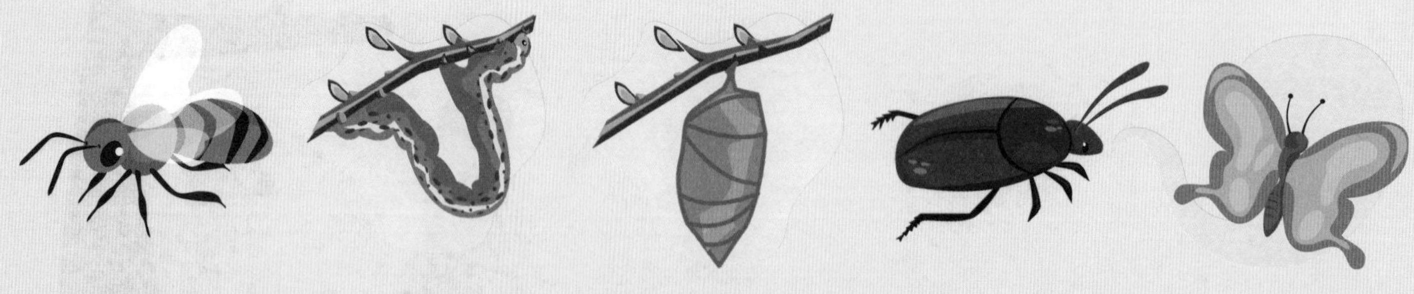

________ 1 ________ 2 ________ 3 ________ 4 ________ 5

Blank Out

FINISH each sentence with a word from the word box.

antennae	caterpillars	hives	larva
butterflies	cocoon	insects	sting

1. My arm still hurts from that bee ______________.
2. Some bugs use their ______________ to smell.
3. Teejay draws ______________ with giant, beautiful wings.
4. That wormy maggot is the ______________ of a fly.
5. Bears get honey from bee ______________ they find in the trees.
6. Some insects put their eggs in a ______________ to keep them safe.
7. I don't kill ______________ because one day they'll be butterflies!
8. Nate loves nature, but he hates ______________ that bite.

Criss Cross

READ the clues. FILL IN the boxes with the right word for each clue.

Across

2. A bug
5. A bug's feelers
6. A nest of bees

Down

1. A sharp pain
3. A safe, silky place
4. A baby bug

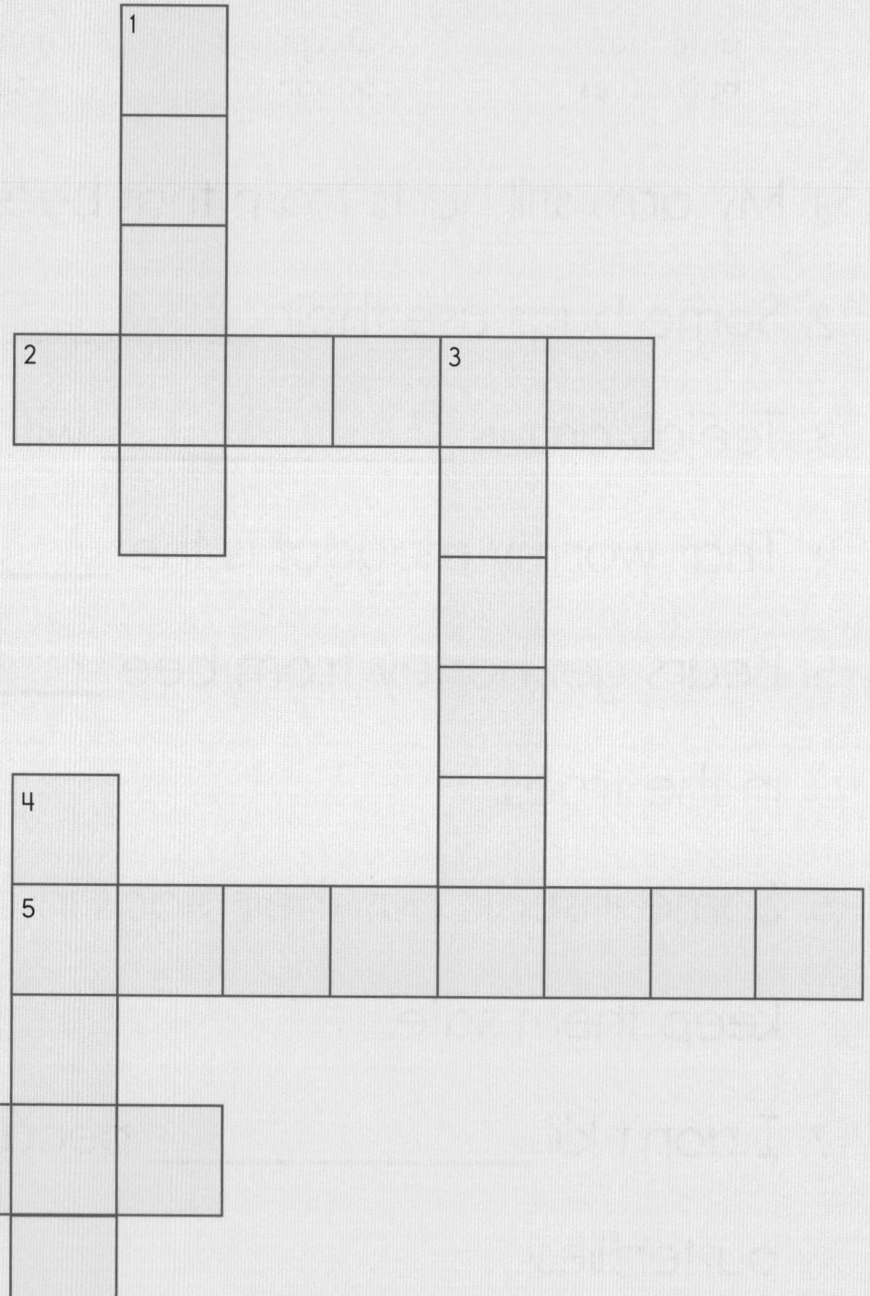

Maze Crazy!

DRAW a line through the words about **bugs** to get to the beehive.

Start at the green arrow.

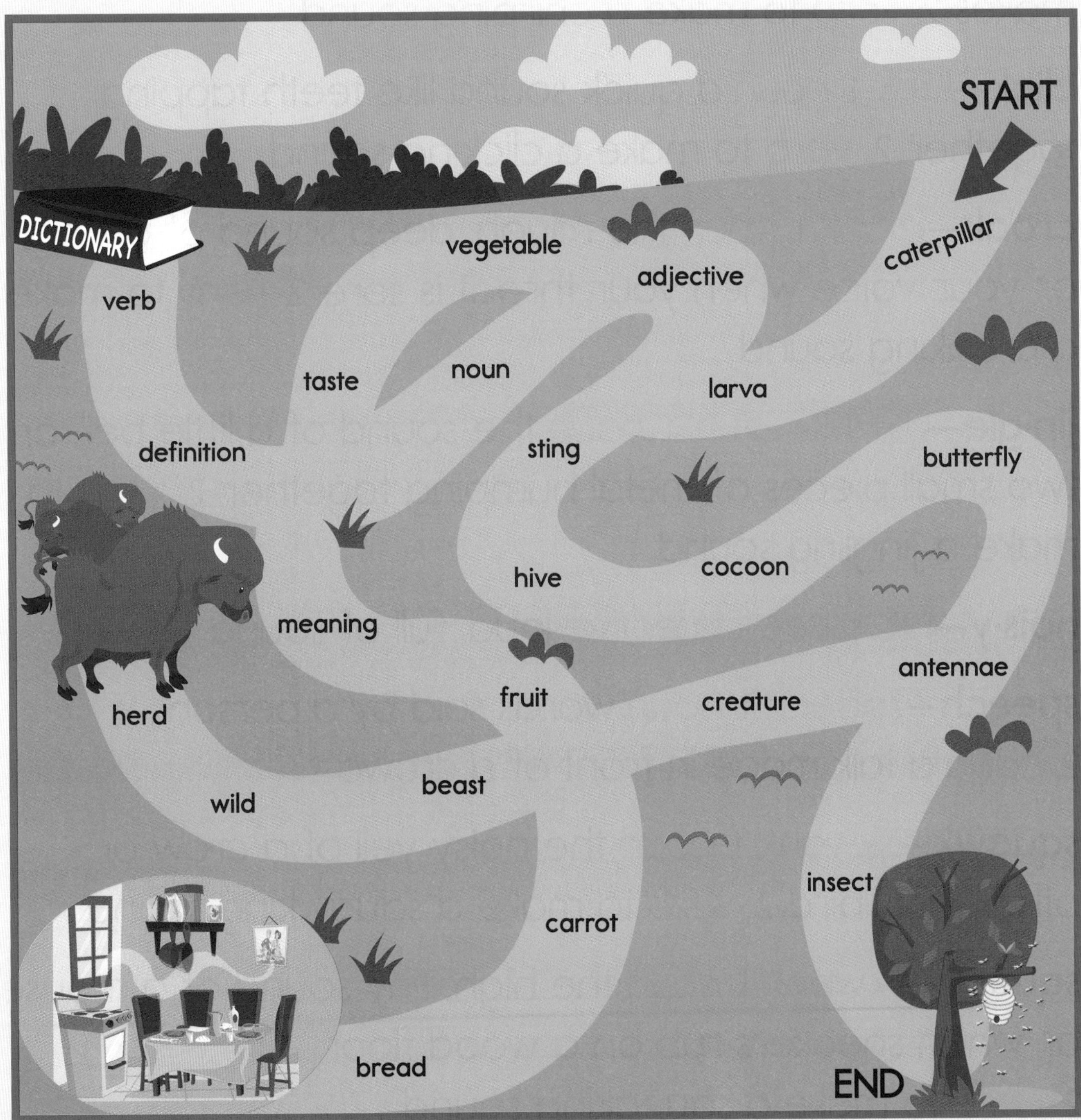

Word List

READ the words and their meanings.

chirp—cherp 1. *noun* the short, pretty sound a small bird makes 2. *verb* to make a chirping sound

click—klihk 1. *noun* a quick sound like teeth tapping together 2. *verb* to make a clicking sound

croak—krohk 1. *noun* the rough, deep sound of a frog, or your voice when your throat is sore 2. *verb* to make a croaking sound

jin·gle—JIHNG-guhl 1. *noun* the sound of a little bell, or two small pieces of metal bumping together 2. *verb* to make a jingling sound

nois·y—NOY-zee *adjective* loud, full of sound

speech—speech 1. *noun* words said by a person 2. *noun* a talk made in front of a crowd

squawk—skwahk 1. *noun* the noisy yell of a crow or other loud bird 2. *verb* to make a squawking sound

squeak—skweek 1. *noun* the high, tiny sound of a mouse, or when sneakers rub on a wood floor 2. *verb* to make a squeaking sound

Match the Meaning

WRITE the words next to their definitions. LOOK at the word box for help.

click	croak	noisy	squawk
chirp	jingle	speech	squeak

1. ____________________ loud
2. ____________________ the sound a little bird makes
3. ____________________ a high, tiny sound
4. ____________________ a sound like teeth tapping together
5. ____________________ the sound of a shaking bell
6. ____________________ words said out loud
7. ____________________ the yell of a loud bird
8. ____________________ the sound of a frog

Criss Cross

READ the clues. FILL IN the boxes with the right word for each clue.

Across

3. Your teeth can make this sound.
5. Full of sound
6. A mousy sound

Down

1. A sudden bird yell
2. Sounds like a tiny bell
4. A deep frog sound

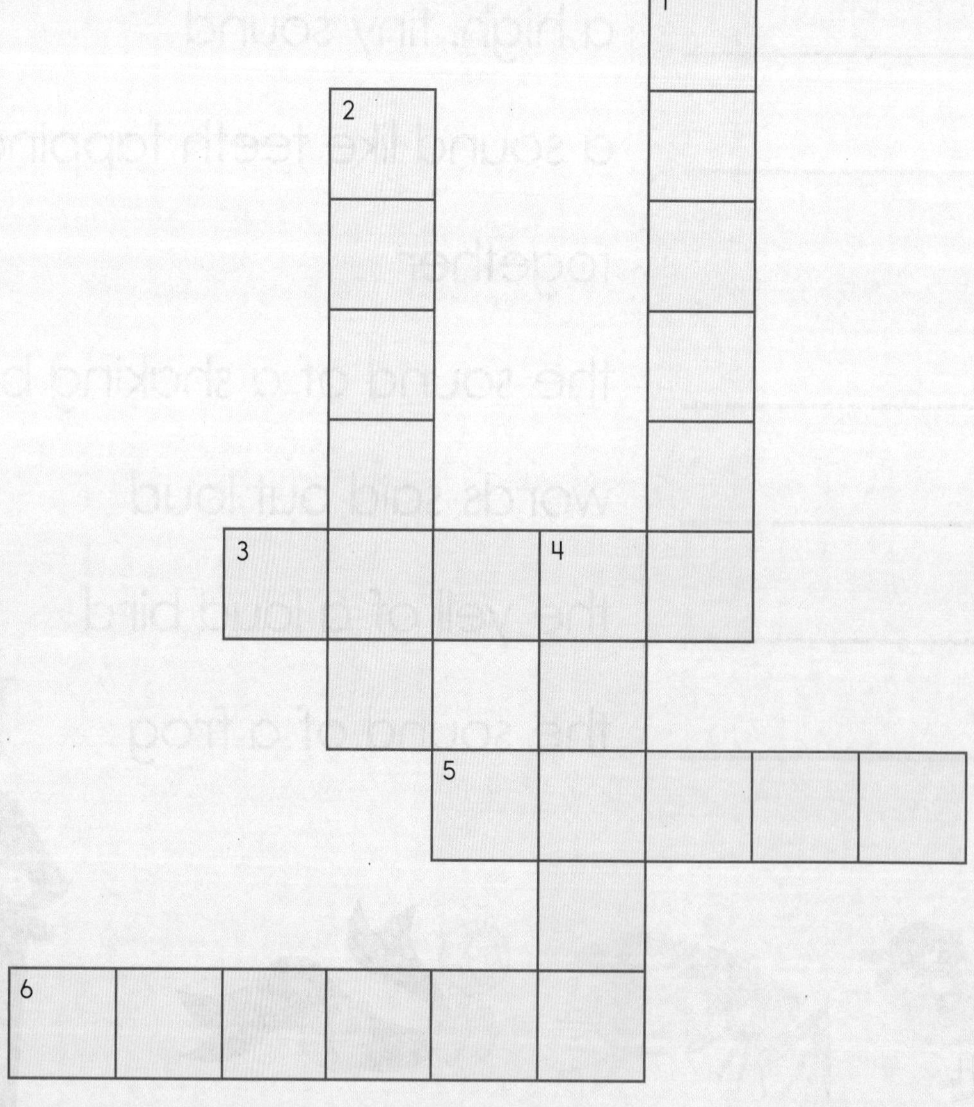

Blank Out

FINISH each sentence with a word from the word box.

clicking	croak	noisy	squawks
chirping	jingle	speech	squeaking

1. Ben had a bad cold, so his voice sounded like a ________________.
2. The crowd was talking and clapping. It was very ________________.
3. Jess says we have mice. She hears them ________________ in the walls.
4. Mom gave a long, boring ________________ about doing chores.
5. I shivered so hard, my teeth were ________________ together.
6. Dad likes to ________________ his keys while he walks to the car.
7. The big parrot always ________________ when I come into the pet shop.
8. It was a nice morning. The sun was shining and the birds were ________________.

Pick the One

CIRCLE the sound that fits best for each word.

1. **lion**	roar	squeak	speech
2. **dog toy**	crash	bark	squeak
3. **car horn**	bang	honk	buzz
4. **carrot**	chirp	squeak	crunch
5. **crow**	squawk	roar	bark
6. **push button**	shout	quack	click
7. **bird**	bark	chirp	roar
8. **frog**	speech	croak	squeak

Cross Out

CROSS OUT the words that are **not** sounds.

1. click	carrot	larva	hoot
2. paint	teen	roar	squawk
3. honk	chirp	taste	kneel
4. squeak	cheek	screech	frown

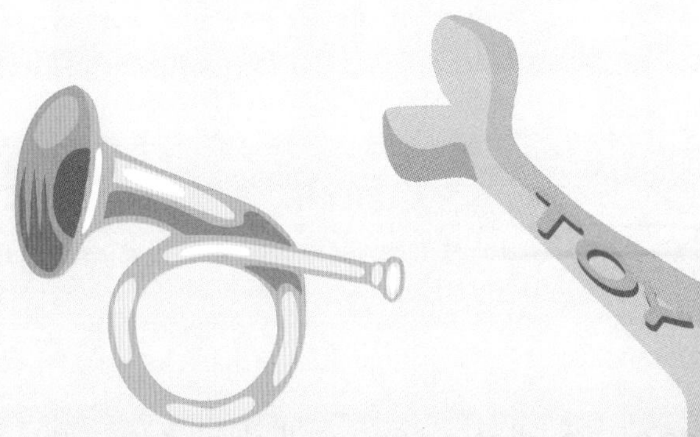

Blank Out

READ each word. Then WRITE the number of syllables in the blank.

HINT: Some of these have more syllables than you might think!

1. antennae ____________
2. cocoon ____________
3. caterpillar ____________
4. everywhere ____________
5. exercise ____________
6. favorite ____________
7. squawk ____________
8. taste ____________

Don't forget—a dictionary will show you the syllable breaks.

Same or Opposite?

READ each word pair. CIRCLE if they are the same or opposites.

1. squeak	roar	same	opposite
2. wild	tame	same	opposite
3. stuffed	full	same	opposite
4. noisy	quiet	same	opposite
5. speak	talk	same	opposite
6. beast	animal	same	opposite
7. borrow	return	same	opposite
8. insect	bug	same	opposite

Criss Cross

WRITE the word for each clue in the grids.

agree	captain	exercise	respect	share	speech

Across

1. Give to others
2. What you do at the gym
3. Leader of the team
5. Honor someone

Down

1. All talk
4. Say yes

Dictionary Dare

READ the guide words. CIRCLE the word in each row that comes between them.

1. **commercial → communicate**

   commentary | commodity | community

2. **whippoorwill → whiten**

   whisper | whinny | whittle

3. **shoelace → shortening**

   shovel | shoal | shoplifter

4. **guard → guillotine**

   guacamole | gullible | guidance

5. **mischief → missile**

   misunderstand | miser | misuse

6. **insolent → instrument**

   insulin | inspire | insight

7. **referendum → refugee**

   reforest | referee | refund

8. **presently → president**

   presence | preserve | presume

Nature

Word List

READ the words and their meanings.

crop—krahp *noun* a planting of something, like corn, that a farmer is growing in a field

field—feeld *noun* a wide space of ground that has plants growing in it, like grass or a crop

flood—fluhd 1. *noun* a lot of water that overflows from a river, or fills an area like a house 2. *verb* to fill an area with water

moun·tain—MOWN-tuhn *noun* a tall peak of land, much higher than a hill

nat·u·ral—NATCH-er-uhl 1. *adjective* the way nature made it, not changed by humans 2. *adjective* not fake

shade—shad *noun* a place where the sun is blocked by something, like under a tree

soil—soyl 1. *noun* dirt that is used for growing plants 2. *verb* to make something dirty

val·ley—VAL-ee *noun* a low spot between hills or mountains

Match the Meaning

WRITE the words in the box next to their definitions.

crop	flood	natural	soil
field	mountain	shade	valley

1. ____________________ a really tall hill
2. ____________________ a cool, dark spot
3. ____________________ a bunch of plants, like corn
4. ____________________ a low spot between hills
5. ____________________ a place to grow crops
6. ____________________ not changed
7. ____________________ a lot of water
8. ____________________ dirt

Blank Out!

FINISH each sentence with a word from the box.

crops	flooded	natural	soiled
field	mountain	shade	valley

1. The plastic tree in the living room doesn't look ____________.
2. Next to our house is a big ____________ full of weeds.
3. On a hot day, it's nice to sit in the ____________ of a tree.
4. We live in a deep ____________ that follows a river.
5. After Zan walked in the mud, his socks were all ____________.
6. Farmer Ned grows three ____________: corn, wheat, and oats.
7. Last year, my Uncle Jaime climbed a tall ____________.
8. We had to stay in a hotel because our house ____________ in the storm.

Right or Wrong?

UNDERLINE the sentence that matches the picture.

1.

Vernon is sitting in the shake.

Vernon is sitting in the shade.

2.

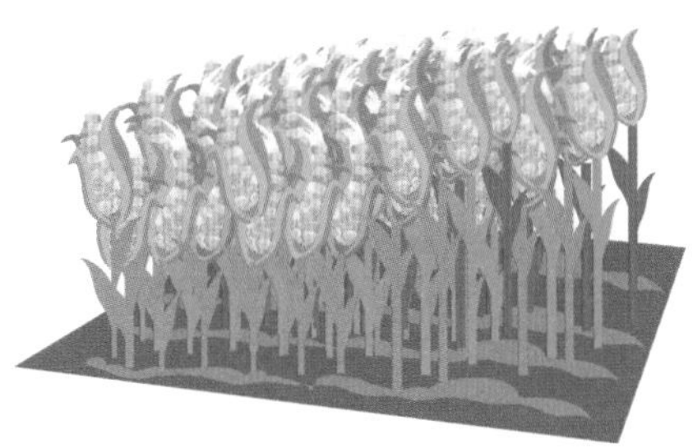

Corn is growing in this field.

Corn is growing in this feel.

3.

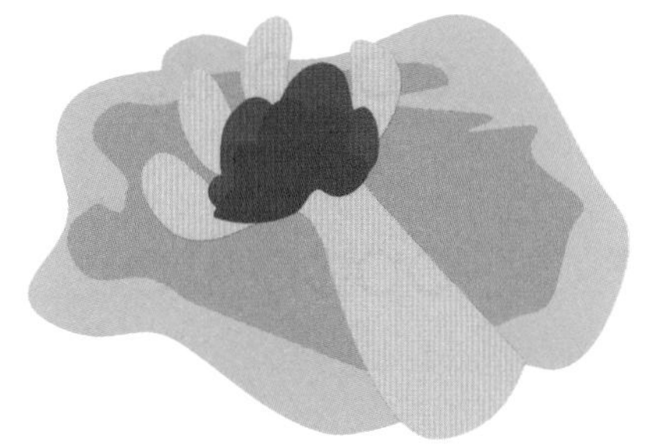

This soil is good for growing things.

This soap is good for growing things.

4.

The house is on the mountain.

The house is in the valley.

Same or Opposite?

READ each word pair. CIRCLE if they are the same or opposites.

HINT: Look up any words you don't know.

1. mountain	valley	same	opposite
2. fake	natural	same	opposite
3. soil	dirt	same	opposite
4. field	meadow	same	opposite
5. natural	unchanged	same	opposite
6. flooded	dry	same	opposite
7. soiled	clean	same	opposite
8. shady	sunny	same	opposite

Word Pictures

COLOR the spaces that show words for things in nature.

HINT: Don't forget to look up any words you don't know.

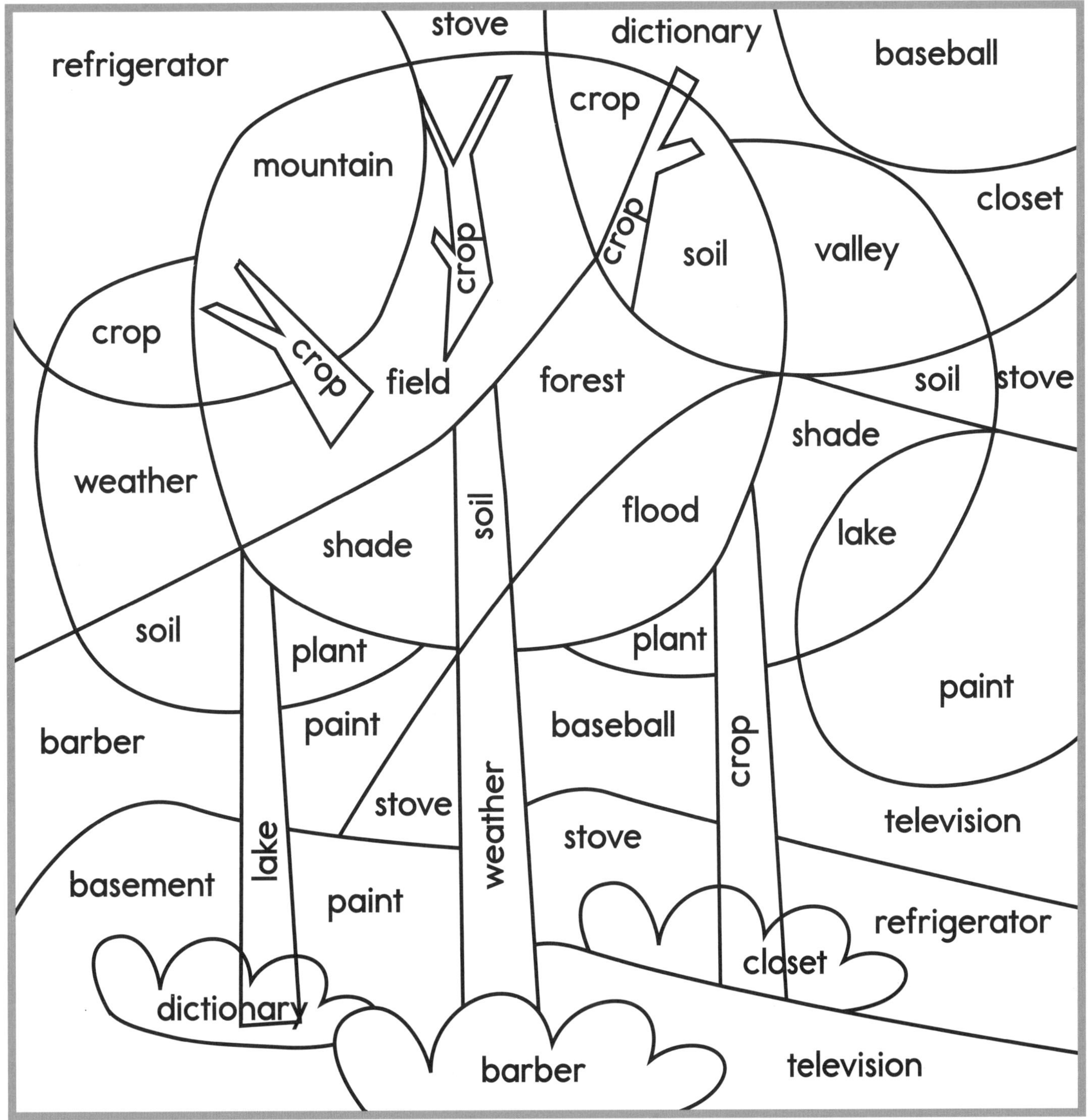

Word List

READ the words and their meanings.

el•e•va•tor—EHL-uh-vay-ter *noun* a moving box that takes you up to the high floors of a building

lit•ter—LIHT-er 1. *noun* trash that is on the ground 2. *verb* to leave trash on the ground

lone•ly—LOHN-lee *adjective* sad because there's nobody around

mod•ern—MAHD-dern *adjective* very new and up to date, not old

mon•u•ment—MAHN-yuh-muhnt *noun* anything that is put up to honor a person or event

neigh•bor•hood—NAY-ber-hud *noun* an area where people live

rude—rood *adjective* not nice, makes other people feel bad

spend—spehnd *verb* to use up, like money or time

Match the Meaning

WRITE the words next to their definitions. LOOK at the word box for help.

elevator	lonely	monument	rude
litter	modern	neighborhood	spend

1. ______________ the area where you live
2. ______________ to leave trash on the street
3. ______________ not old fashioned
4. ______________ a box that takes you up
5. ______________ to use up
6. ______________ sad and alone
7. ______________ something to honor a person
8. ______________ not nice

Finish the Story

READ the story. FILL IN the blanks with words from the box.

elevator	modern	neighborhood	spend
lonely	monument	rude	

A New Friend

I get a little ______________ (1) in the summer when all the kids in my ______________ (2) go to camp. I ______________ (3) a lot of time playing at the park by myself. There's a ______________ (4) there, of a big, stone soldier. One day, I saw a girl sitting on the soldier's foot. At first she was ______________ (5) and wouldn't talk to me. But now we hang out all the time! She lives in a new, ______________ (6) apartment building with an ______________ (7) to take you to her floor. I hope we stay friends when the summer is over!

Criss Cross

READ the clues. FILL IN the boxes with the right word for each clue.

HINT: Look up words you don't know.

Across

1. New
2. By yourself and sad
3. Lets you skip the stairs

Down

1. A statue that honors someone
2. Trash on the street

1

2

3

Word List

READ the words and their meanings.

back•ward—BAK-werd 1. *adverb* back in the direction you came from 2. *adjective* pointing the wrong way, so the front is facing back

coun•try—KUHN-tree 1. *noun* the nation where you live, like the United States or Canada 2. *noun* a place far away from any city, where there is more nature

di•rec•tion—duh-REHK-shuhn 1. *noun* the way you're going, like left or north 2. *noun* an order, like "go to bed now"

for•ward—FOR-werd *adverb* in a straight direction

is•land—I-luhnd *noun* a piece of land that is in the ocean, with water on all sides

lan•guage—LANG-gwihj *noun* the kind of speech used in different countries, like English or French

trav•el—TRAV-uhl 1. *noun* a visit to another place 2. *verb* to go somewhere

va•ca•tion—vay-KAY-shuhn 1. *noun* a break from work or school 2. *verb* to take a break, maybe travel

Match the Meaning

WRITE the words next to their definitions. LOOK at the word box for help.

backward	direction	island	travel
country	forward	language	vacation

1. ________________ like France or England
2. ________________ land with water all around
3. ________________ the opposite of *forward*
4. ________________ to take a trip
5. ________________ an order from someone
6. ________________ time off from work
7. ________________ keep going straight
8. ________________ what speech you use

Find the Friend

READ the clues. Then WRITE the friends' names next to the corresponding numbers.

Jorge lives in the country of France.

Chantal's shirt is backward.

Simon lives on an island.

Fiona is traveling.

Mona is on vacation in Germany.

Who am I?

1. ____________________

2. ____________________

3. ____________________

4. ____________________

5. ____________________

Blank Out

FINISH each sentence with a word from the word box.

backward	directions	islands	traveled
country	forward	language	vacation

1. In chorus, we have to face ____________ and smile at the crowd.
2. At our school, we get two months of ____________ in the summer.
3. I'm from India. What ____________ are you from?
4. Last year, my uncle ____________ all over the world!
5. People who look ____________ when they walk will bump into things.
6. Hawaii is a string of ____________.
7. North, south, east, and west are all ____________ on a map.
8. Sometimes I think my math teacher is speaking another ____________.

Right or Wrong?

UNDERLINE the sentence that matches the picture.

1.

Staci is walking forward.

Staci is walking backward.

2.

Martin is on an island.

Martin is on a mountain.

3.

Xyqx speaks a different langor.

Xyqx speaks a different language.

4.

Joel is in the country.

Joel is in the city.

Maze Crazy!

DRAW a line through words about **travel** to get to the train.
Start at the green arrow.

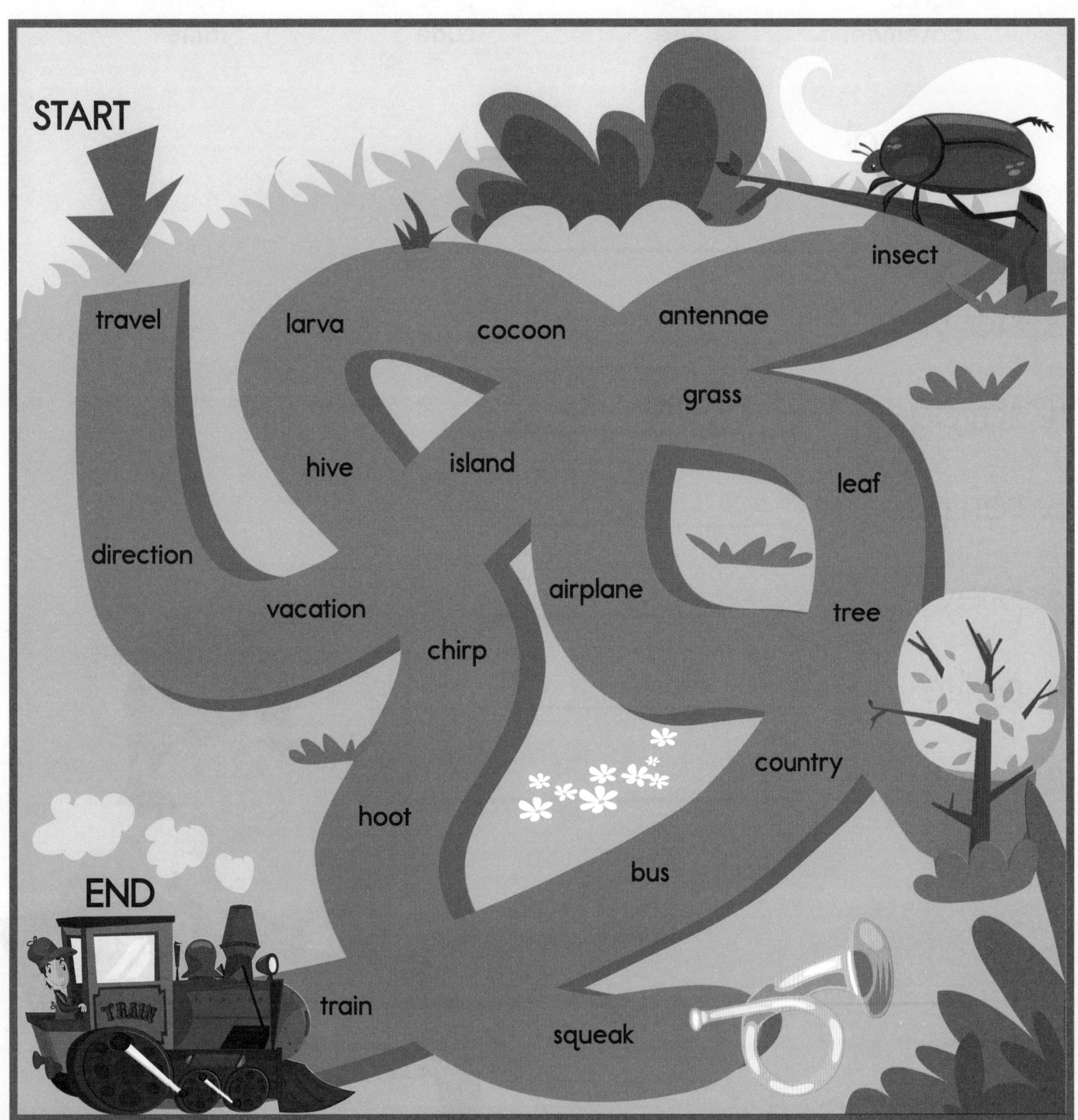

Dictionary Dare

LOOK UP the words in a dictionary. Then FILL IN the blanks with words from the box that mean the **opposite**.

agree	crowd	predator	stuffed
basement	noise	rude	tame

1. individual ____________
2. attic ____________
3. starving ____________
4. savage ____________
5. refuse ____________
6. prey ____________
7. polite ____________
8. silence ____________

Blank Out

FINISH each sentence with a word from the word box.

adjectives	country	dictionary	opposite
compound	definition	language	verb

1. Canada is a ________________.

2. *Pretty* and *purple* are ________________.

3. Every word has a ________________.

4. You can look up a word's meaning in the ________________.

5. A word that names an action is a ________________.

6. *Night* is the ________________ of *day*.

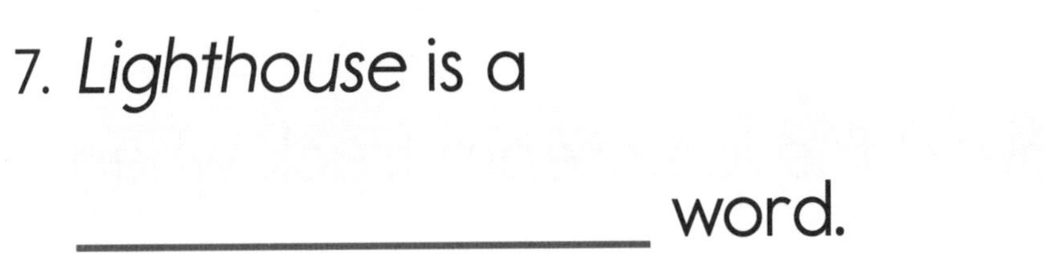

7. *Lighthouse* is a ________________ word.

8. English is a ________________.

Pick the One

READ each sentence. CIRCLE the correct part of speech for each word in green.

HINT: Some words are tricky because they can be nouns, verbs, or adjectives!

1. That man **littered** the sidewalk with his lunch bag.

   noun verb adjective

2. This is Gerri's second **attempt** at that skateboard trick.

   noun verb adjective

3. The door **clicked** as it slid open.

   noun verb adjective

4. Mom cried when she saw our **flooded** basement.

   noun verb adjective

5. Do you have time to **braid** my hair?

   noun verb adjective

6. All the kids **flock** around the ice cream truck when it comes.

   noun verb adjective

7. Can I have a **taste** of that cake?

   noun verb adjective

Cross Out

CROSS OUT the words that are **not** nouns.

1. comfortable monument forgive toothpaste
2. flight lonely stomach borrow
3. succeed wife basement empty
4. arrive elevator rude neighborhood

Index

ac•tor—AK-ter *noun* a person who acts on stage or screen

ad•jec•tive—AJ-ihk-tihv *noun* a word that describes something, like *pretty* or *blue*

a•dult—uh-DUHLT 1. *noun* a person who is grown up 2. *adjective* fully grown

a•gree—uh-GREE 1. *verb* to think the same way as someone else 2. *verb* to say yes to something

an•ten•nae—an-TEHN-ee *noun* two thin feelers that help a bug sense the world

ar•rive—uh-RIV *verb* to come to a place

at•tempt—uh-TEHMPT *verb* to try to do something

aunt—ant 1. *noun* the sister of your mother or father 2. *noun* the wife of your uncle

back•ward—BAK-werd 1. *adverb* back in the direction you came from 2. *adjective* pointing the wrong way, so the front is facing back

ba•nan•a—buh-NAN-uh *noun* a long, curved fruit with a yellow peel

bar•ber—BAHR-ber *noun* a person who cuts hair

base•ball—BAYS-bahl 1. *noun* a game played with a bat, a ball, and four bases 2. *noun* a ball used for playing baseball

base•ment—BAS-muhnt *noun* a room or rooms under a house or building

bath•room—BATH-room *noun* a room for bathing and using the toilet

beast—beest *noun* an animal or other creature that is not human and doesn't act human

beau•ti•ful—BYOO-tuh-fuhl *adjective* very pretty

bor•row—BAHR-oh *verb* when someone allows you to take something for a short time, then give it back

braid—brayd 1. *noun* hair in a rope-like style 2. *verb* to put hair in a rope-like style

bread—brehd *noun* a baked food made with flour that's used for toast and sandwiches

breathe—breeth *verb* to take in air through your mouth or nose

broth•er—BRUH*TH*-er *noun* a boy whose mother and father have another child

but•ter•fly—BUHT-er-fli *noun* an insect with large wings that are sometimes very colorful

cap•tain—KAP-tihn 1. *noun* the leader of a sports team 2. *noun* the leader of a ship or airplane 3. *noun* the leader of firefighters, police, or the military

car•rot—KEHR-uht *noun* a skinny orange vegetable that grows underground

cat•er•pil•lar—KAT-er-pihl-er *noun* an insect like a worm that turns into a butterfly or a moth

cheek—cheek *noun* the side of your face between your nose and your ear. You have two cheeks.

chew—choo *verb* to use your teeth to bite food in your mouth

chirp—cherp 1. *noun* the short, pretty sound a small bird makes 2. *verb* to make a chirping sound

click—klihk 1. *noun* a quick sound like teeth tapping together 2. *verb* to make a clicking sound

clos•et—CLAHZ-iht *noun* a very small room to keep clothes and shoes

co•coon—kuh-KOON *noun* a silk wrap or bag made by an insect to keep its body or eggs safe. A caterpillar goes into a cocoon while turning into a moth.

com•fort•a•ble—KUHM-fer-tuh-buhl 1. *adjective* very soft or easy, 2. *adjective* with no pain or fear

coun•try—KUHN-tree 1. *noun* the nation where you live, like the United States or Canada 2. *noun* a place far away from any city, where there is more nature

crea•ture—KREE-cher *noun* a living animal or human

croak—krohk 1. *noun* the rough, deep sound of a frog, or your voice when your throat is sore 2. *verb* to make a croaking sound

crop—krahp *noun* a planting of something, like corn, that a farmer is growing in a field

crowd—krowd *noun* a lot of people all together

def•i•ni•tion—dehf-uh-NIHSH-uhn *noun* the meaning of a word

de•scribe—dih-SKRIB *verb* to make a picture with words, like "a pretty girl in a blue dress"

dic•tion•ar•y—DIHK-shuh-nehr-ee *noun* a book filled with definitions of words

di•rec•tion—duh-REHK-shuhn 1. *noun* the way you're going, like left or north 2. *noun* an order, like "go to bed now"

el•e•va•tor—EHL-uh-vay-ter *noun* a moving box that takes you up to the high floors of a building

emp•ty—EHMP-tee *adjective* having nothing inside

en•e•my—EHN-uh-mee *noun* someone who is working against you, a foe

eve•ry•where—EHV-ree-wehr *adverb* in all places

ex•er•cise—EHK-ser-siz 1. *noun* a set of moves that work out your body 2. *noun* an activity that helps practice a lesson 3. *verb* to move your body to make it strong and fit

ex•plain—ihk-SPLAYN *verb* to tell or teach someone about something

eye•brow—I-brow *noun* the strip of hair above your eye

fail—fayl *verb* to lose, to not get what you tried for

fa•vor•ite—FA-ver-iht *adjective* the one that is liked the most

feath•er—FEH*TH*-er *noun* one of the soft pieces that cover a bird's body and wings

field—feeld *noun* a wide space of ground that has plants growing in it, like grass or a crop

flight—flit 1. *noun* a trip through the air, like on a plane 2. *noun* a fast getaway, escape

flock—flahk 1. *noun* a group of birds 2. *verb* to make a group, like a flock of birds

flood—fluhd 1. *noun* a lot of water that overflows from a river, or fills an area like a house 2. *verb* to fill an area with water

for•give—fer-GIHV *verb* to stop being mad and make up after a fight with someone

for•ward—FOR-werd *adverb* in a straight direction

freck•les—FREHK-lz *noun* spots on skin from the sun

fright•en—FRIT-uhn *verb* to scare somebody

frown—frown 1. *noun* a sad or mad face, the opposite of a smile 2. *verb* to make a sad or mad face

fruit—froot 1. *noun* a food that can be juicy and sweet, like an apple 2. *noun* the part of a plant that holds the seeds

gi•ant—JI-uhnt 1. *noun* a huge person or other creature out of a fairy tale 2. *adjective* very big

grand•fa•ther—GRAND-fah-*th*er 1. *noun* the father of your father or mother 2. *noun* your grandmother's husband

grand•moth•er—GRAND-muh*th*-er 1. *noun* the mother of your father or mother 2. *noun* your grandfather's wife

herd—herd 1. *noun* a group of land animals like cows 2. *verb* to make a group of animals go somewhere

hive—hiv *noun* a nest of bees, where they make honey

hus•band—HUHZ-buhnd *noun* a man who is married

in•sect—IHN-sehkt *noun* a small creature with no backbone (a bug)

is•land—I-luhnd *noun* a piece of land that is in the ocean, with water on all sides

jin•gle—JIHNG-guhl 1. *noun* the sound of a little bell, or two small pieces of metal bumping together 2. *verb* to make a jingling sound

kneel—neel *verb* to get down on your knees

lan•guage—LANG-gwihj *noun* the kind of speech used in different countries, like English or French

lar•va—LAHR-vuh *noun* a baby insect that looks like a worm. A caterpillar is the larva of a butterfly.

lawn—lawn *noun* the grass around a house

light•house—LIT-hows *noun* a tall building with a big light that helps boats see the shore

lit•ter—LIHT-er 1. *noun* trash that is on the ground 2. *verb* to leave trash on the ground

lone•ly—LOHN-lee *adjective* sad because there's nobody around

may•or—MAY-er *noun* the leader of a town or city

mean•ing—MEE-nihng *noun* the idea of a word, what it means

mod•ern—MAHD-dern *adjective* very new and up to date, not old

mon•u•ment—MAHN-yuh-muhnt *noun* anything that is put up to honor a person or event

moun•tain—MOWN-tuhn *noun* a tall peak of land, much higher than a hill

mouth—mowth 1. *noun* the hole in your face where you put your food 2. *verb* to talk with your lips without making a sound

nat•u•ral—NATCH-er-uhl 1. *adjective* the way nature made it, not changed by humans 2. *adjective* not fake

neigh•bor—NAY-ber *noun* a person who lives next door to or near you

neigh•bor•hood—NAY-ber-hud *noun* an area where people live

nois•y—NOY-zee *adjective* loud, full of sound

noun—nown *noun* a word that stands for a person, place, or thing

paint—peynt 1. *noun* color that can be put on walls or objects 2. *verb* to put color on something using paint

pred•a•tor—PREHD-uh-ter *noun* an animal or insect that hunts others for its food

reach—reech 1. *verb* to put out your hand to get something 2. *verb* to arrive at a place

re•frig•er•a•tor—rih-FRIHJ-uh-ray-ter *noun* a metal box that keeps food and drinks cold

re•spect—rih-SPEHKT 1. *noun* a feeling that you honor someone 2. *verb* to honor and show consideration for someone

rude—rood *adjective* not nice, makes other people feel bad

shade—shad *noun* a place where the sun is blocked by something, like under a tree

share—shehr 1. *noun* one person's part of something that can be split 2. *verb* to let other people use your things or eat your food 3. *verb* to use something with other people

shiv•er—SHIHV-er 1. *noun* a shake of the body 2. *verb* to shake your body, like when it's cold

side•walk—SID-wawk *noun* a smooth, hard walkway

sis•ter—SIHS-ter *noun* a girl whose mother and father have another child

skate—skayt 1. *noun* a shoe with a sharp blade that helps you slide on ice 2. *noun* a shoe with wheels that help you roll on the sidewalk 3. *verb* to use skates to move along the ground or on ice

soil—soyl 1. *noun* dirt that is used for growing plants 2. *verb* to make something dirty

speech—speech 1. *noun* words said by a person 2. *noun* a talk made in front of a crowd

spend—spehnd *verb* to use up, like money or time

spread—sprehd 1. *verb* to put something all over, like jam on bread 2. *verb* to open wide

squawk—skwahk 1. *noun* the noisy yell of a crow or other loud bird 2. *verb* to make a squawking sound

squeak—skweek 1. *noun* the high, tiny sound of a mouse, or when sneakers rub on a wood floor 2. *verb* to make a squeaking sound

squirm—skwerm *verb* to move around in a twisty-turny way

sting—stihng 1. *noun* the feeling of a bug bite or pin prick 2. *verb* to use a stinger or other sharp object to break someone's skin

Index

stom•ach—STUHM-uhk *noun* your tummy, or belly, that tells you when you're hungry or full

stop•light—STAHP-lit *noun* a light that helps move traffic safely where two roads cross

stuffed—stuhft *adjective* filled with something, like a pillow is filled with fluff, or a belly is filled with food

suc•ceed—suhk-SEED *verb* to win, to get what you wanted

sug•gest—suhg-JEHST 1. *verb* to hint at something 2. *verb* to give an idea or plan as an option

sun•rise—SUHN-riz *noun* the time of day when the sun comes up

swal•low—SWAHL-oh *verb* to let food go from your mouth into your throat and stomach

tame—taym 1. *adjective* quiet, safe, and nice 2. *verb* to make a wild animal be nice to humans

taste—tayst 1. *noun* the way a food is salty, sweet, or icky 2. *verb* to put a bit of food in your mouth to see if you like it

teen—teen *noun* a person who is older than a child but younger than an adult

throat—throht 1. *noun* the front part of your neck 2. *noun* the tube inside your neck that goes to your stomach and your lungs

tooth•paste—TOOTH-payst *noun* a cream used to clean teeth

trav•el—TRAV-uhl 1. *noun* a visit to another place 2. *verb* to go somewhere

un•cle—UHNG-kuhl *noun* 1. the brother of your mother or father 2. *noun* the husband of your aunt

va•ca•tion—vay-KAY-shuhn 1. *noun* a break from work or school 2. *verb* to take a break, maybe travel

val•ley—VAL-ee *noun* a low spot between hills or mountains

veg•e•ta•ble—VEHJ-tuh-buhl *noun* a food that comes from a plant's leaves or roots

verb—verb *noun* a word that stands for an action, like *run*

wife—wif *noun* a woman who is married

wild—wild 1. *adjective* not tame, not safe, not able to live with humans 2. *noun* a place where people don't live, like the jungle

Answers

Page 127
1. describe
2. meaning
3. verb
4. noun
5. adjective
6. dictionary
7. definition

Page 128
1. angry
2. balloon
3. jelly
4. learn
5. machine
6. octopus
7. trouble
8. whisper

Page 129
1. verb
2. adjective
3. verb
4. noun
5. adjective
6. verb
7. noun
8. noun

Page 130
1. food
2. present
3. traffic
4. rock
5. bagpipes
6. monarch
7. unique
8. hawk

Page 131
1. 3
2. 4
3. 2
4. 4
5. 2
6. 1
7. 3
8. 1

Page 133
1. giant
2. fail
3. succeed
4. predator
5. arrive
6. beautiful
7. attempt
8. enemy

Page 134
1. opposite
2. same
3. opposite
4. opposite
5. same
6. same
7. opposite
8. same

Page 135
1. Kira
2. Joe
3. Larry
4. Darla
5. Talia

Page 136

ACROSS	DOWN
2. arrive	1. beautiful
4. giant	3. enemy
5. fail	

Page 137
1. 3
2. NO
3. **Suggestion:** I don't skate very well.

Page 139
1. everywhere
2. sunrise
3. baseball
4. sidewalk
5. lighthouse
6. toothpaste
7. bathroom
8. stoplight

Page 140
1. sunrise
2. baseball
3. toothpaste
4. bathroom
5. sidewalk
6. stoplight

Page 141
1. grand + father = grandfather
2. skate + board = skateboard
3. play + ground = playground
4. news + paper = newspaper
5. green + house = greenhouse

Page 142
sunrise → sunset
troublemaker → peacemaker
somebody → nobody
downstairs → upstairs
nighttime → daytime
everything → nothing
bedtime → playtime
highway → sidewalk

Page 143
1. starfish, football, ~~adjective,~~ ~~predator~~
2. ~~enemy,~~ playground, everybody, ~~arrive~~
3. lighthouse, ~~beautiful,~~ ~~dictionary,~~ blueberry
4. stoplight, ~~unhappy,~~ nothing, ~~syllable~~

Page 144
1. adjective
2. arrive
3. attempt
4. definition
5. describe
6. dictionary
7. sidewalk
8. stoplight

Page 145
1. adjective
2. noun
3. verb
4. noun
5. verb
6. adjective
7. verb
8. noun

Page 146
1. opposite
2. same
3. same
4. opposite
5. same
6. same
7. opposite
8. opposite

Page 147

ACROSS	DOWN
3. succeed	1. describe
4. verb	2. adjective
	3. syllable

Page 149
1. frown
2. throat
3. mouth
4. braid
5. freckles
6. eyebrow
7. stomach
8. cheek

Page 150

ACROSS	DOWN
3. throat	1. frown
5. cheek	2. stomach
	4. freckles

Page 151
1. finger, throat, ~~verb,~~ ~~definition~~
2. ~~sunrise,~~ ~~fail,~~ freckles, mouth
3. arm, ~~sidewalk~~, stomach, ~~attempt~~
4. ~~syllable,~~ eyebrow, ~~giant~~, cheek

Page 152
1. Tyara
2. Connor
3. Carly
4. Jordan
5. Doug

Page 153
1. cheek
2. mouth
3. stomach
4. eyebrow
5. freckles
6. throat

Page 155
1. squirm
2. kneel
3. shiver
4. chew
5. swallow
6. reach
7. breathe
8. exercise

Page 156
1. Maddy is chewing gum.
2. Mr. Santos is exercising.
3. Ty kneels on the ground.
4. The baby reaches for her bottle.

Page 157
1. shiver
2. exercise
3. reach
4. squirming
5. swallow
6. kneel
7. chew
8. breathe

Page 158
1. squirm
2. breathe
3. beautiful
4. reach
5. shiver
6. swallow
7. chew
8. enemy

Page 159

Page 161
1. teen
2. adult
3. crowd
4. actor
5. barber
6. mayor
7. captain
8. neighbor

Page 162
1. crowd
2. mayor
3. captain
4. actor
5. barber
6. neighbor

Answers

Page 163

ACROSS	DOWN
2. teen	1. neighbor
4. adult	3. mayor
5. barber	

Page 164
1. Leena
2. Serena
3. Hunter
4. Cyrus
5. Bart

Page 165

Page 167
1. respect
2. share
3. borrow
4. explain
5. suggest
6. agree
7. frighten
8. forgive

Page 168
1. Tom does not respect Donna.
2. Jean shares her pizza with Mike.
3. Sondra frightens Neal.
4. Neal forgives Sondra.

Page 169
1. borrow
2. explain
3. respect
4. beautiful
5. share
6. neighbor
7. enemy
8. agree

Page 170
1. explain
2. forgive
3. respect
4. suggests
5. agree
6. shares
7. frighten
8. borrow

Page 171
1. ~~enemy~~, ~~beautiful~~, forgive, attempt
2. frighten, ~~scary~~, exercise, ~~definition~~
3. ~~verb~~, share, ~~throat~~, borrow
4. respect, ~~sidewalk~~, suggest, ~~idea~~

Page 172
1. ginger
2. outsmart
3. spindle
4. aunt
5. country
6. north
7. wear
8. incomplete

Page 173
1. scare → frighten
2. succeed → win
3. hunter → predator
4. try → attempt
5. meaning → definition
6. come → arrive
7. tummy → stomach
8. shake → shiver

Page 174

ACROSS	DOWN
1. suggest	1. swallow
3. chew	2. squirm
4. explain	
5. crowd	

Page 175

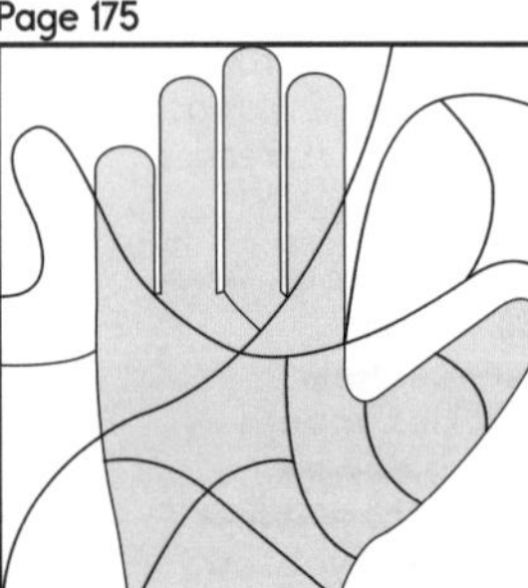

Page 177
1. husband
2. grandfather
3. sister
4. uncle
5. wife
6. brother
7. aunt
8. grandmother

Page 178

ACROSS	DOWN
2. grandfather	1. brother
3. husband	

parent: a mother or father
sibling: a brother or sister
spouse: a husband or wife

Page 179
1. grandmother
2. grandfather
3. wife
4. husband
5. aunt
6. uncle
7. brother
8. sister

Page 180
1. Jen is Peter's sister.
2. Stan is Sheila's husband.
3. Greg is Karl's grandfather.
4. This is my aunt.

Page 181
1. grandfather, daughter, ~~frighten~~, ~~frown~~
2. son, ~~bathroom~~, ~~suggest~~, sister
3. ~~predator~~, ~~agree~~, mother, aunt
4. ~~respect~~, uncle, brother, ~~elephant~~

Page 183
1. empty
2. closet
3. basement
4. favorite
5. refrigerator
6. paint
7. comfortable
8. lawn

Page 184
1. refrigerator
2. empty
3. favorite
4. comfortable
5. lawn

Page 185

ACROSS	DOWN
3. closet	1. paint
4. empty	2. basement
5. lawn	

Page 186
1. The box is empty.
2. The lawn is green.
3. That chair looks comfortable.
4. That's Dipti's favorite doll.

Page 187

Page 189
1. taste
2. carrot
3. banana
4. vegetable
5. stuffed
6. fruit
7. spread
8. bread

Page 190
1. Crispin
2. Lyle
3. Shama
4. Mai
5. Val

Page 191
1. vegetable
2. vegetable
3. fruit
4. fruit
5. vegetable
6. vegetable
7. fruit
8. vegetable

Page 192
1. carrots
2. taste
3. spread
4. bread
5. fruit
6. stuffed
7. banana
8. vegetables

Page 193

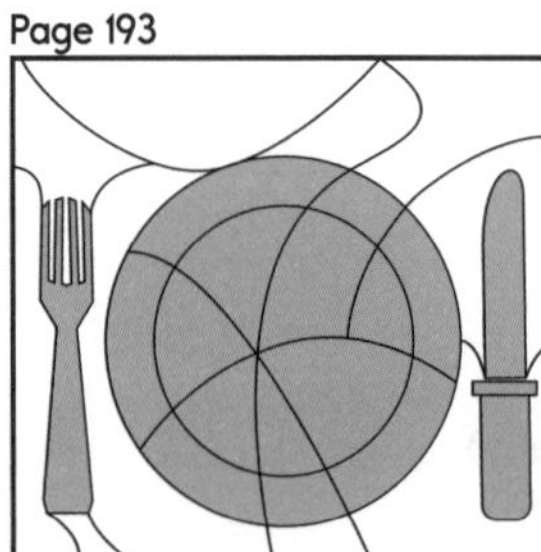

Page 194
1. noun
2. noun
3. adjective
4. verb
5. noun
6. verb
7. adjective
8. verb

Page 195

ACROSS	DOWN
3. freckles	1. uncle
6. teen	2. frown
	4. spread
	5. enemy

Answers

Page 196
1. ~~beautiful~~, empty, braid, ~~comfortable~~
2. ~~predator~~, ~~enemy~~, bathroom, toothpaste
3. meaning, ~~adjective~~, freckles, ~~everywhere~~
4. ~~grandmother~~, throat, ~~definition~~, lighthouse

Page 197
1. forgive
2. taste
3. frown
4. frighten
5. teen
6. actor
7. explain
8. comfortable

Page 199
1. flock
2. wild
3. beast
4. flight
5. creature
6. tame
7. feather
8. herd

Page 200
1. beasts
2. tame
3. wild
4. flocks
5. feathers
6. herds

Page 201

ACROSS	DOWN
1. flock	2. creature
3. herd	4. feather
4. flight	

Page 202
1. A flock of geese flew by.
2. Mr. Tibbles is tame.
3. This bird has green feathers.
4. We are in the wild.

Page 203

Page 205
1. cocoon
2. insect
3. antennae
4. caterpillar
5. sting
6. butterfly
7. larva
8. hive

Page 206
1. Tinky
2. Slinky
3. Binky
4. Dinky
5. Pinky

Page 207
1. sting
2. antennae
3. butterflies
4. larva
5. hives
6. cocoon
7. caterpillars
8. insects

Page 208

ACROSS	DOWN
2. insect	1. sting
5. antennae	3. cocoon
6. hive	4. larva

Page 209

Page 211
1. noisy
2. chirp
3. squeak
4. click
5. jingle
6. speech
7. squawk
8. croak

Page 212

ACROSS	DOWN
3. click	1. squawk
5. noisy	2. jingle
6. squeak	4. croak

Page 213
1. croak
2. noisy
3. squeaking
4. speech
5. clicking
6. jingle
7. squawks
8. chirping

Page 214
1. roar
2. squeak
3. honk
4. crunch
5. squawk
6. click
7. chirp
8. croak

Page 215
1. click, ~~carrot~~, ~~larva~~, hoot
2. ~~paint~~, ~~teen~~, roar, squawk
3. honk, chirp, ~~taste~~, ~~kneel~~
4. squeak, ~~cheek~~, screech, ~~frown~~

Page 216
1. 3
2. 2
3. 4
4. 3
5. 3
6. 3
7. 1
8. 1

Page 217
1. opposite
2. opposite
3. same
4. opposite
5. same
6. same
7. opposite
8. same

Page 218

ACROSS	DOWN
1. share	1. speech
2. exercise	4. agree
3. captain	
5. respect	

Page 219
1. commodity
2. whisper
3. shoplifter
4. guidance
5. miser
6. inspire
7. reforest
8. preserve

Page 221
1. mountain
2. shade
3. crop
4. valley
5. field
6. natural
7. flood
8. soil

Page 222
1. natural
2. field
3. shade
4. valley
5. soiled
6. crops
7. mountain
8. flooded

Page 223
1. Vernon is sitting in the shade.
2. Corn is growing in this field.
3. This soil is good for growing things.
4. The house is in the valley.

Page 224
1. opposite
2. opposite
3. same
4. same
5. same
6. opposite
7. opposite
8. opposite

Page 225

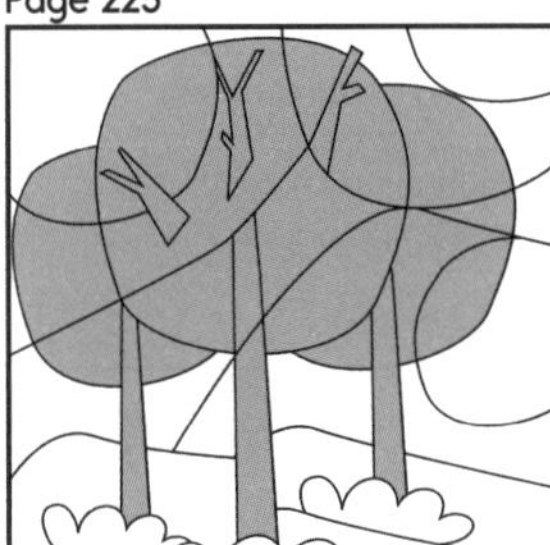

Page 227
1. neighborhood
2. litter
3. modern
4. elevator
5. spend
6. lonely
7. monument
8. rude

Page 228
1. lonely
2. neighborhood
3. spend
4. monument
5. rude
6. modern
7. elevator

Page 229

ACROSS	DOWN
1. modern	1. monument
2. lonely	2. litter
3. elevator	

Answers

Page 231
1. country
2. island
3. backward
4. travel
5. direction
6. vacation
7. forward
8. language

Page 232
1. Fiona
2. Chantal
3. Jorge
4. Mona
5. Simon

Page 233
1. forward
2. vacation
3. country
4. traveled
5. backward
6. islands
7. directions
8. language

Page 234
1. Staci is walking forward.
2. Martin is on a mountain.
3. Xyqx speaks a different language.
4. Joel is in the country.

Page 235

Page 236
1. crowd
2. basement
3. stuffed
4. tame
5. agree
6. predator
7. rude
8. noise

Page 237
1. country
2. adjectives
3. definition
4. dictionary
5. verb
6. opposite
7. compound
8. language

Page 238
1. verb
2. noun
3. verb
4. adjective
5. verb
6. verb
7. noun

Page 239
1. ~~comfortable~~, monument, ~~forgive~~, toothpaste
2. flight, ~~lonely~~, stomach, ~~borrow~~
3. ~~succeed~~, wife, basement, ~~empty~~
4. ~~arrive~~, elevator, ~~rude~~, neighborhood

2nd Grade Math Games & Puzzles

Contents

Hidden Design

COUNT the hundreds, tens, and ones. Then COLOR the squares that match the numbers to see the hidden design.

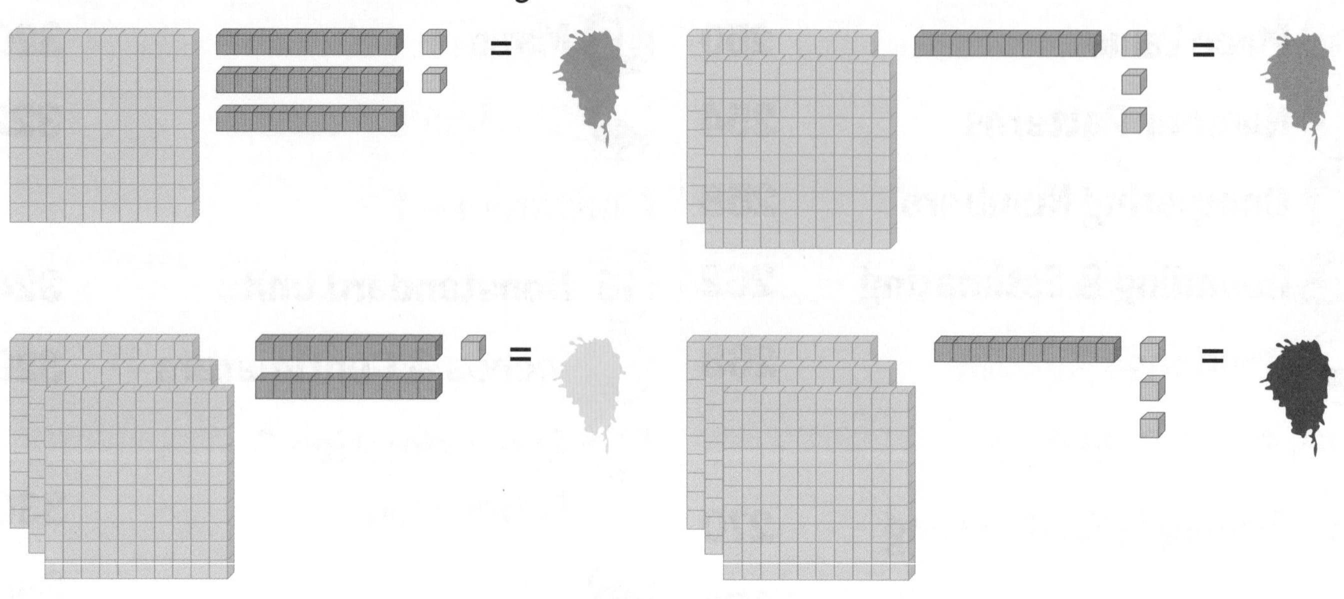

313	213	132	321	132	213	313	321
213	132	321	313	321	132	213	313
132	321	313	213	313	321	132	213
321	313	213	132	213	313	321	132
313	213	132	321	132	213	313	321
213	132	321	313	321	132	213	313
132	321	313	213	313	321	132	213
321	313	213	132	213	313	321	132

Safe Crackers

WRITE the number for each picture. Then WRITE the digit from the hundreds place of each number from left to right to find the combination for the safe.

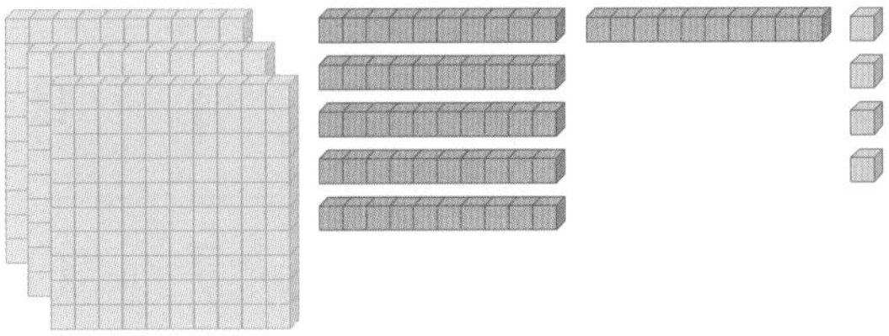

364

1

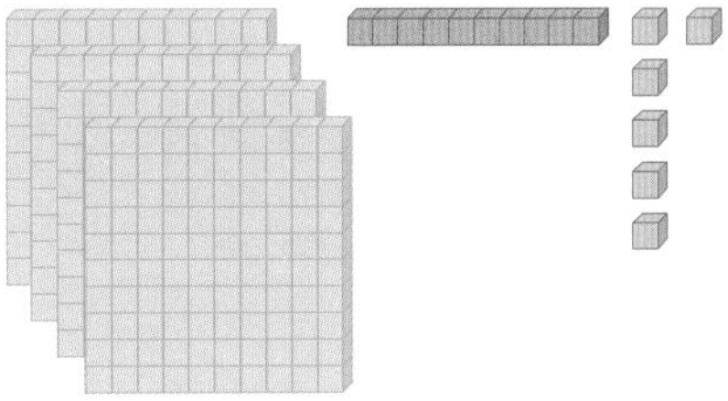

2

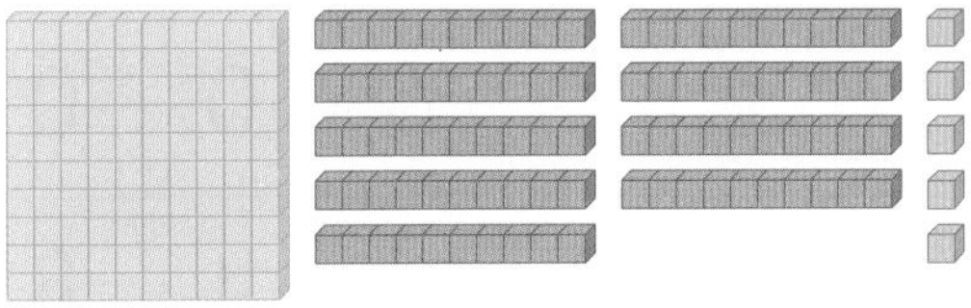

3

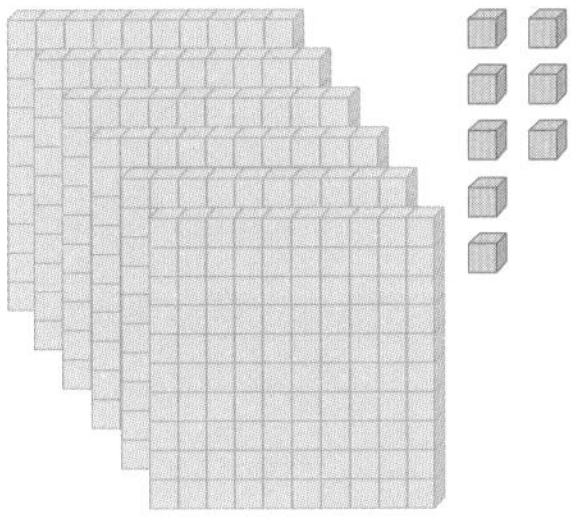

4

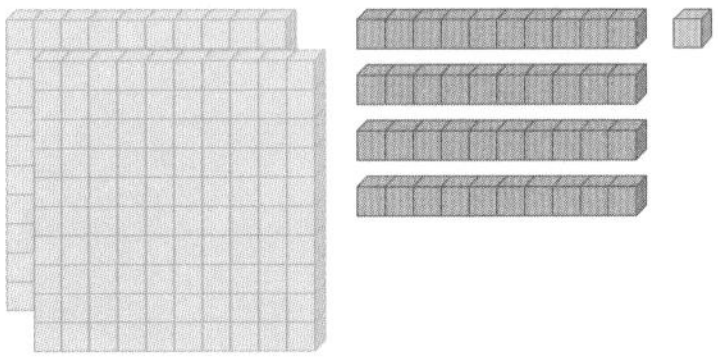

5

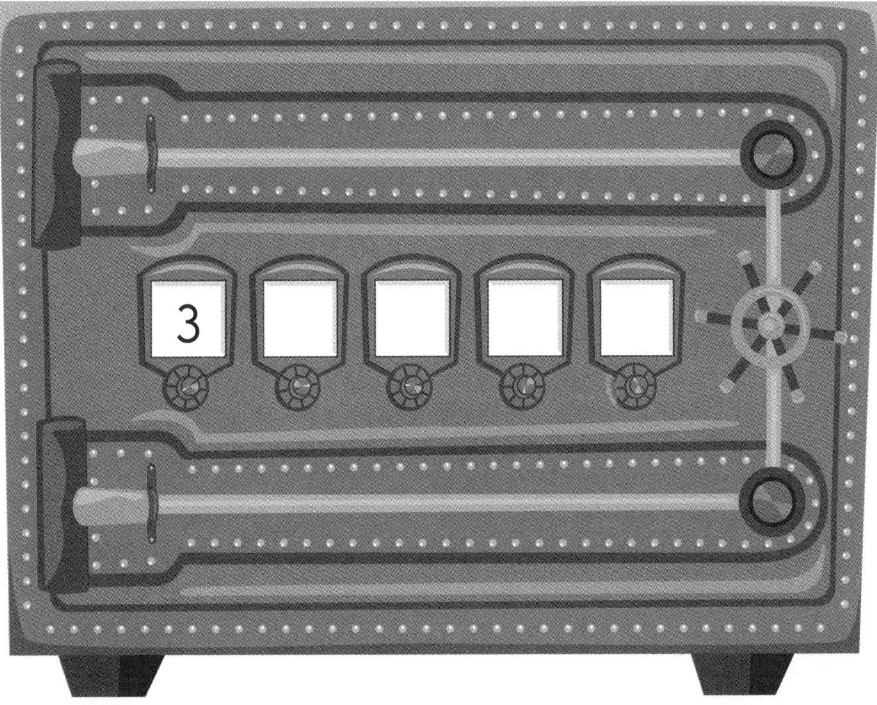

Number Search

WRITE the number for each picture. Then CIRCLE it in the puzzle.

HINT: Numbers are across and down only.

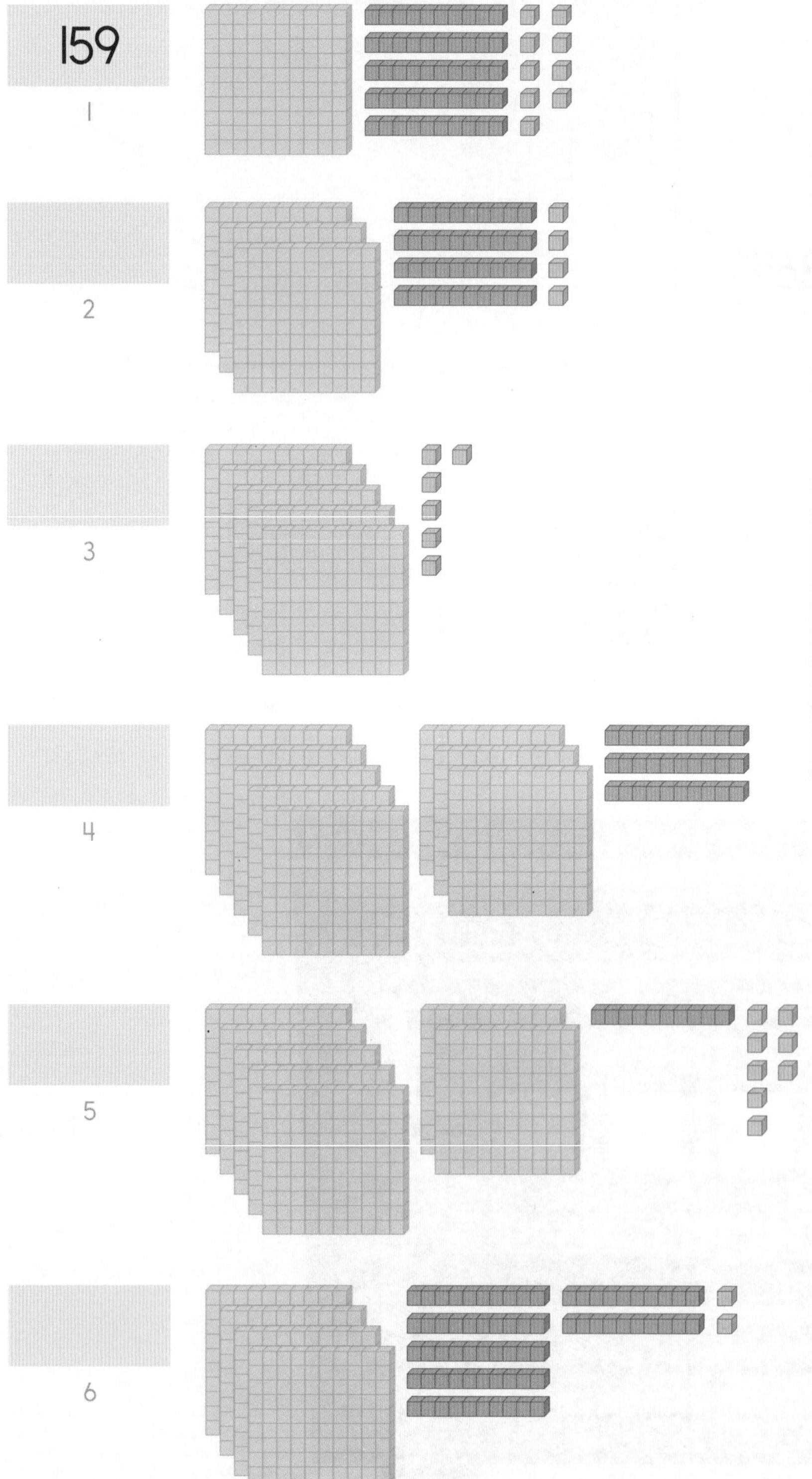

5	8	0	3	1	4
2	1	5	4	7	0
0	5	0	6	8	3
8	9	3	1	3	5
3	3	7	6	0	0
1	5	2	3	4	8
7	1	8	4	2	1
1	9	6	4	7	2

Roll It

ROLL a number cube, and WRITE the number in the first box. ROLL the number cube two more times, and WRITE the numbers in the second and third boxes. Then COLOR the hundreds, tens, and ones to match the number.

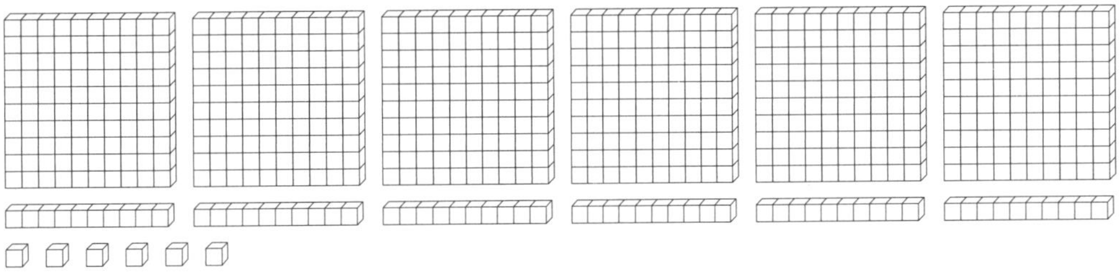

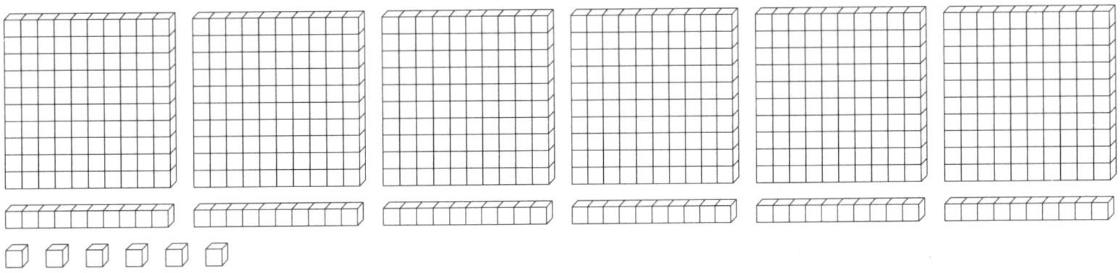

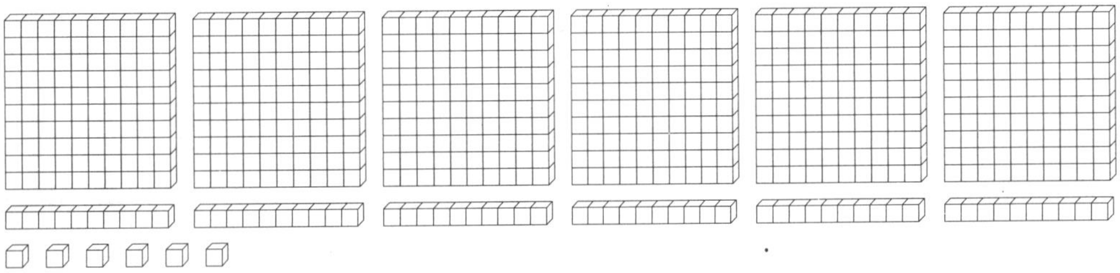

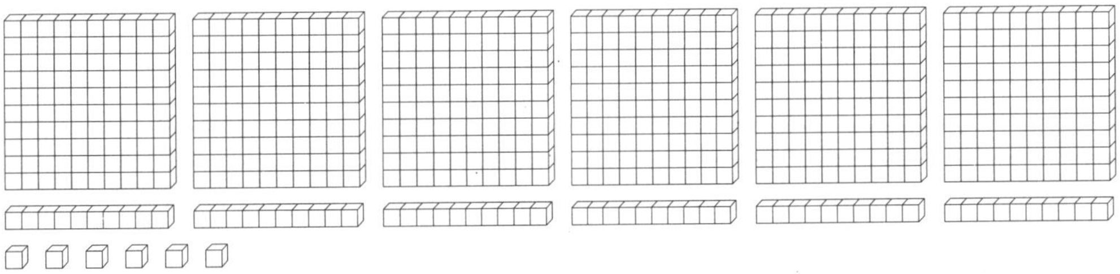

Code Breaker

WRITE the missing numbers. Then WRITE the letter that matches each number to solve the riddle.

1.

97	98	99		101	102		104
B			Y			K	

2.

213	214		216	217		219	
		I			R		U

3.

		748	749	750	751		
T	O					L	E

What did the zero say to the eight?

___	___	___	___	___
215	752	215	103	753

___	___	___	___		B	___	___	___	!
100	747	220	218		97	753	752	746	

Skipping Stones

DRAW a path by skip counting by 5 to cross the river.

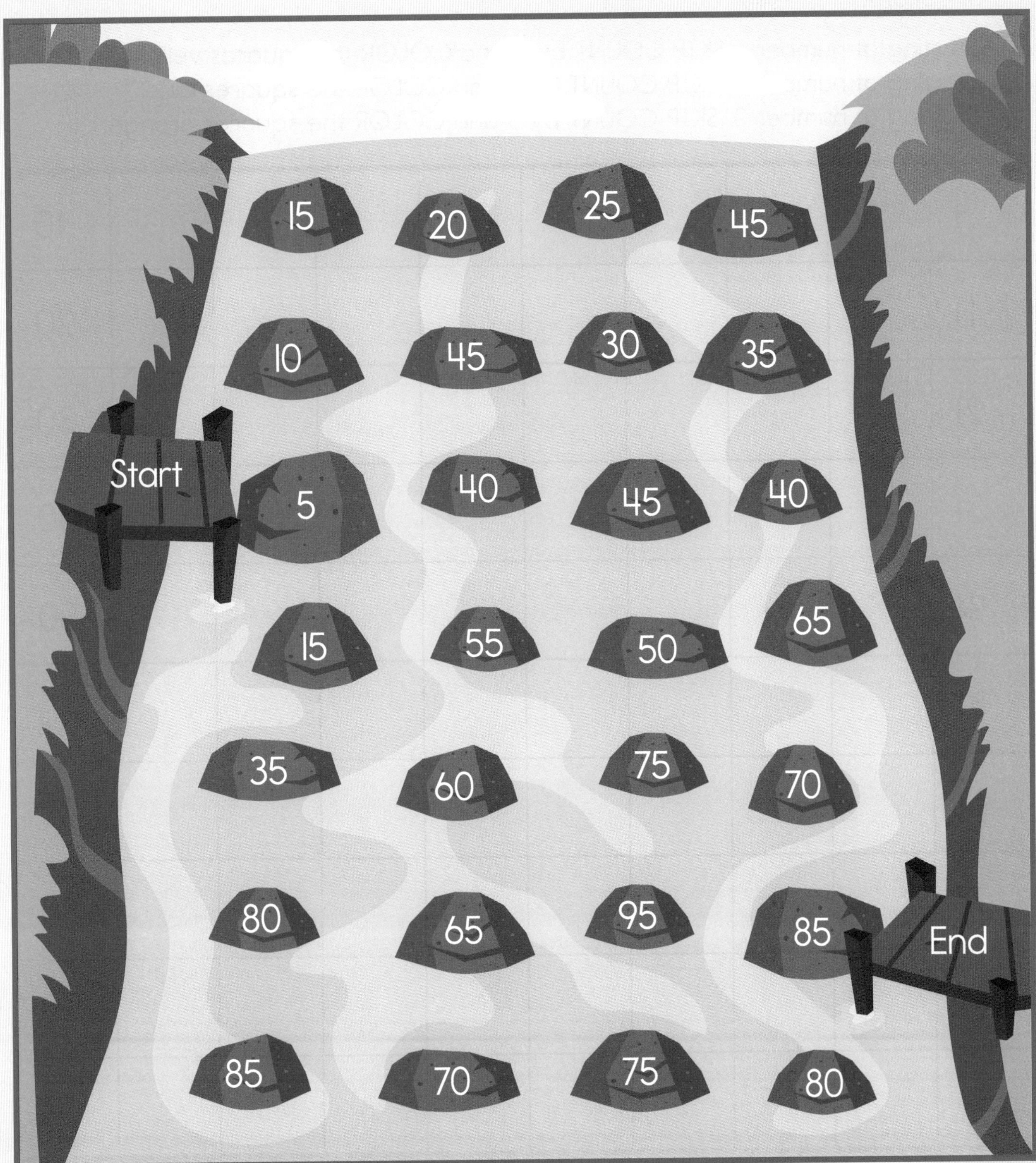

Three for Thrills

WRITE the numbers in the hundreds chart. Then COLOR the chart by following the directions.

1. Starting at number 1, SKIP COUNT by 3 and COLOR the squares yellow.
2. Starting at number 2, SKIP COUNT by 3 and COLOR the squares blue.
3. Starting at number 3, SKIP COUNT by 3 and COLOR the squares orange.

1	2								10
11									20
21									30
31									40
41									50
51									60
61									70
71									80
81									90
91									100

Skip to My Loo

SKIP COUNT by 10, 4, and 7, and WRITE the numbers along each track.

Skip count by:

Finish

10	4	7				
10	4	7				
20						

Just Right

WRITE each number next to a smaller blue number.

HINT: There may be more than one place to put a number, but you need to use every number.

742 113 981 187 256 677 409 556 823 399

599	1	98	2
724	3	545	4
750	5	251	6
830	7	400	8
178	9	398	10

Totally Tangled

Each numbered circle is connected to another numbered circle. FIND the pairs of numbers, and COLOR the circle with the smaller number.

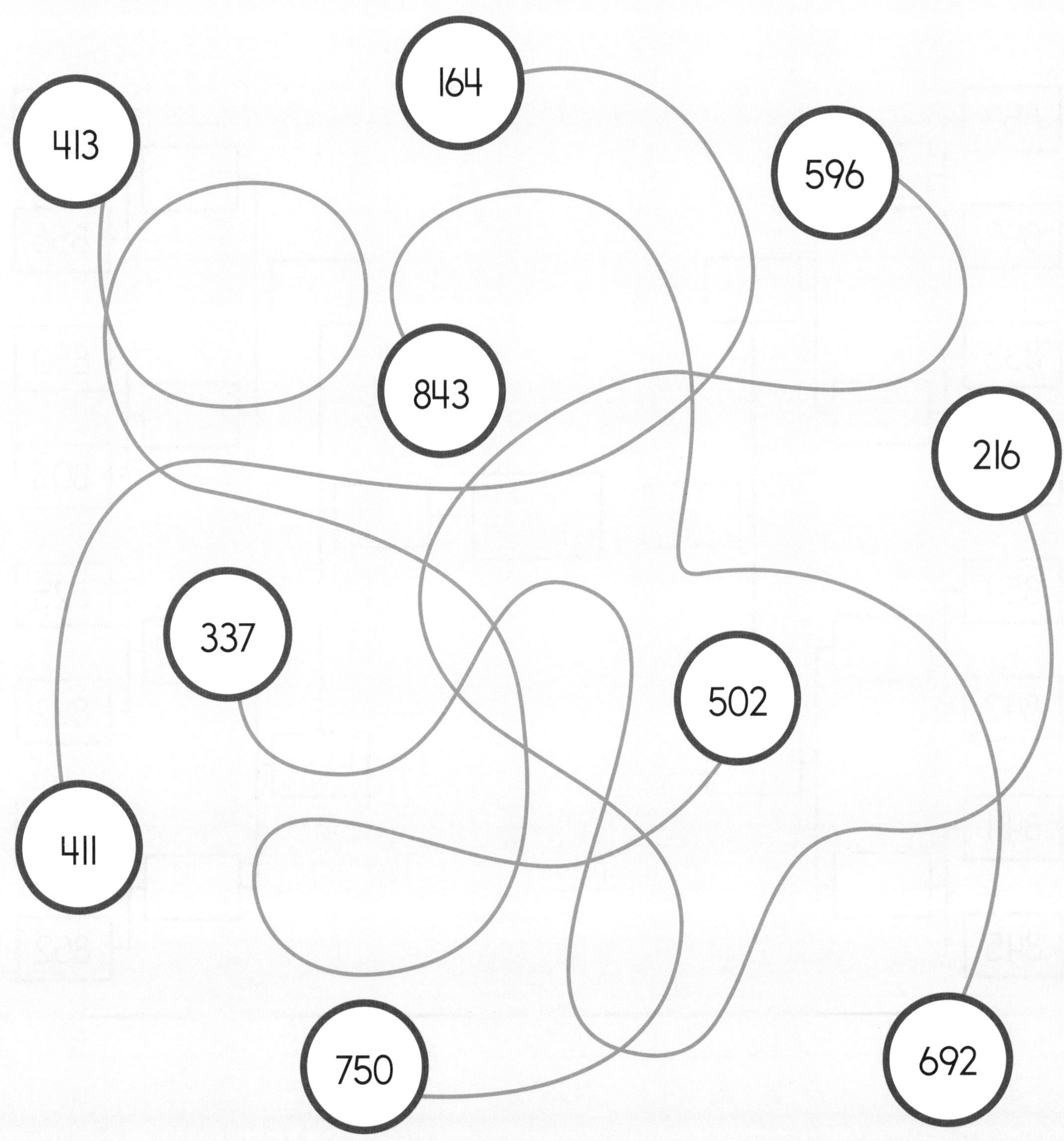

Win Big

Wherever two boxes point to one box, WRITE the larger number. Start at the sides and work toward the center to see which number will win big.

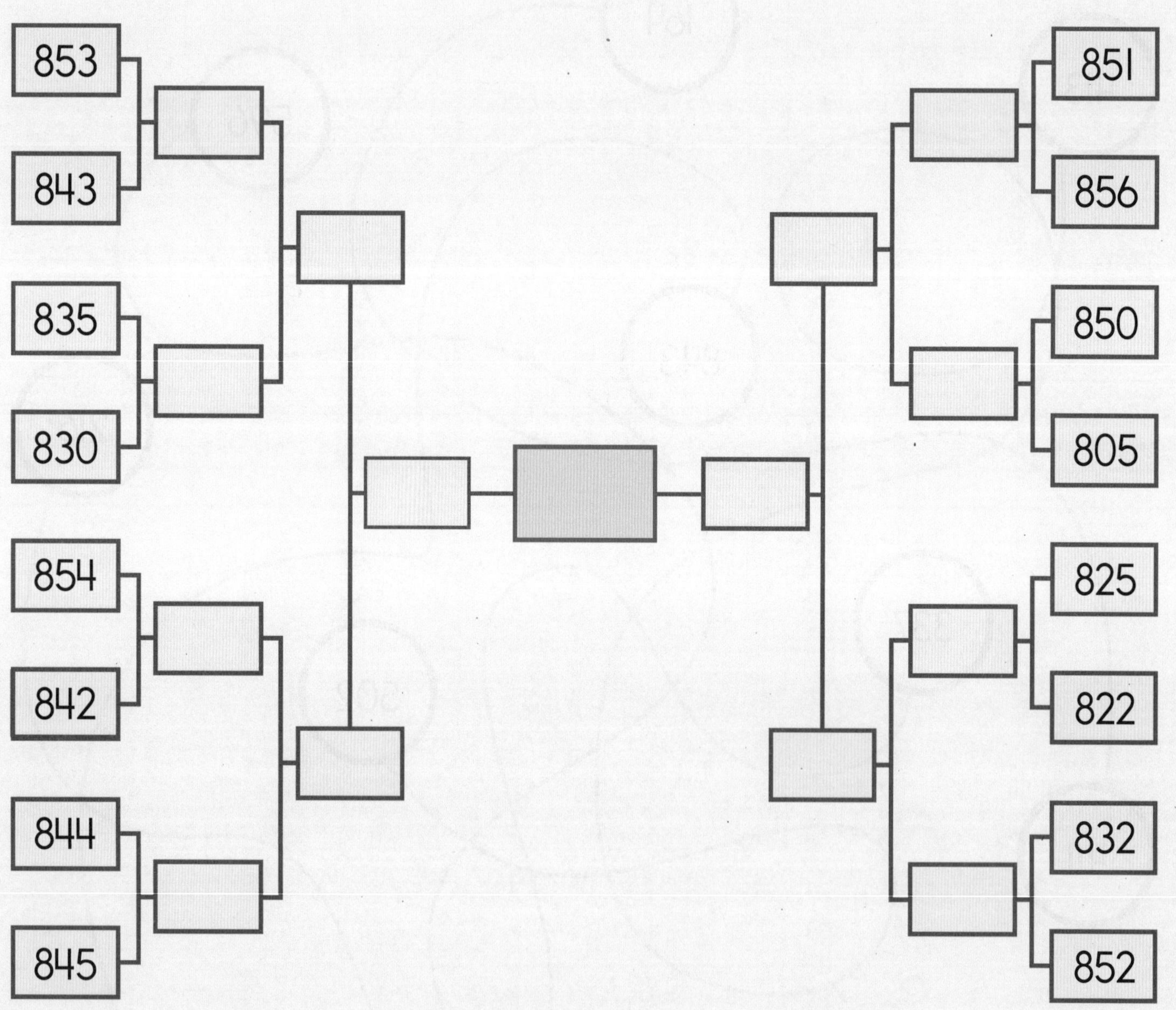

Totally Tangled

Each numbered circle is connected to another numbered circle. FIND the pairs of numbers, and COLOR the circle with the larger number.

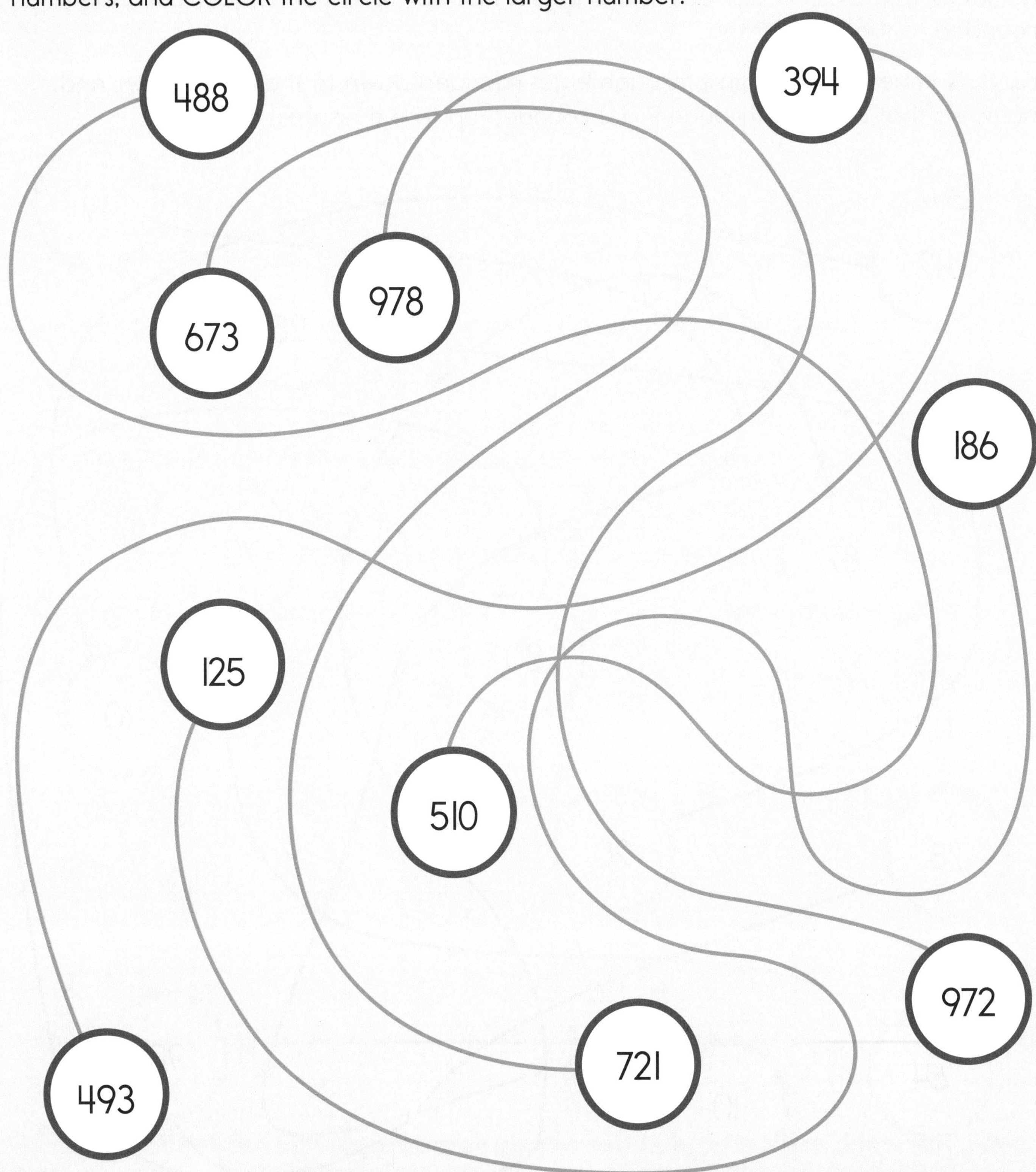

Totally Tangled

Each numbered circle is connected to another numbered circle. FIND the pairs of numbers, and COLOR any pair that shows a number with that number correctly rounded to the nearest ten.

HINT: Numbers that end in 1 through 4 get rounded down to the nearest ten, and numbers that end in 5 through 9 get rounded up to the nearest ten.

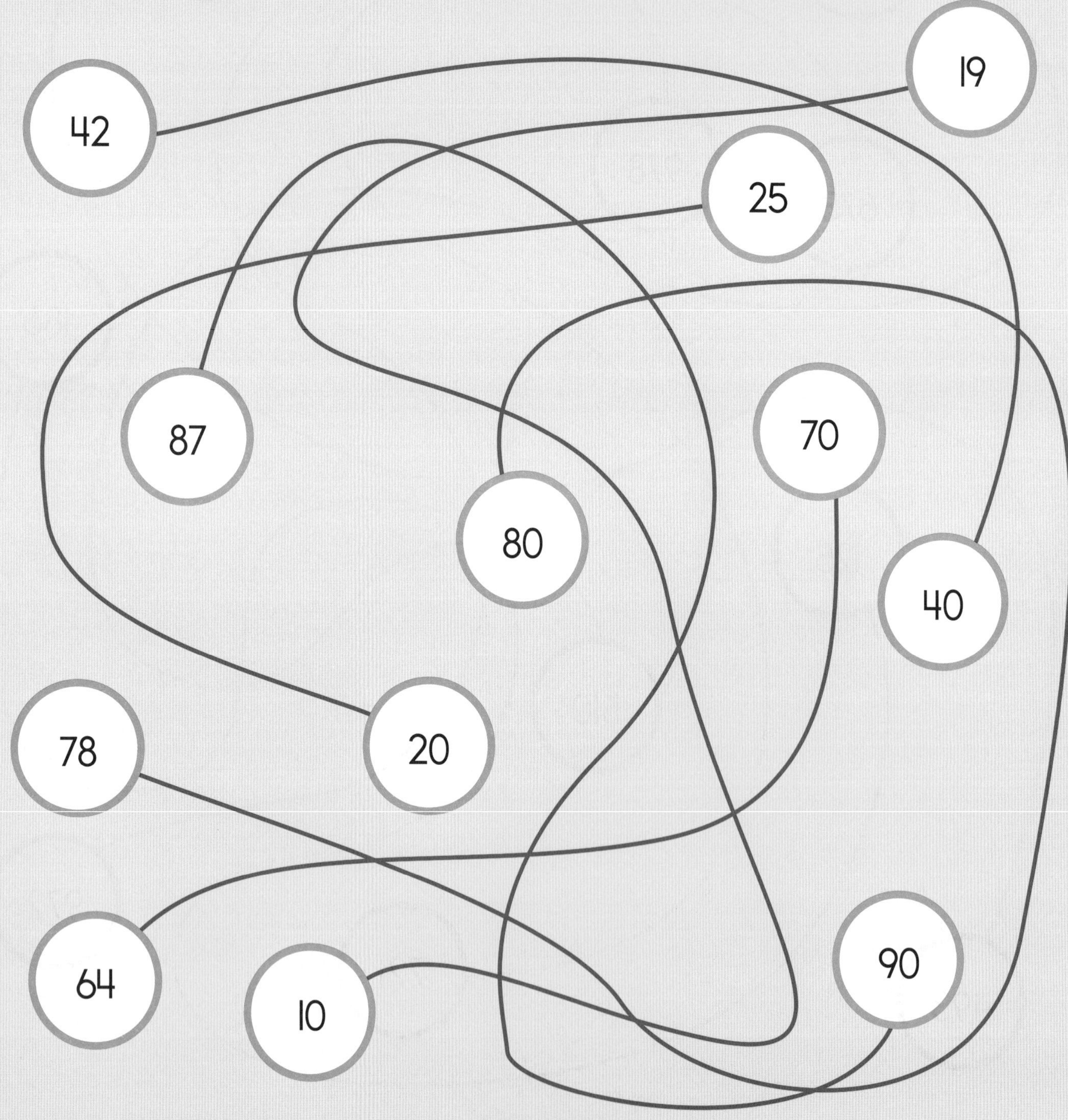

Roll It

ROLL a number cube, and WRITE the number in the first box. ROLL the number cube two more times, and WRITE the numbers in the second and third boxes. Then ROUND each number to the nearest ten and the nearest hundred.

HINT: Numbers that end in 1 through 49 get rounded down to the nearest hundred, and numbers that end in 50 through 99 get rounded up to the nearest hundred.

			Nearest Ten	Nearest Hundred

Just Right

WRITE each of the numbers to correctly complete the sentences. There may be more than one place to put a number, but you need to use every number.

HINT: Numbers that end in 1 through 49 get rounded down to the nearest hundred, and numbers that end in 50 through 99 get rounded up to the nearest hundred.

549	278	709	751	952
717	932	285	544	

1. ________ rounded to the nearest hundred is 300.
2. ________ rounded to the nearest ten is 540.
3. ________ rounded to the nearest hundred is 700.
4. ________ rounded to the nearest ten is 950.
5. ________ rounded to the nearest hundred is 500.
6. ________ rounded to the nearest ten is 280.
7. ________ rounded to the nearest hundred is 900.
8. ________ rounded to the nearest ten is 720.
9. ________ rounded to the nearest hundred is 800.

Fitting In

GUESS how many marbles are needed to fill the circle. WRITE your guess. Then turn the page to CHECK your guess.

Guess: ______ marbles

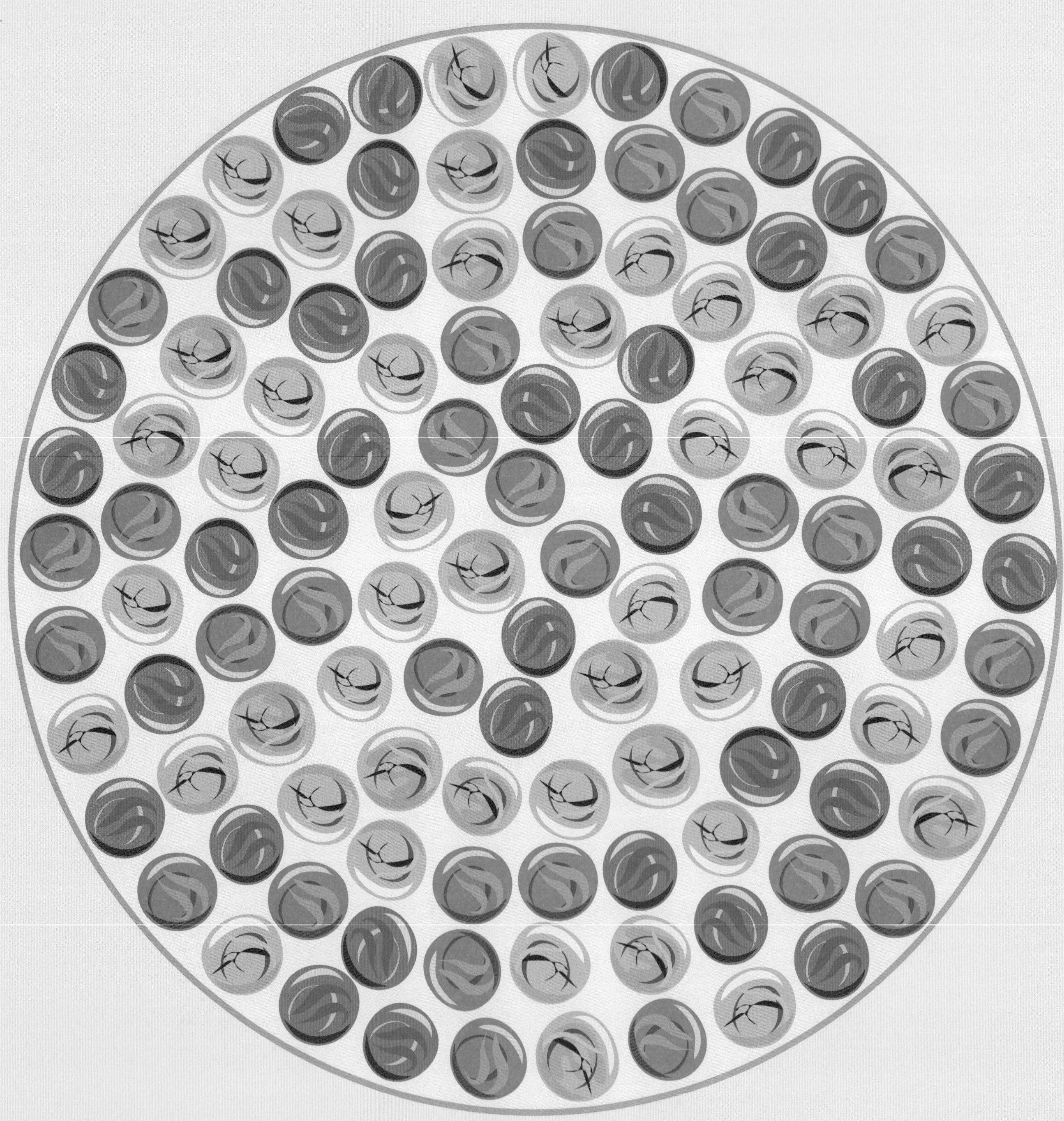

Check: marbles

Fitting In

GUESS how many pennies are needed to fill the square. WRITE your guess. Then fill the square with pennies to CHECK your guess.

Guess: ______ pennies   Check: ______ pennies

Spiraling Sequence

SKIP COUNT by 6, and WRITE the numbers. Can you finish the spiral to the center?

6	12	18				

Who Am I?

READ the clues, and CIRCLE the mystery number.

HINT: Cross out any number that does not match the clues.

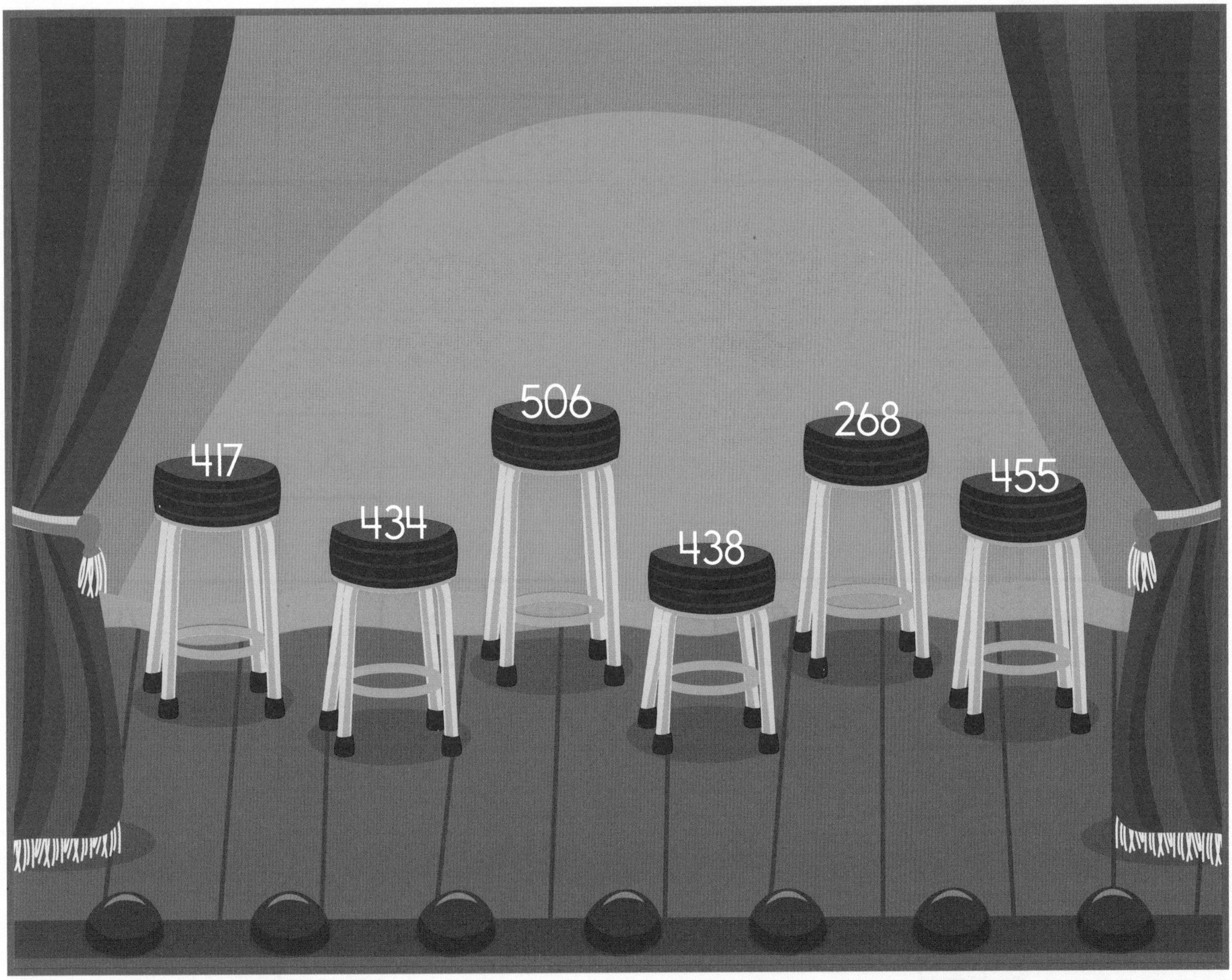

417 434 506 438 268 455

I am more than 300.

I am less than 500.

When rounded to the nearest hundred, I'm 400.

I have a 3 in the tens place.

When rounded to the nearest ten, I'm 440.

Who am I?

Missing Middles

WRITE the number missing from the center square.

1.

32
+
17 + = 38
=
53

2.

43
+
50 + = 66
=
59

3.

12
+
44 + = 89
=
57

4.

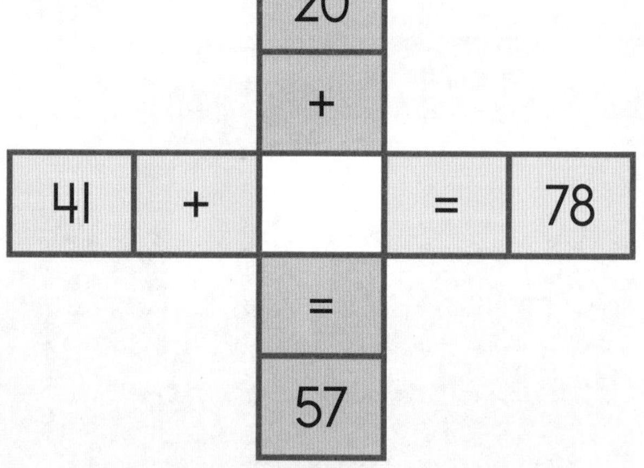

5.

31
+
23 + = 85
=
93

6.

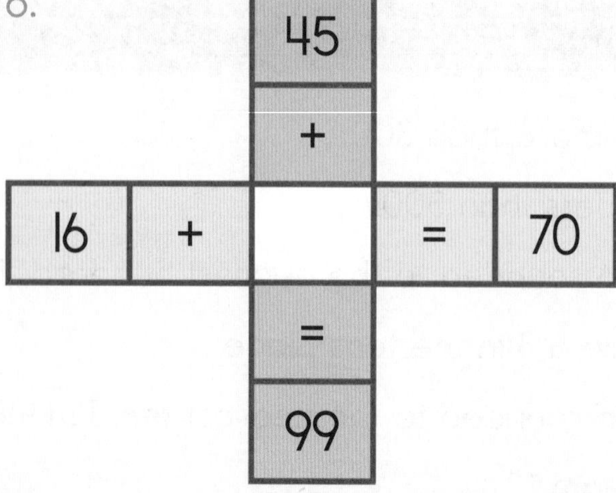

Crossing Paths

WRITE the missing numbers.

3 + 11 = ___ + 23 = ___ + 20 = ___ + 18 = ___ + 14 = ___

5 + 11 = ___ + 23 = ___ + 20 = ___ + 18 = ___ + 14 = ___

4 + 37 = ___ + 12 = ___ + 8 = ___ + 25 = ___ + 14 = ___

2 + 37 = ___ + 12 = ___ + 8 = ___ + 25 = ___ + 14 = ___

Super Square

WRITE numbers in the empty squares to finish all of the addition problems.

3	+	12	=	
+		+		+
9	+		=	
=		=		=
	+	37	=	

Code Breaker

SOLVE each problem. WRITE the letter that matches each sum to solve the riddle.

1	2	3	4
11 + 26 = ___ O	38 + 30 = ___ L	46 + 13 = ___ V	21 + 58 = ___ C

5	6	7	8
43 + 52 = ___ P	17 + 31 = ___ I	81 + 12 = ___ N	67 + 10 = ___ A

9	10	11	12
29 + 34 = ___ T	13 + 58 = ___ G	62 + 18 = ___ E	77 + 14 = ___ S

Where does the pencil go on vacation?

___ ___   ___ ___ ___ ___   ___ ___

48 63   71 37 80 91   63 37

___ ___ ___ ___ ___ ___ ___ ___ ___ ___ ___.

95 80 93 79 48 68 59 77 93 48 77

Pipe Down

WRITE each number. Then FOLLOW the pipe, and WRITE the same number in the next problem.

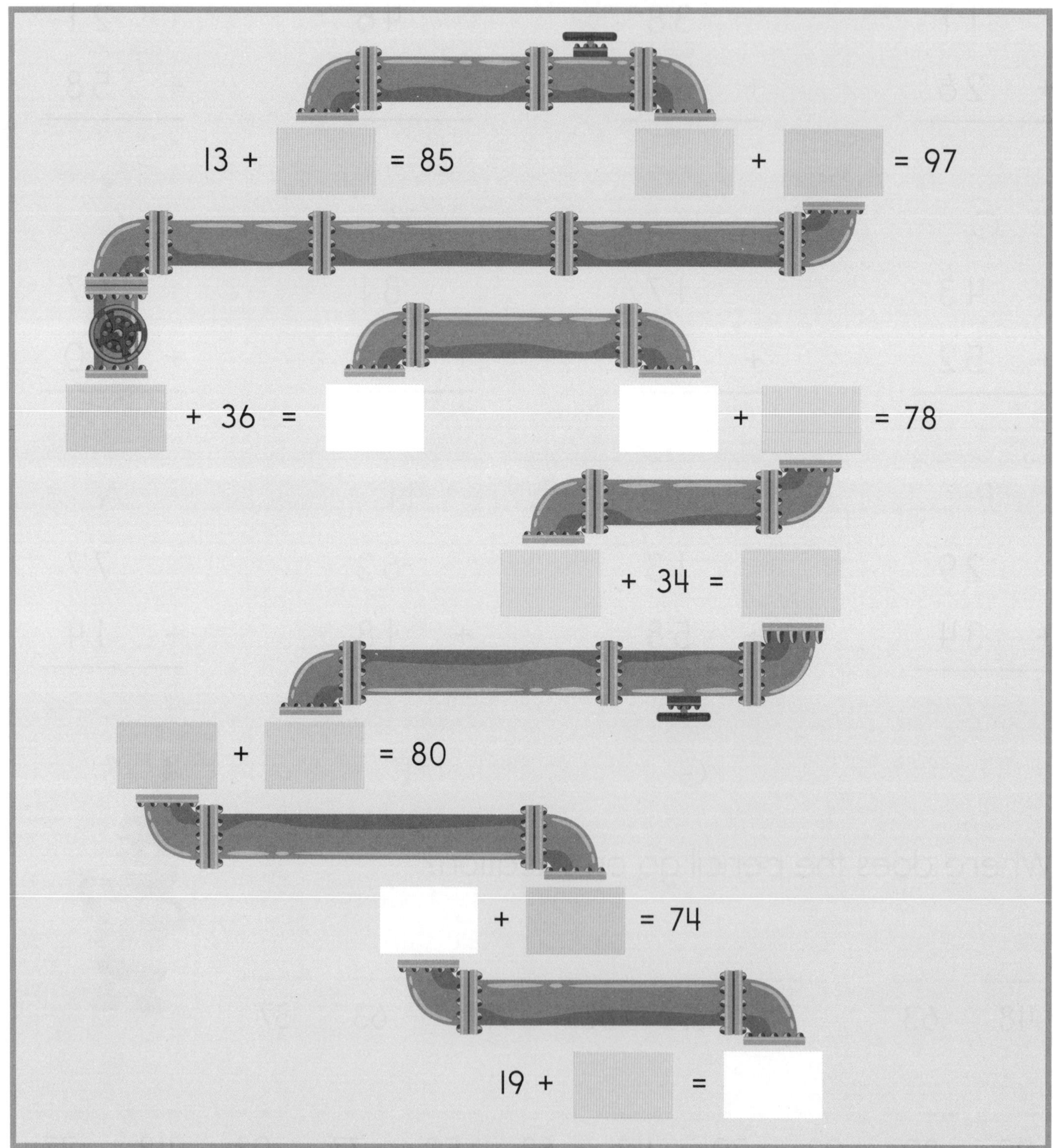

Ground Floor

DRAW a line connecting one of the numbers in the windows at the top with the sum on the ground floor. CHOOSE one operation from each floor on the way down.

HINT: When you're done, can you find more ways to the ground floor?

Missing Middles

WRITE the number missing from the center square.

1.

		48		
		–		
25	–		=	13
		=		
		36		

2.

		37		
		–		
78	–		=	45
		=		
		4		

3.

		86		
		–		
99	–		=	28
		=		
		15		

4.

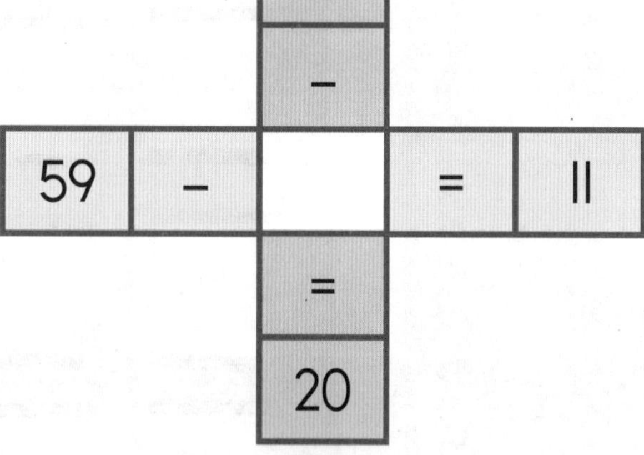

5.

		95		
		–		
44	–		=	22
		=		
		73		

6.

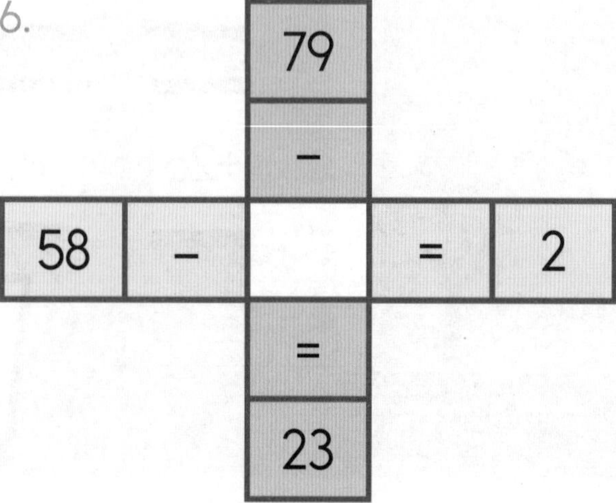

Crossing Paths

WRITE the missing numbers.

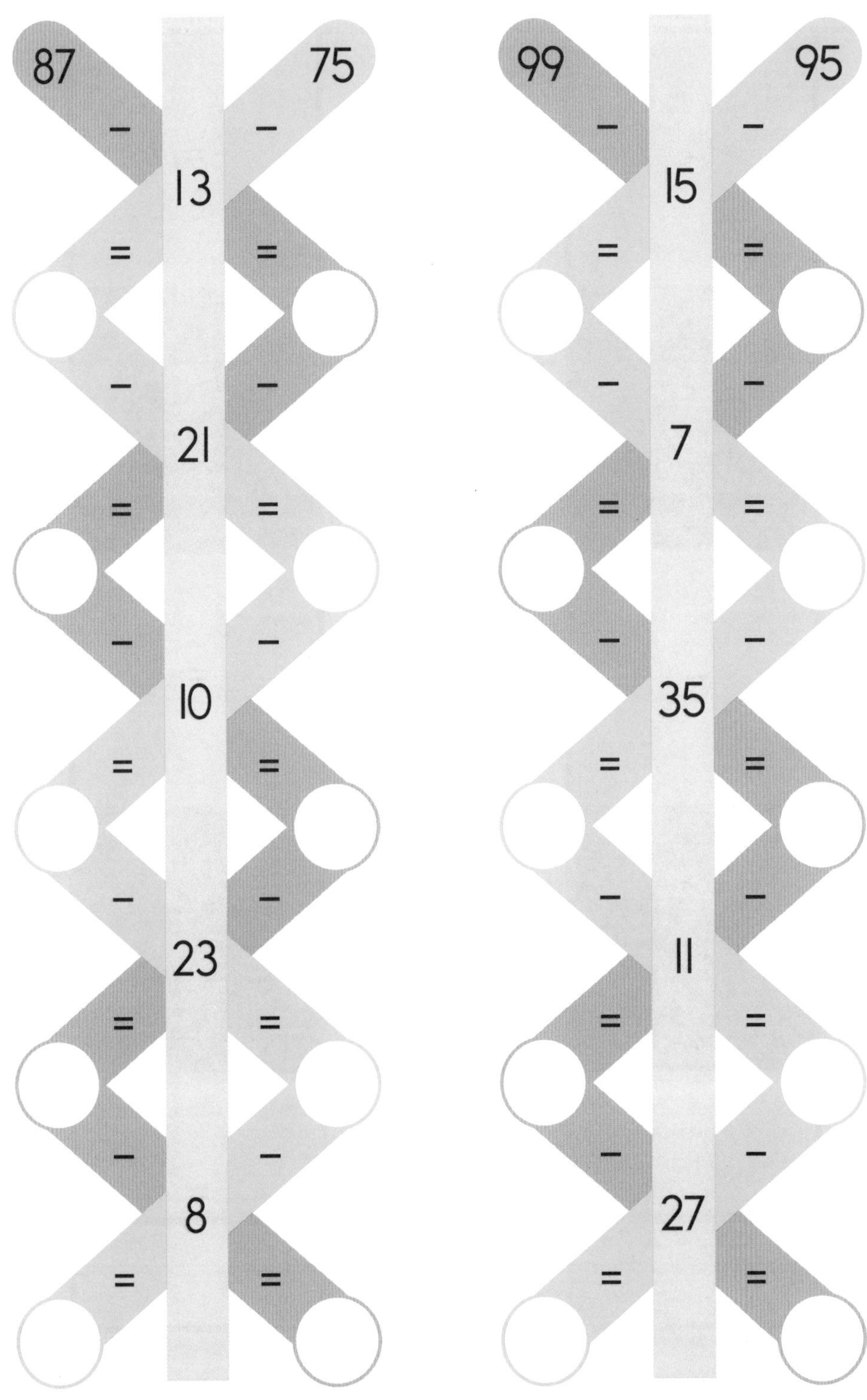

Super Square

WRITE numbers in the empty squares to finish all of the subtraction problems.

95	–		=	32
–		–		–
47	–		=	
=		=		=
	–	46	=	

Code Breaker

SOLVE each problem. WRITE the letter that matches each difference to solve the riddle.

1	2	3	4	5	6
42 − 11	75 − 52	18 − 16	84 − 62	91 − 45	72 − 23
W	D	O	A	L	V

7	8	9	10	11	12
63 − 37	71 − 19	72 − 59	96 − 49	60 − 24	52 − 36
U	T	S	Y	E	H

If you took two toys away from seven toys, how many toys would you have?

___ ___ ___   ___ ___ ___ ___ ___
47 2 26   31 2 26 46 23

___ ___ ___ ___   ___ ___ ___
16 22 49 36   52 31 2

___ ___ ___ ___.
52 2 47 13

Pipe Down

WRITE each number. Then FOLLOW the pipe, and WRITE the same number in the next problem.

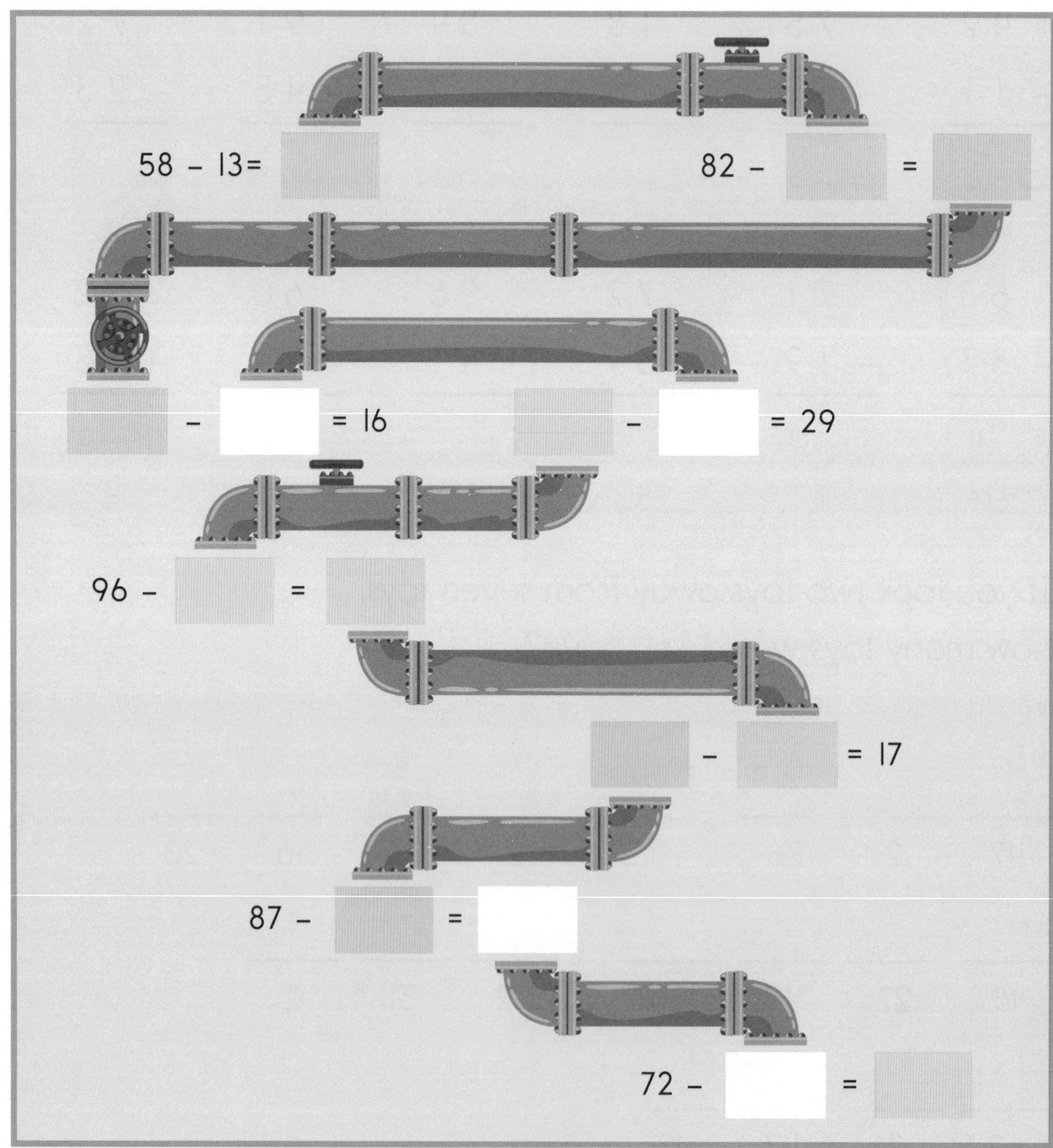

Ground Floor

DRAW a line connecting one of the numbers in the windows at the top with the difference on the ground floor. CHOOSE one operation from each floor on the way down.

HINT: When you're done, can you find more ways to the ground floor?

Crossing Paths

WRITE the missing numbers.

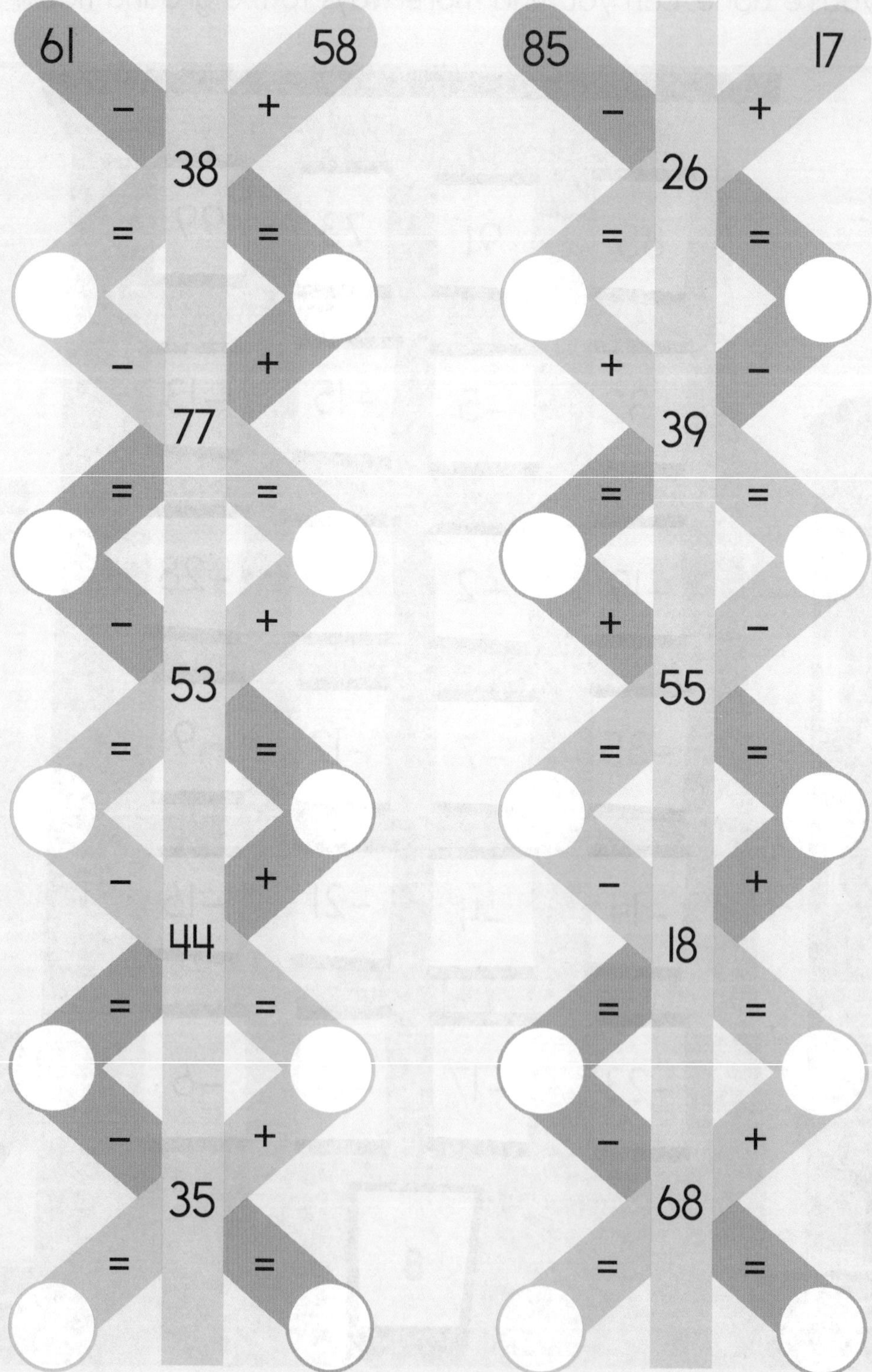

Ground Floor

DRAW a line connecting one of the numbers in the windows at the top with the answer on the ground floor. CHOOSE one operation from each floor on the way down.

HINT: When you're done, can you find more ways to the ground floor?

15	62	28	87
+35	−18	+65	−38
+12	−17	+47	−9
−13	+15	−25	+56
+22	−91	−75	+16
+45	+39	−19	−27

53

Sandy Shore

DRAW two straight lines in the sand to create four equal sets of shells.

Car Clubs

FIND each kind of car in the picture. WRITE the number of groups that can be made from each kind of car.

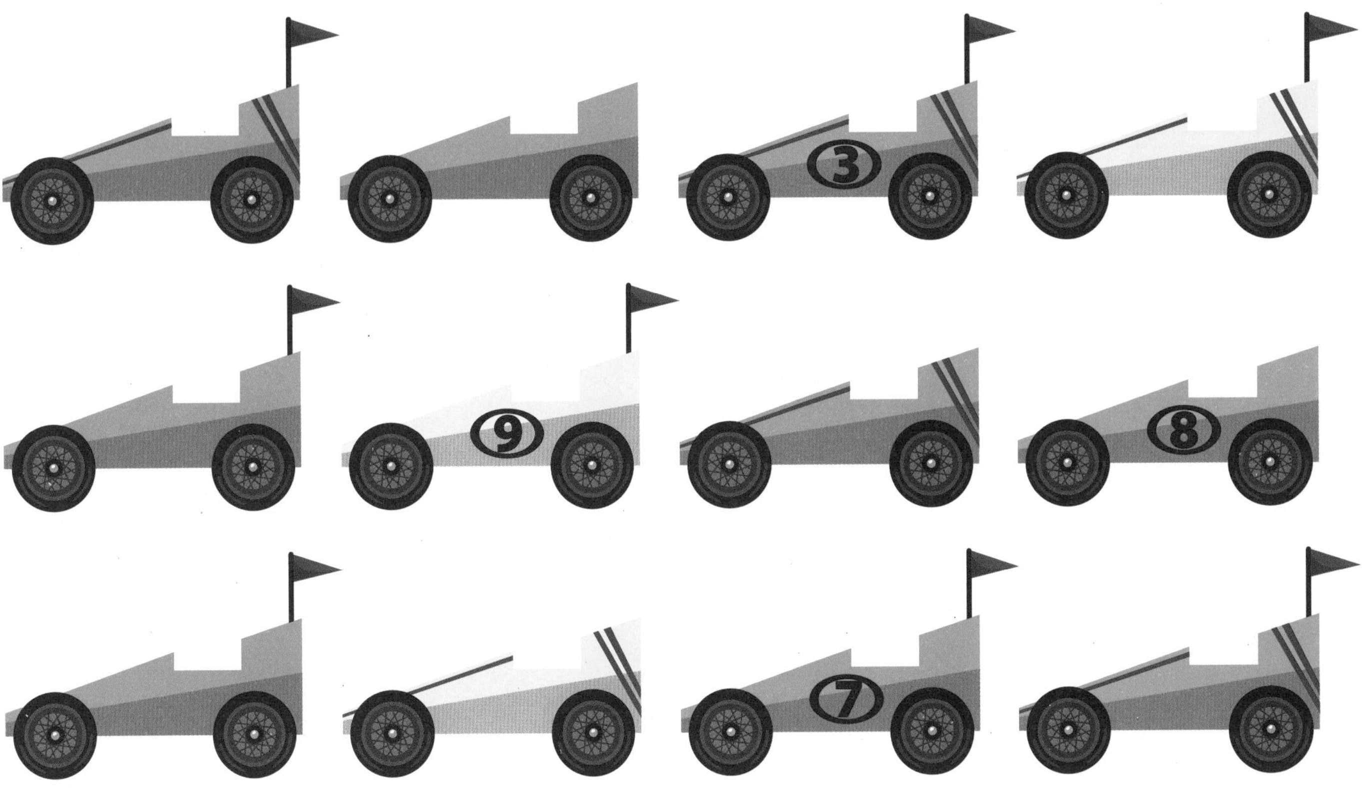

1. Groups of three blue cars 3
2. Groups of two cars with numbers ______
3. Groups of two cars with black wheels ______
4. Groups of four cars with flags ______
5. Groups of three yellow cars ______
6. Groups of two cars with red stripes ______

Sandy Shore

DRAW three straight lines in the sand to create six equal sets of shells.

Bug Buddies

FIND each kind of bug in the picture. WRITE the number of groups that can be made from each kind of bug.

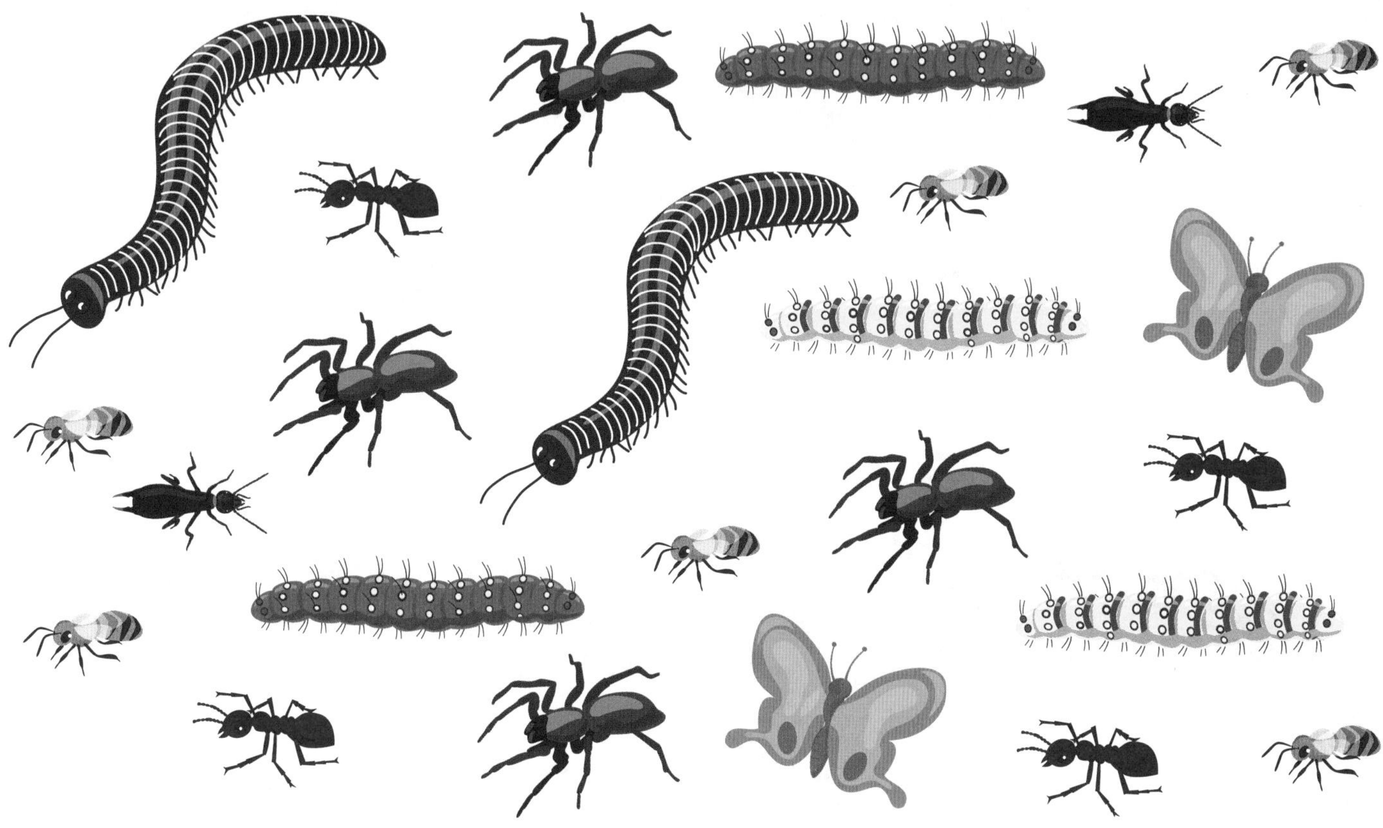

1. Groups of four brown bugs ______

2. Groups of two bugs with wings ______

3. Groups of three bugs with more than eight legs ______

4. Groups of two striped bugs ______

5. Groups of four bugs that can't fly ______

6. Groups of two bugs with eight legs ______

Bean Counter

Use the beans from page 359, and SHARE them equally among the bowls. Start with the number of beans listed, then WRITE how many beans will be in each bowl when the beans are shared equally. (Save the beans to use again later in the workbook.)

1. 9 beans: _______ per bowl
2. 15 beans: _______ per bowl
3. 6 beans: _______ per bowl
4. 18 beans: _______ per bowl
5. 24 beans: _______ per bowl
6. 12 beans: _______ per bowl

Going Bananas

The monkeys want bananas! DRAW a line from each monkey at the top to his basket at the bottom to collect the bananas. You can only cross each banana once, and the monkeys must each end up with the same number of bananas. You must use all of the bananas.

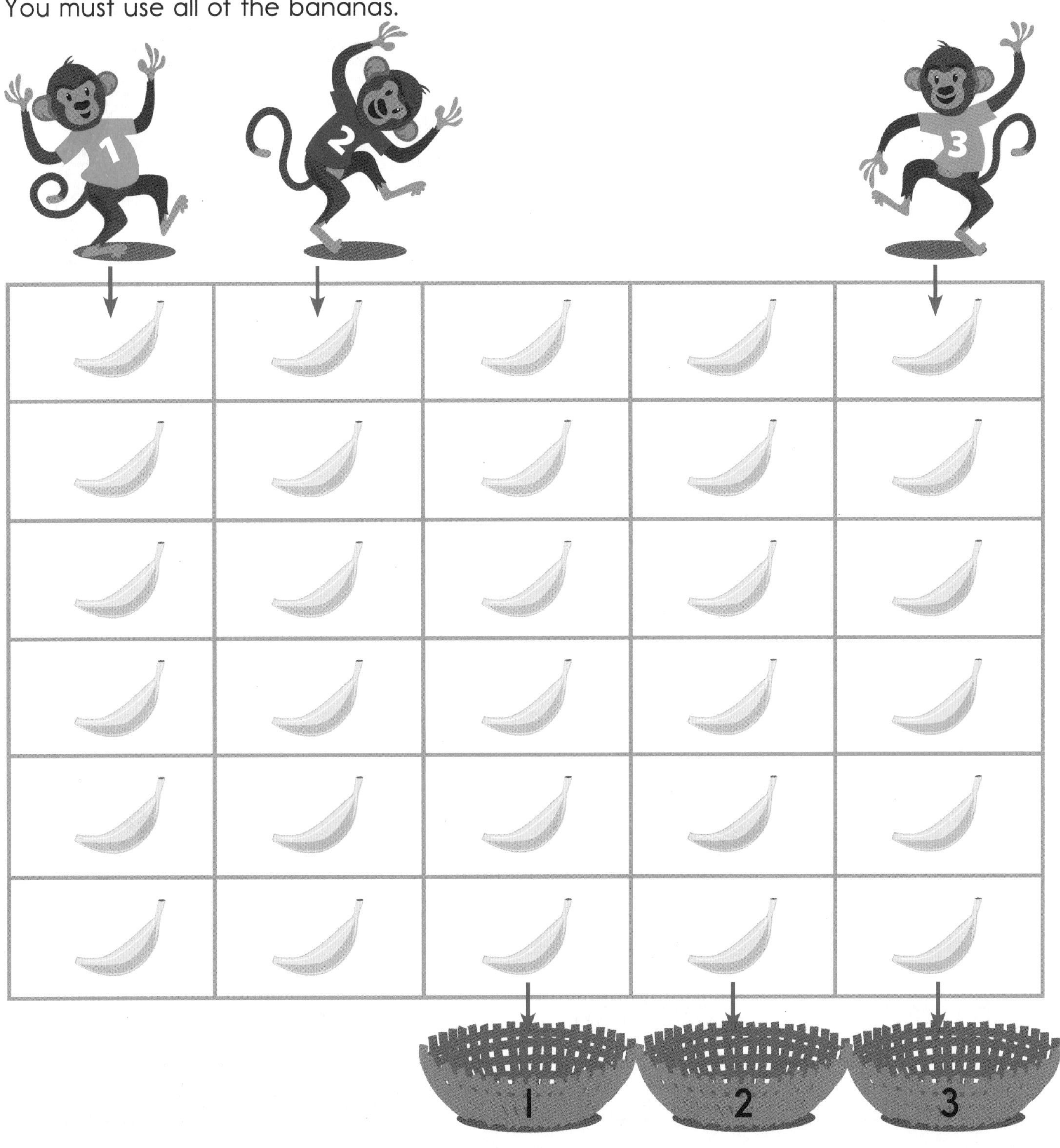

Bean Counter

Use the beans from page 359, and SHARE them equally among the bowls. Start with the number of beans listed, then WRITE how many beans will be in each bowl when the beans are shared equally. (Save the beans to use again.)

1. 16 beans: ______ per bowl
2. 32 beans: ______ per bowl
3. 8 beans: ______ per bowl
4. 28 beans: ______ per bowl
5. 20 beans: ______ per bowl
6. 48 beans: ______ per bowl

Count and Capture

The object of the game is to capture the most beans. Use the beans from page 359, an egg carton with the top cut off, and two small bowls. READ the rules. PLAY the game.

1. Set up the game by putting the bowls at either end of the egg carton and placing four beans in each egg carton section. Each player owns the sections on his side.
2. The youngest player goes first. To take a turn, a player scoops up all of the beans from one of his sections, then places one bean at a time in each section, moving to the right (counterclockwise).

   Example: Player 1 scoops up four beans from the yellow section, and places one bean in each orange section that follows to the right.

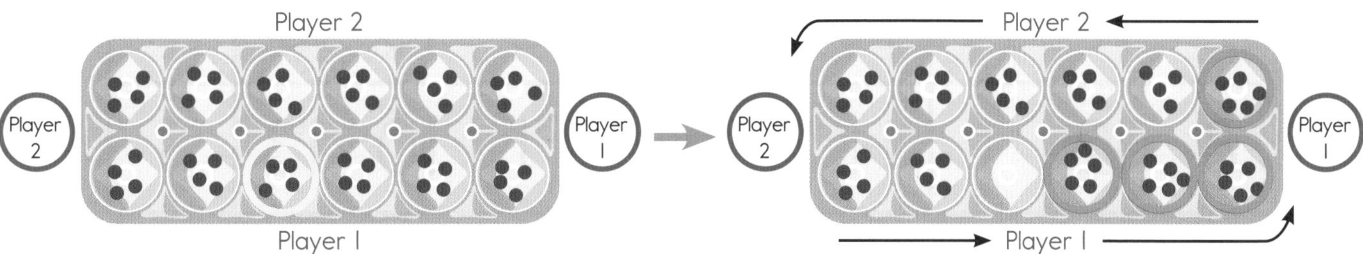

3. A player captures beans when placing a bean in any of the other player's sections to make a total of two or three beans. Captured beans go in the player's bowl.

   Example: Player 1 moves the beans from the yellow section and captures the beans in the two orange sections because the total number of beans is two and three. He then puts all of the captured beans in his bowl.

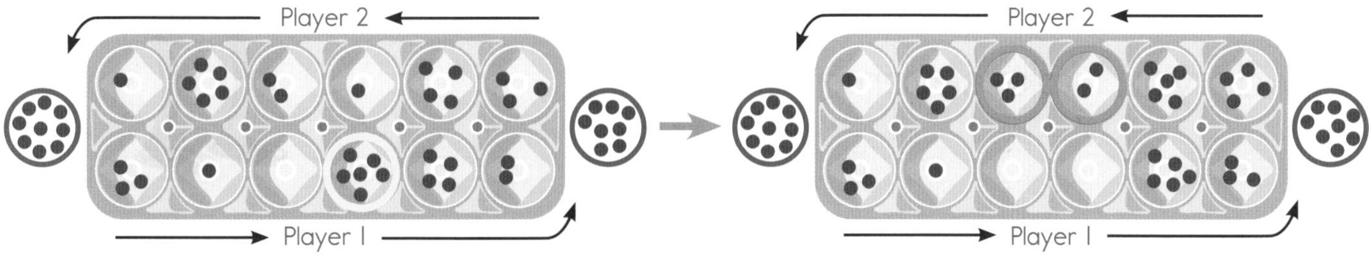

4. Play continues until all of the beans are captured or no more moves can be made.

The player with the most beans wins!

Code Breaker

FIND the odd or even number in each row. Then WRITE the letter that matches each number to solve the riddle.

FIND the odd number in each row.

1.	3	4	8	K
2.	10	7	6	W
3.	2	9	14	A
4.	8	12	1	H

FIND the even number in each row.

5.	7	5	6	E
6.	12	9	11	T
7.	8	15	3	Y
8.	1	10	13	S

How do you make seven even?

____ ____ ____ ____   ____ ____ ____ ____

12 9 3 6   9 7 9 8

____ ____ ____   ____.

12 1 6   10

Odd Way Out

START at the arrow. DRAW a line through only odd numbers to get to the smiley face.

13
8 18
3
7 5 6
14 2 1 12
15 9
20 8 18
11 10
13
24
16 14
17
12 25 13 21
19 3 5
6
22 14

Where's My Brain?

START at the arrow. DRAW a path through only even numbers to reach the brain.

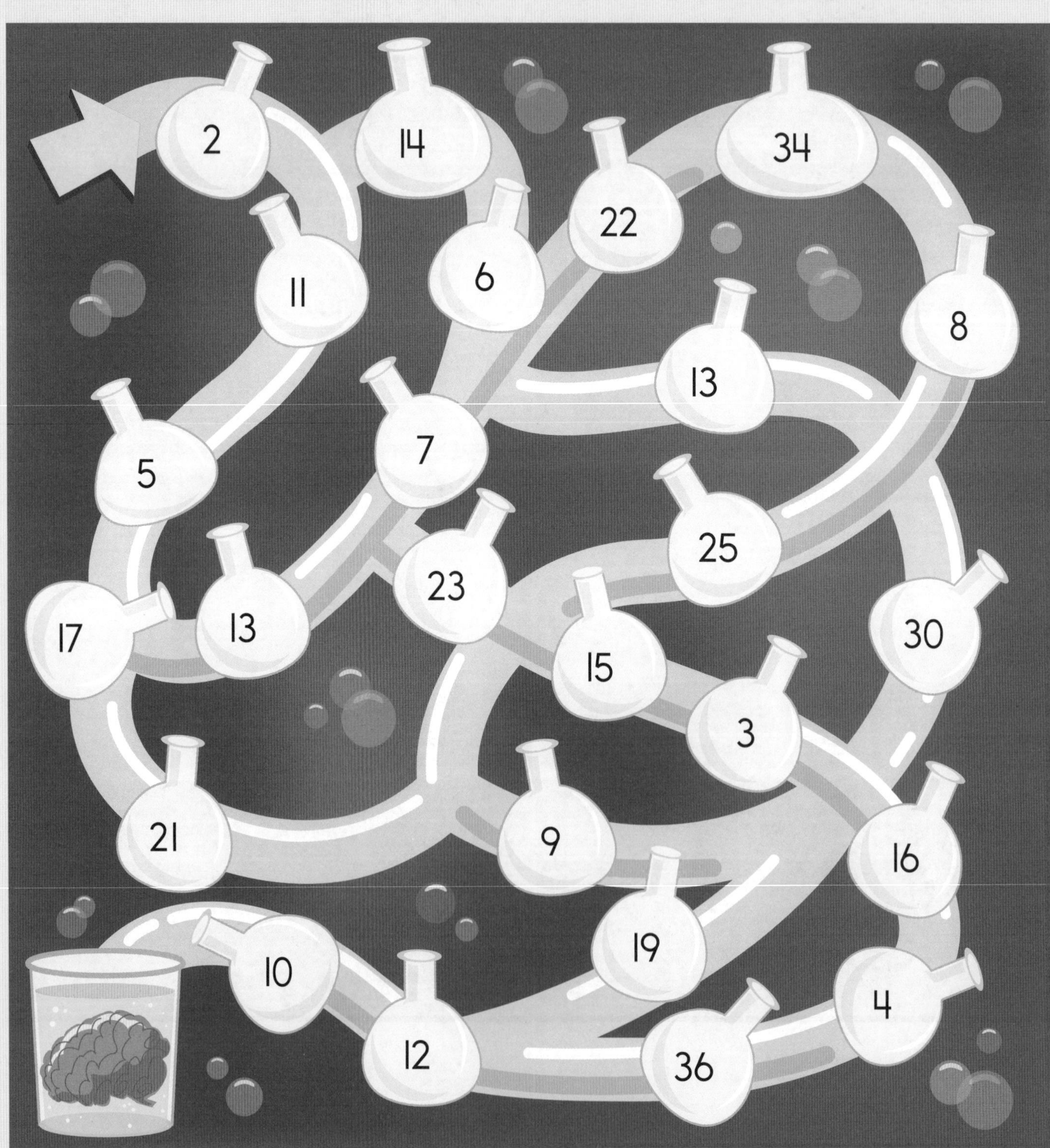

Alien Adventure

Can you be the first alien to reach the spaceship? Use two small objects as playing pieces and the spinner from page 361. READ the rules. PLAY the game! (Save the spinner to use again later in the workbook.)

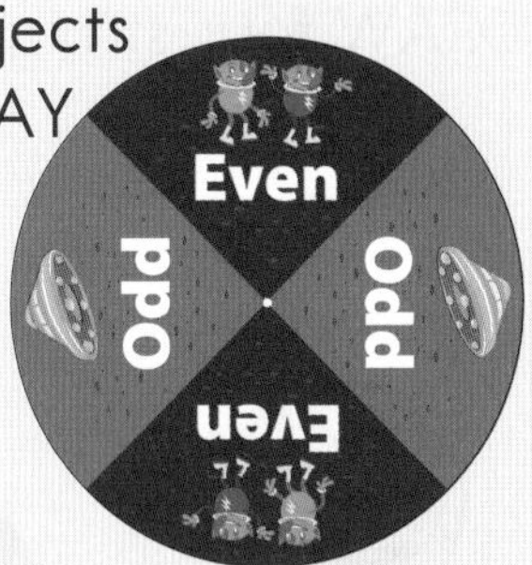

Even
Odd
Even
Odd

Rules: Two players

1. Place the playing pieces at Start.
2. Take turns spinning the spinner. If you spin Odd, move to the next odd number. If you spin Even, move to the next even number.
3. If you land on a space with an asteroid, you lose a turn.

The first player to get to the spaceship wins!

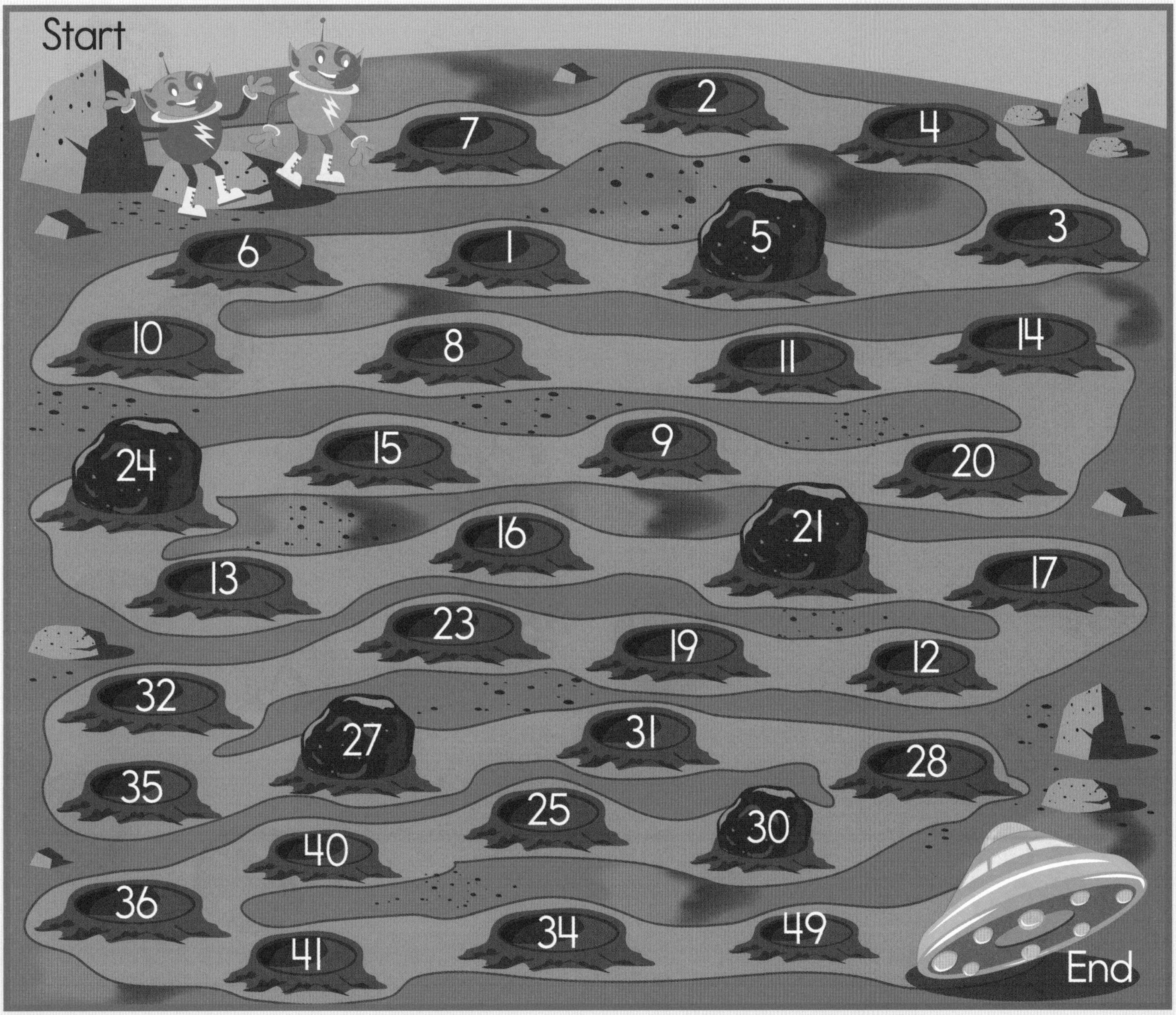

Start

2 7 4
6 1 5 3
10 8 11 14
24 15 9 20
16 21 13 17
23 19 12
32 27 31 28
35 25 30
40 36 34 49 41

End

Button Up

DRAW four straight lines to create nine equal sets of buttons.

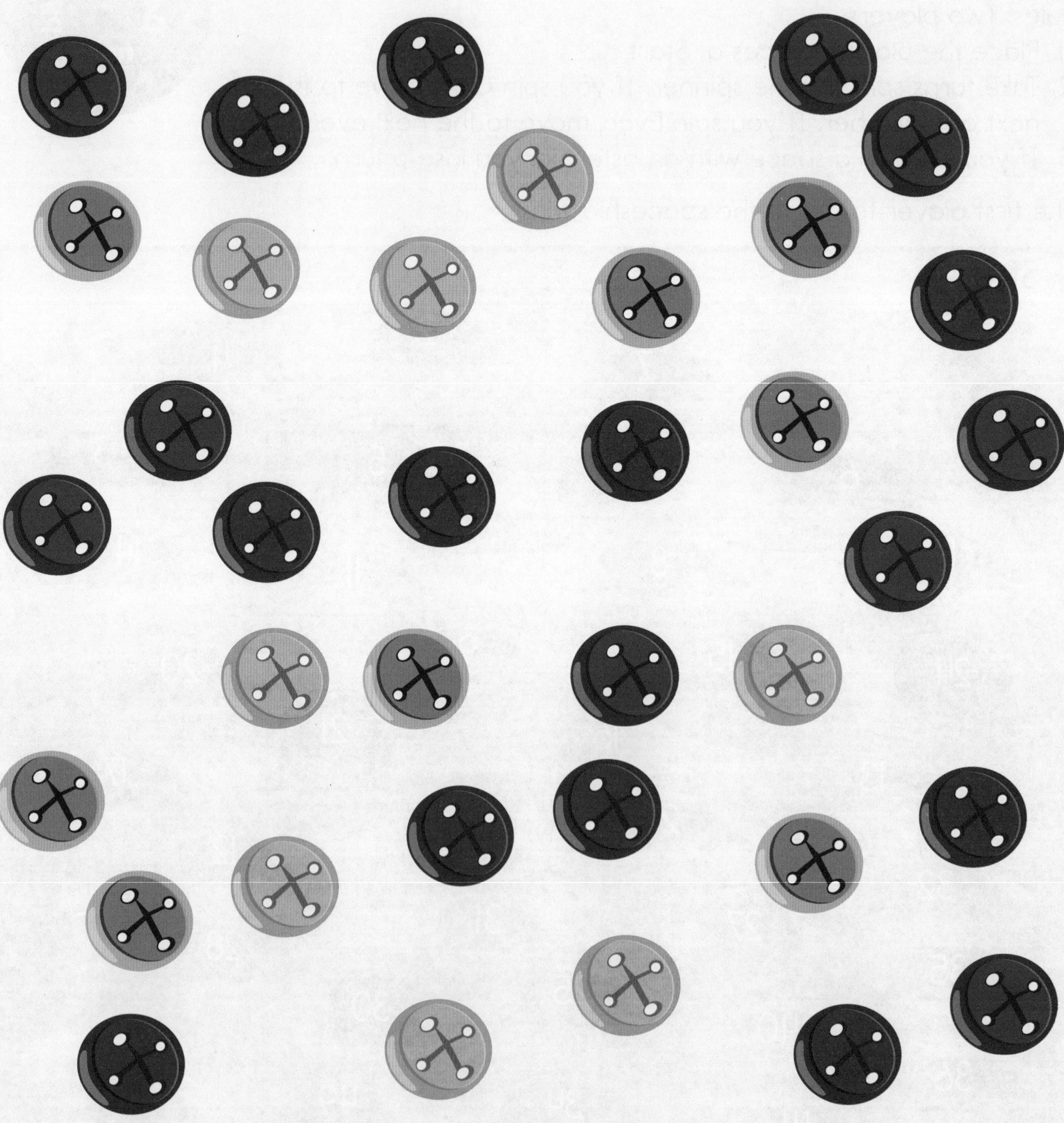

Odd Way Out

START at the arrow. DRAW a line through only odd numbers to get to the end.

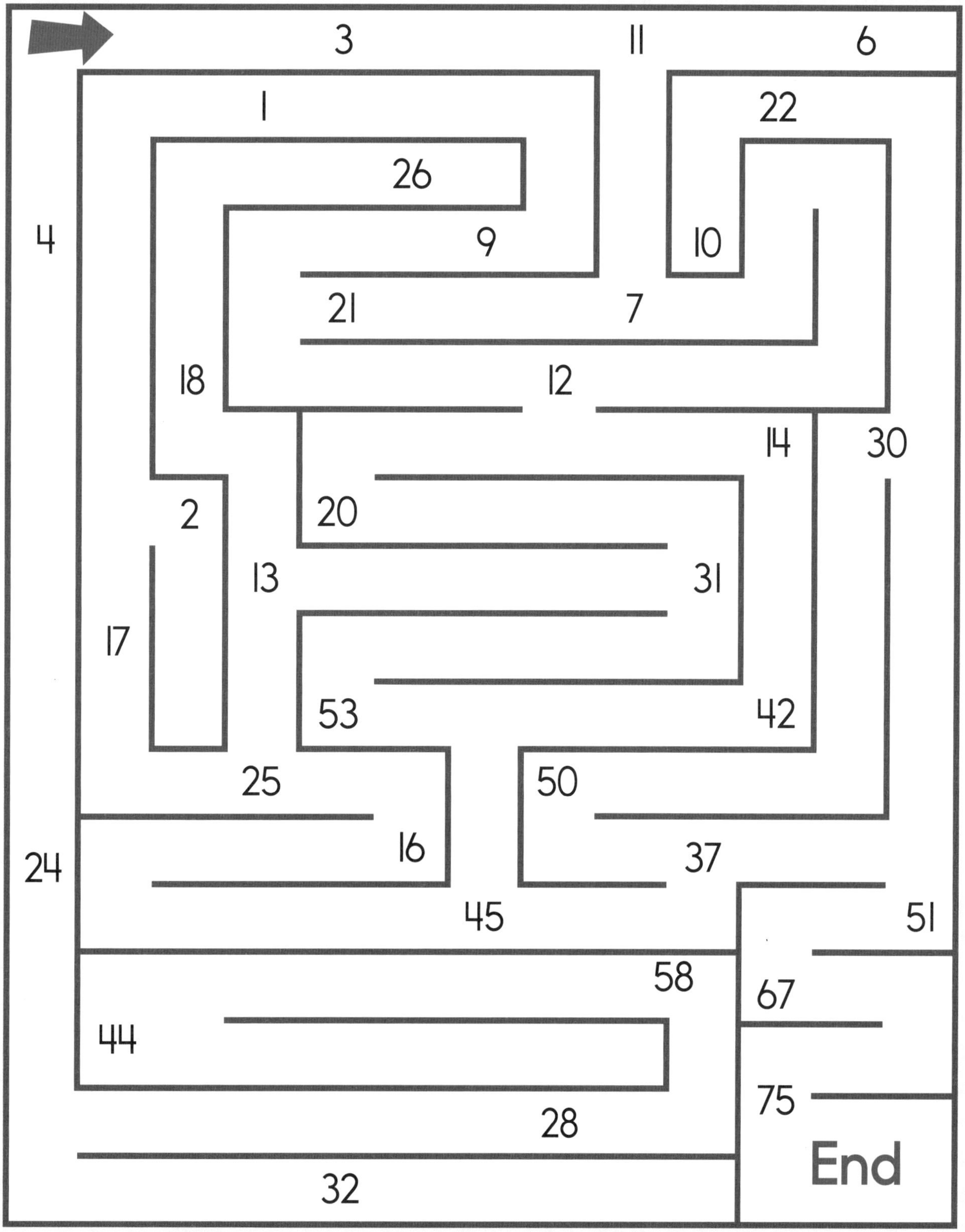

Totally Tangled

FIND the fraction and picture pairs that are connected, and COLOR any fraction that does **not** match the picture.

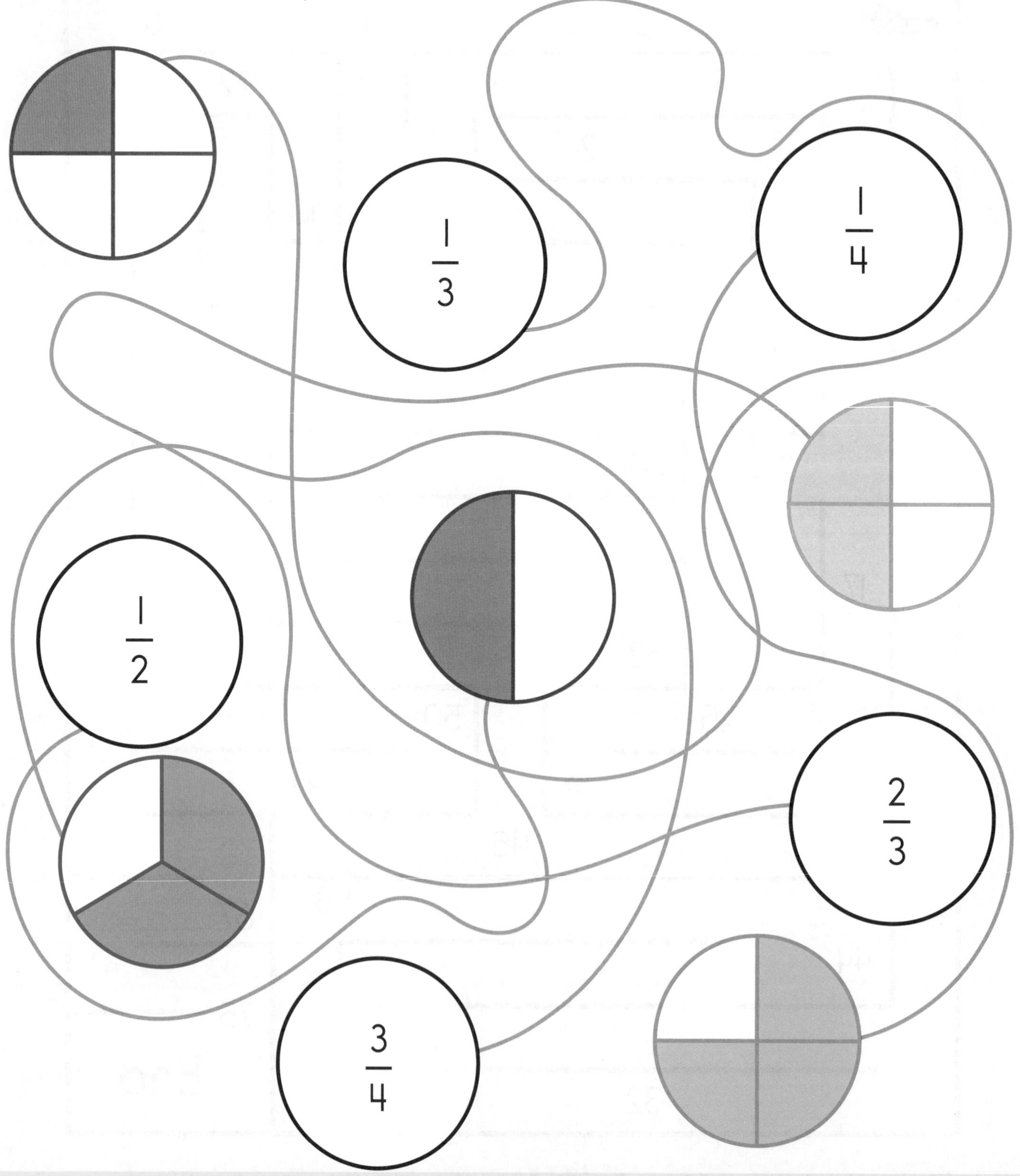

Make a Match

CUT OUT the fractions and pictures. READ the rules. PLAY the game!

Rules: Two players
1. Place the cards face down on a table.
2. Take turns turning over two cards at a time.
3. Keep the cards when you match a fraction and a picture that shows that fraction shaded.

The player with the most matches wins!

$\frac{1}{4}$	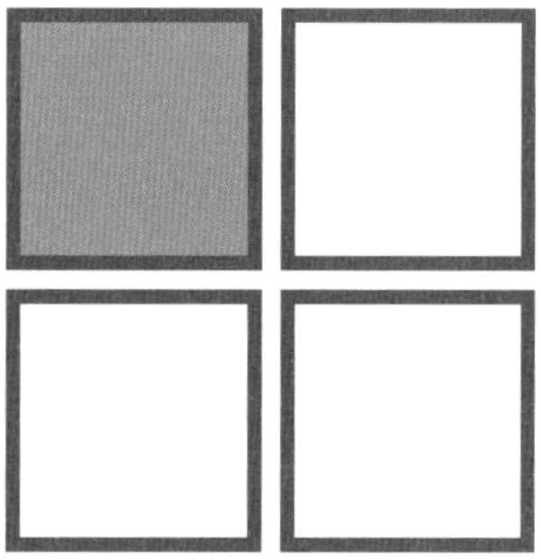	$\frac{1}{3}$	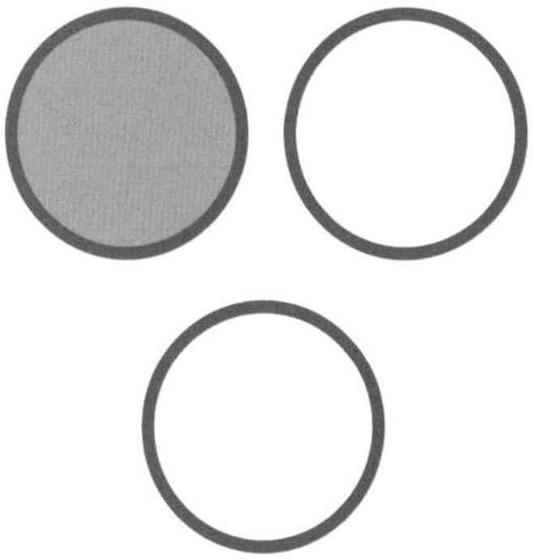
$\frac{1}{2}$		$\frac{2}{3}$	
$\frac{2}{2}$		$\frac{3}{4}$	

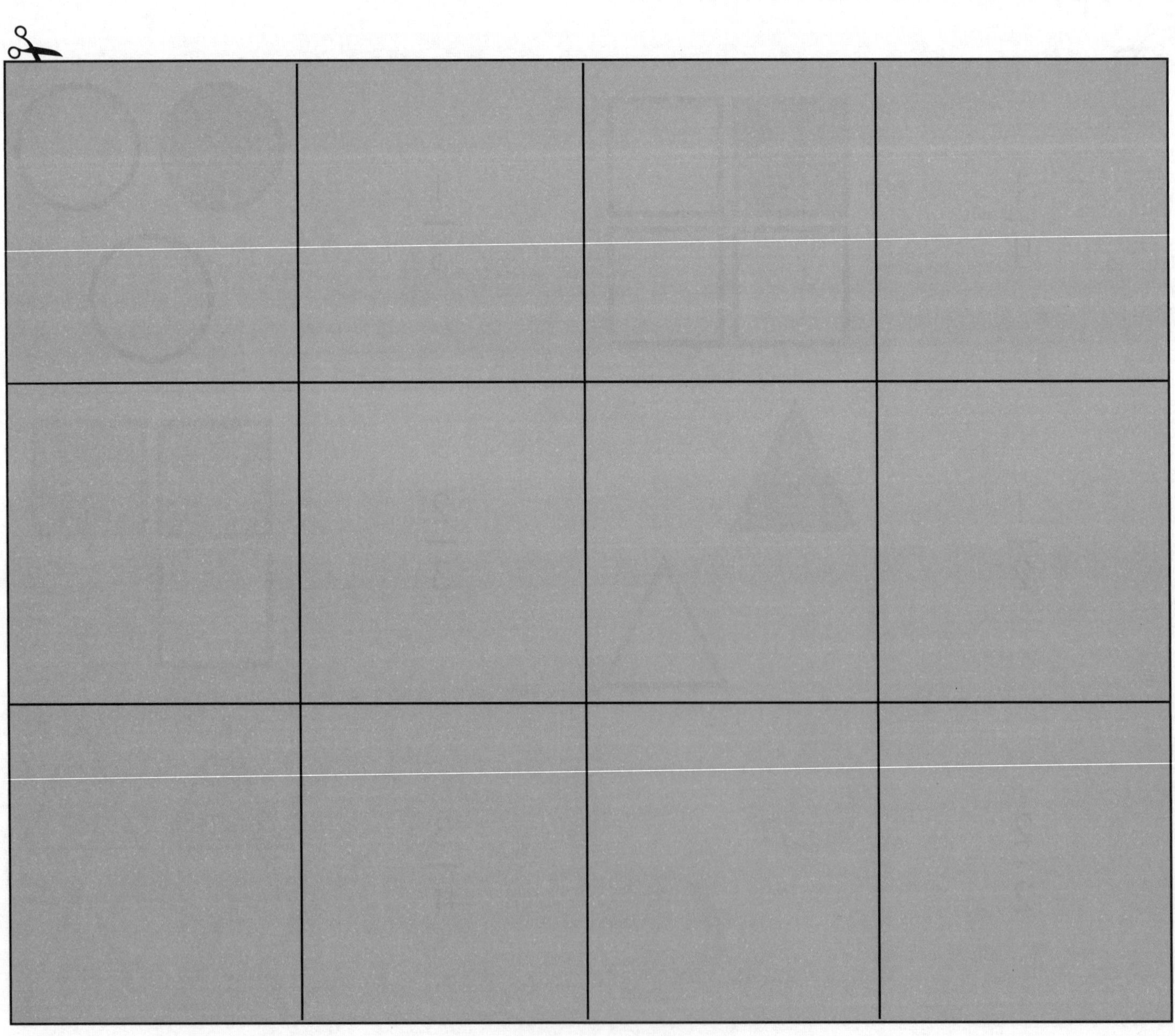

Mystery Picture

COLOR each section according to the fractions to reveal the mystery picture.

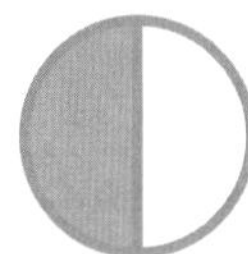

Fraction Factory

Can you be the first to reach the end? Use two small objects as playing pieces and the spinner from page 362. READ the rules. PLAY the game!

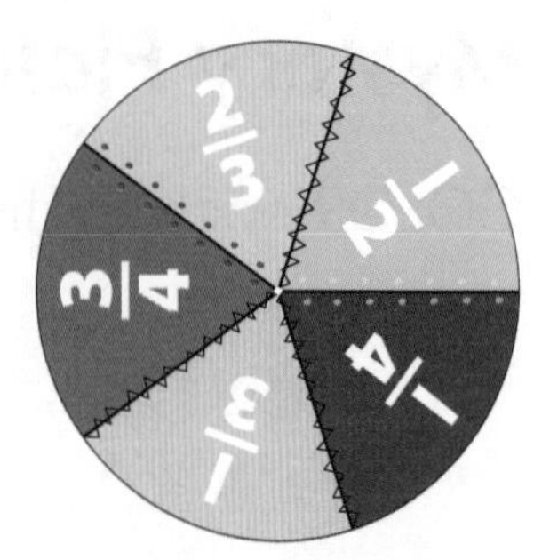

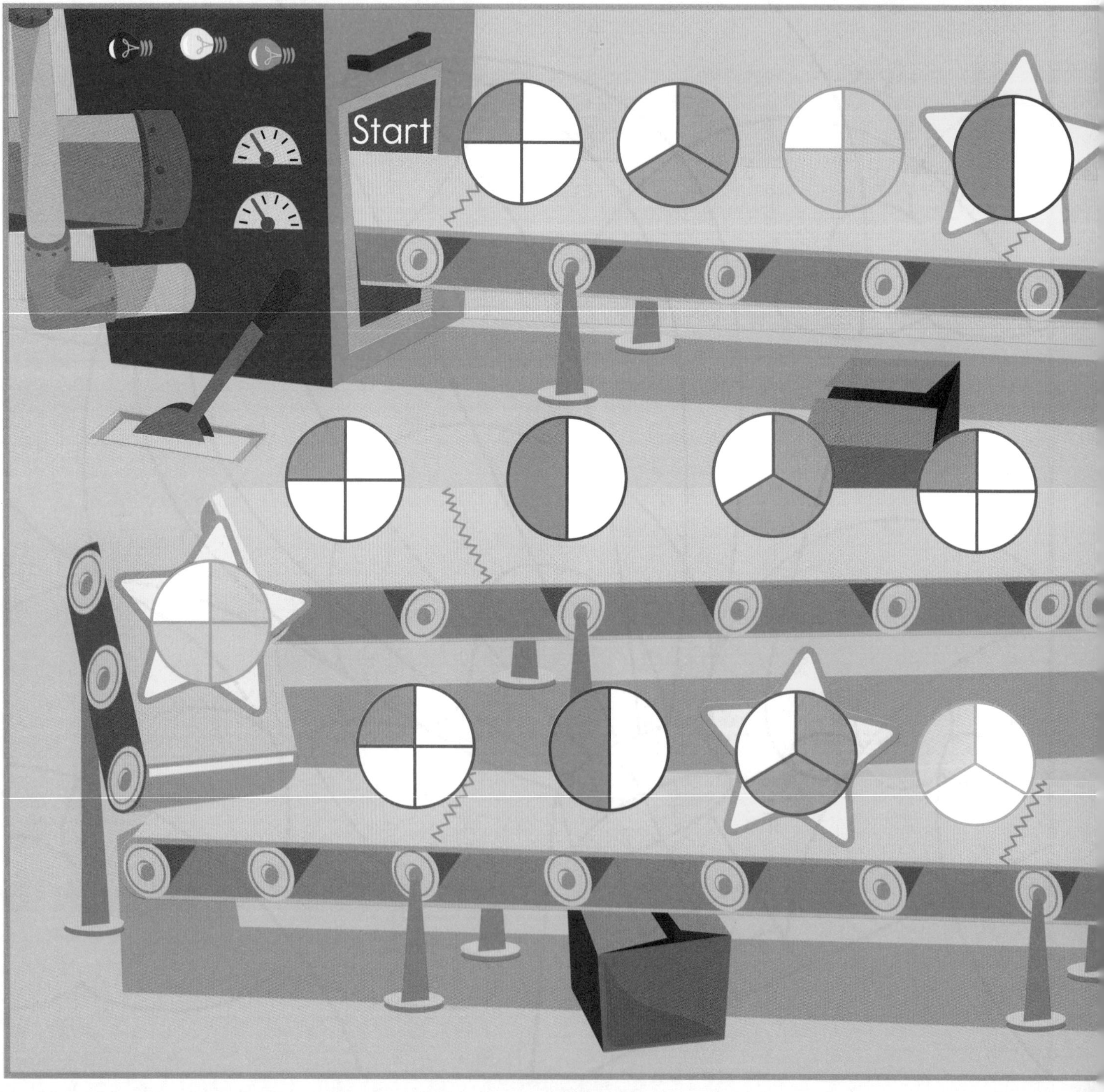

Start

Rules: Two players

1. Place the playing pieces at Start.
2. Take turns spinning the spinner. Move to the closest fraction picture that matches the fraction on the spinner.
3. If you land on a space with a star, you get to spin again.

The first player to get to the End box wins!

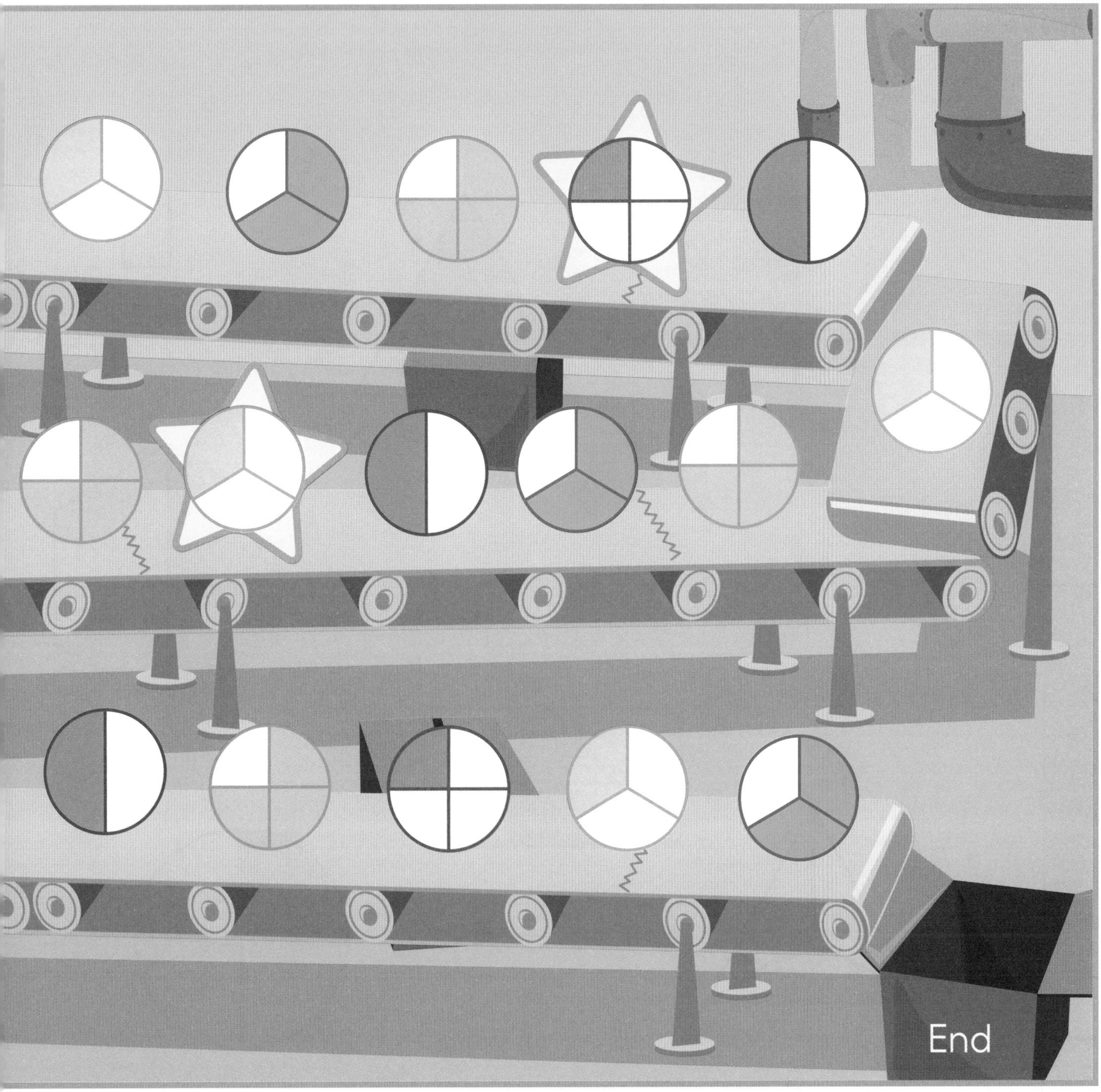

End

Picking Pairs

DRAW a line to connect each equivalent pair of fraction pictures.

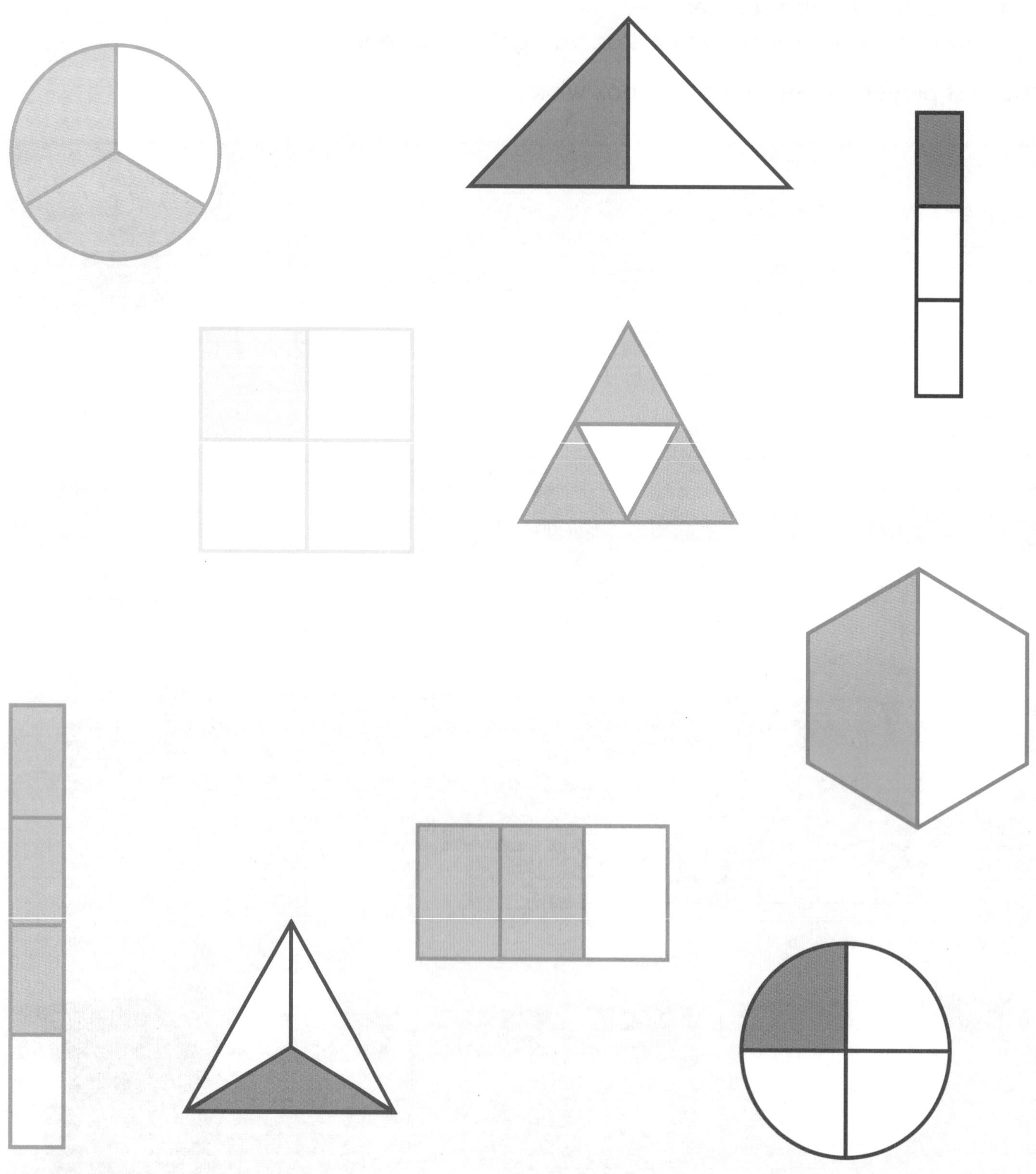

Totally Tangled

Each fraction is connected to another fraction. FIND the pairs of fractions, and COLOR the circle with the larger fraction.

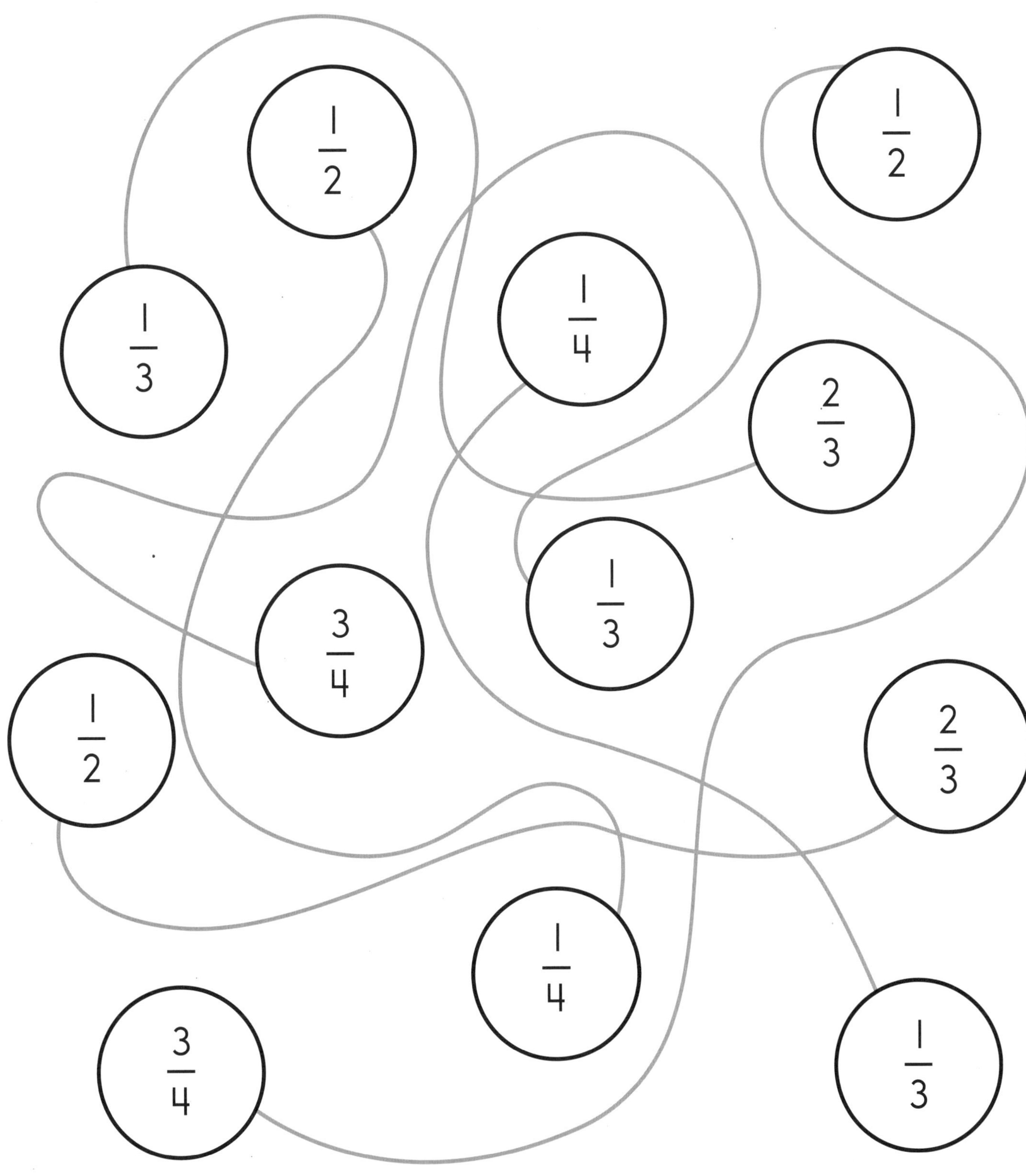

Just Right

WRITE each of these fractions next to a smaller fraction picture.

HINT: There may be more than one place to put a fraction, but you need to use every fraction.

$\frac{1}{3}$ $\frac{3}{4}$ $\frac{2}{3}$ $\frac{1}{2}$ $\frac{4}{4}$

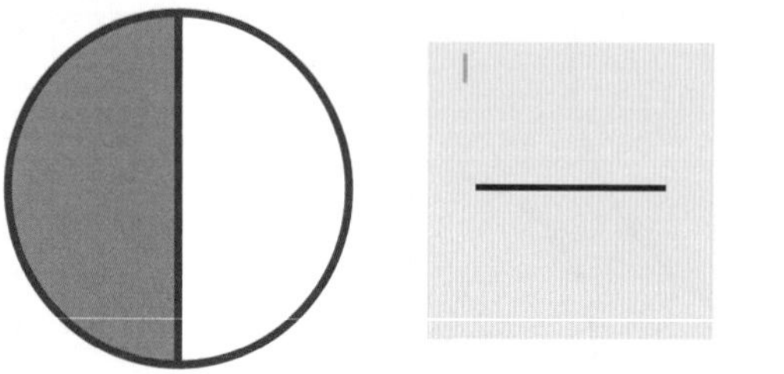

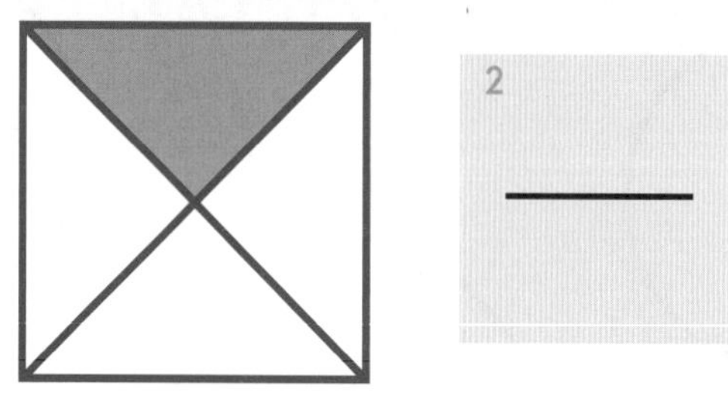

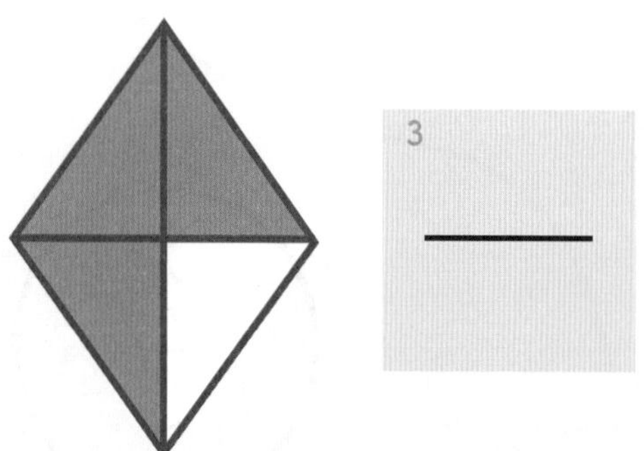

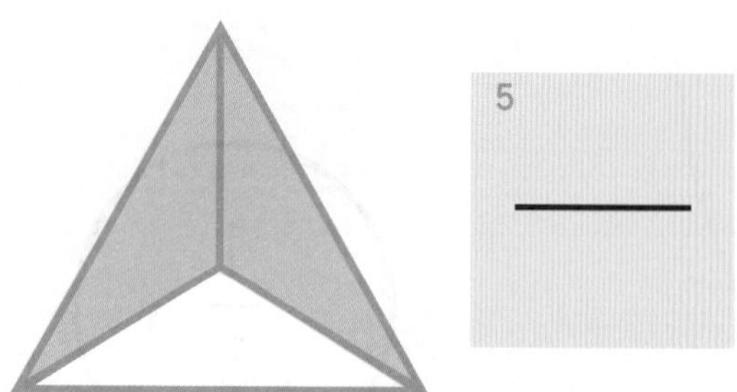

Code Breaker

CIRCLE the larger fraction in each pair. Then WRITE the letter that matches each fraction to solve the riddle.

1		2		3		4	
$\frac{1}{4}$	$\frac{1}{3}$	$\frac{3}{4}$	$\frac{2}{4}$	$\frac{1}{2}$	$\frac{2}{2}$	$\frac{1}{2}$	$\frac{1}{3}$
W		E		T		O	

5		6		7		8	
$\frac{2}{4}$	$\frac{1}{3}$	$\frac{3}{3}$	$\frac{1}{2}$	$\frac{2}{4}$	$\frac{2}{3}$	$\frac{4}{4}$	$\frac{2}{3}$
L		H		I		N	

Why did the boat carrying three thirds sink?

There was a ____ ____ ____ ____ ____

$\frac{1}{3}$ $\frac{3}{3}$ $\frac{1}{2}$ $\frac{2}{4}$ $\frac{3}{4}$

____ ____ ____ ____.

$\frac{2}{3}$ $\frac{4}{4}$ $\frac{2}{3}$ $\frac{2}{2}$

What's the Password?

WRITE the letters that form a fraction of each word. Then WRITE the letters in order to find the secret password.

The first $\frac{1}{2}$ of PECK ______ 1

The last $\frac{1}{4}$ of RAIN ______ 2

The first $\frac{1}{3}$ of COW ______ 3

The middle $\frac{1}{3}$ of CHILLY ______ 4

The last $\frac{1}{4}$ of TAKE ______ 5

The second $\frac{1}{2}$ of OR ______ 6

The first $\frac{2}{3}$ of ASK ______ 7

The last $\frac{1}{3}$ of SINGER ______ 8

Password: ______ ______ ______ ______ ______ ______

______ ______ ______ ______ ______ ______

Who Am I?

READ the clues, and CIRCLE the mystery number.

HINT: Cross out any fraction picture that does not match the clues.

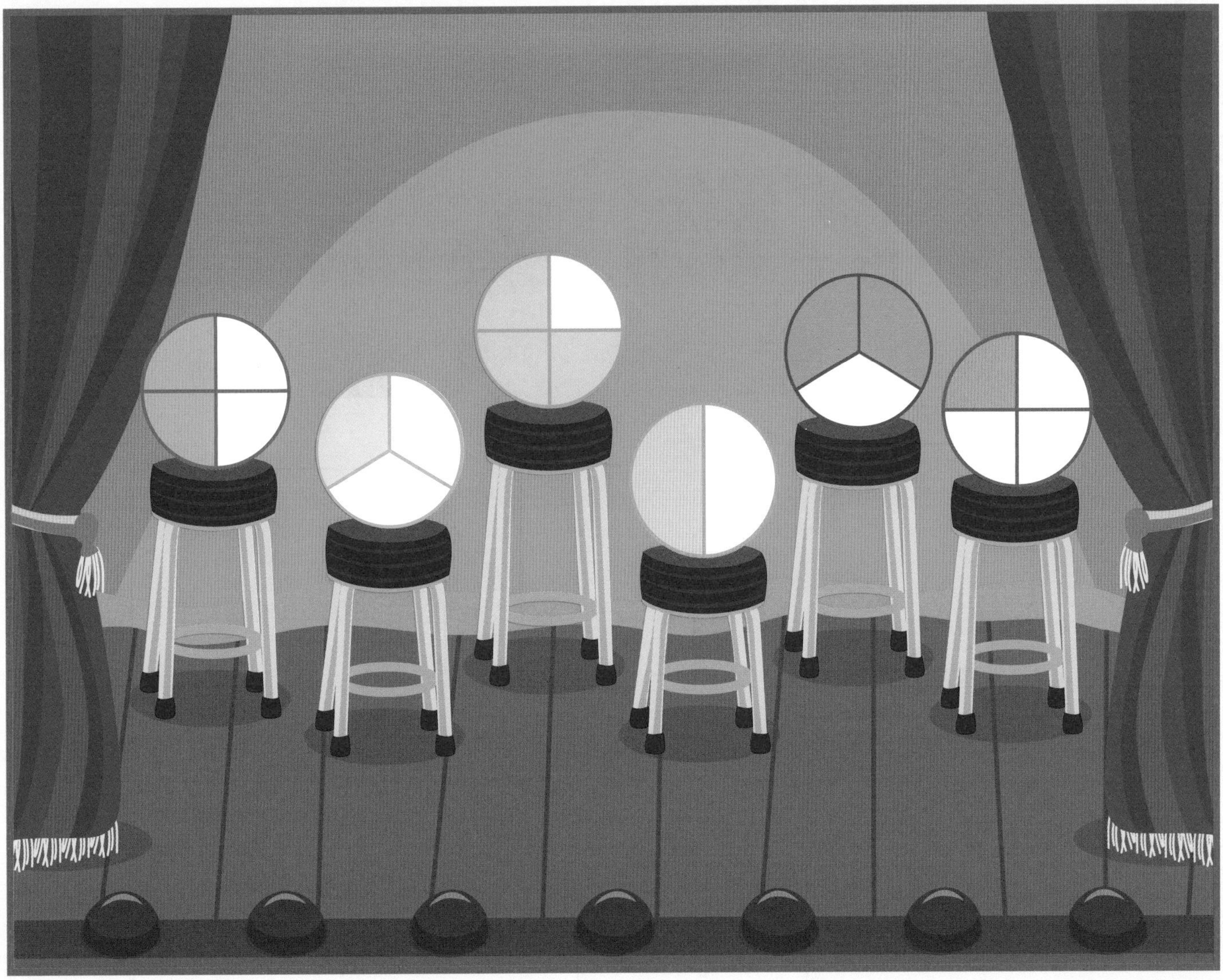

I am larger than $\frac{1}{4}$.

I am smaller than $\frac{3}{4}$.

I have two parts shaded.

I am not equivalent to anyone else.

Who am I?

Hidden Shapes

FIND each shape hidden in the picture. DRAW a line to connect each shape with its location in the picture.

HINT: Be sure to use shapes that match in size.

Doodle Pad

TRACE the shapes. Then DRAW a picture using each shape.

Shape Shifters

A shape has **symmetry** if a line can divide the shape so each half is a mirror image of the other. Use the pattern block pieces from page 363, and PLACE the pieces to make each picture symmetrical without overlapping any pieces. (Save the pattern block pieces to use again later in the workbook.)

Cool Kaleidoscope

COLOR the kaleidoscope so it is symmetrical.

HINT: Make a mirror image across each line.

Shape Shifters

Use the pattern block pieces from page 363, and PLACE the pieces to completely fill each shape without overlapping any pieces. See if you can solve the puzzles different ways. (Save the pattern block pieces to use again.)

Puzzling Pentominoes

Perimeter is the distance around a two-dimensional shape. Use the pentomino pieces from page 365, and PLACE the pieces to completely fill each shape without overlapping any pieces. Then WRITE the perimeter of each shape. (Save the pentomino pieces to use again.)

1. ______ units

2. ______ units

3. ______ units

4. ______ units

Shape Creator

DRAW six different shapes that all have a perimeter of 12 units.

Puzzling Pentominoes

Area is the size of the surface of a shape, and it is measured in square units. Use the pentomino pieces from page 365, and PLACE the pieces to completely fill each shape without overlapping any pieces. Then WRITE the area of each shape. (Save the pentomino pieces to use again.)

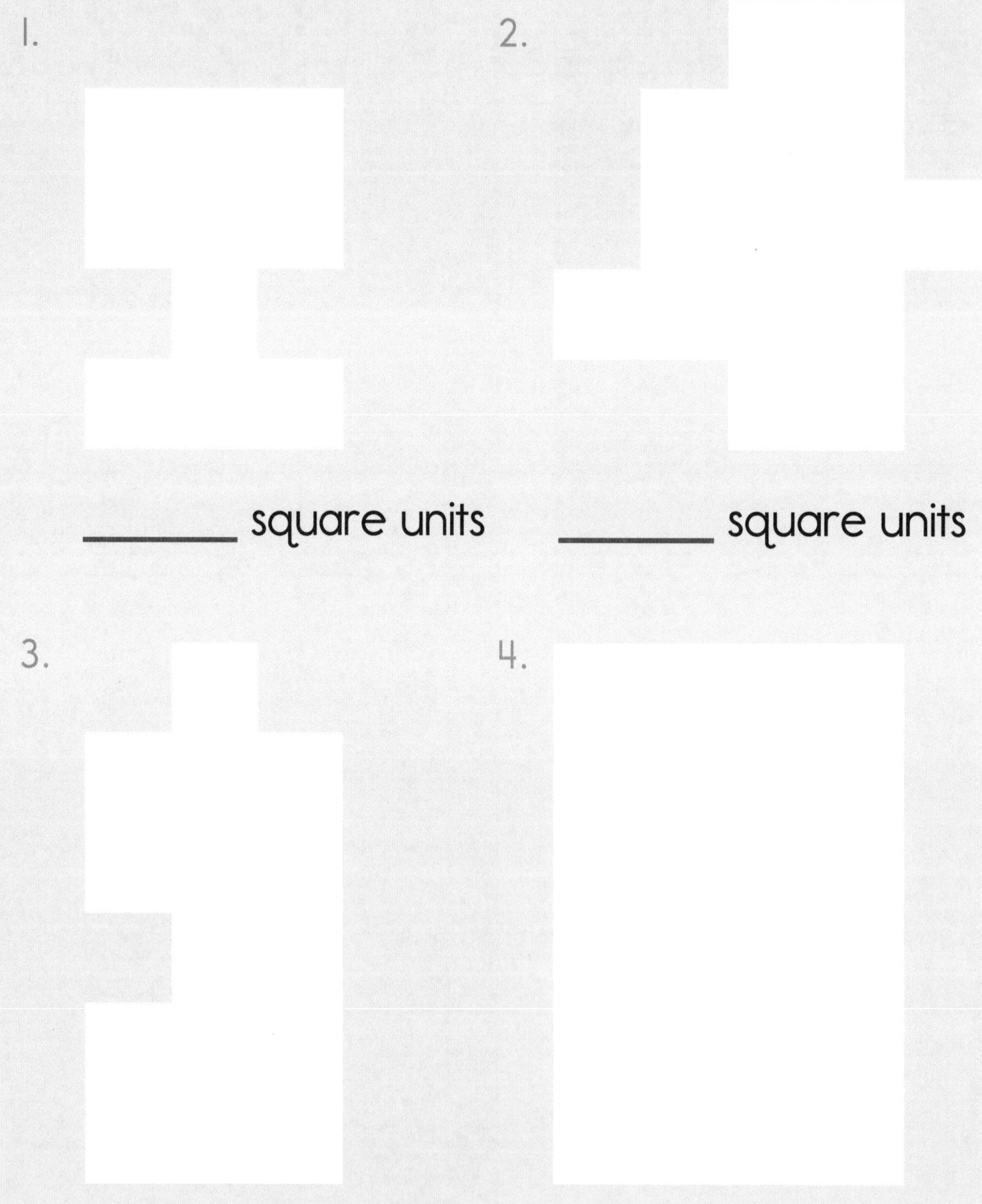

1. ______ square units

2. ______ square units

3. ______ square units

4. ______ square units

Shape Creator

DRAW six different shapes that all have an area of 10 square units.

Animal Adventure

WRITE the name of the animal that can be found at each location on the map.

HINT: Follow the letter and the number and see where the two lines meet.

1. C5 ____________________
2. C1 ____________________
3. E1 ____________________
4. D3 ____________________
5. A6 ____________________
6. A4 ____________________
7. C7 ____________________
8. B2 ____________________
9. E5 ____________________
10. E7 ____________________

Treasure Hunt

Use the squares on the map to find the pirate treasure. FOLLOW the directions. DRAW an X where the treasure is buried.

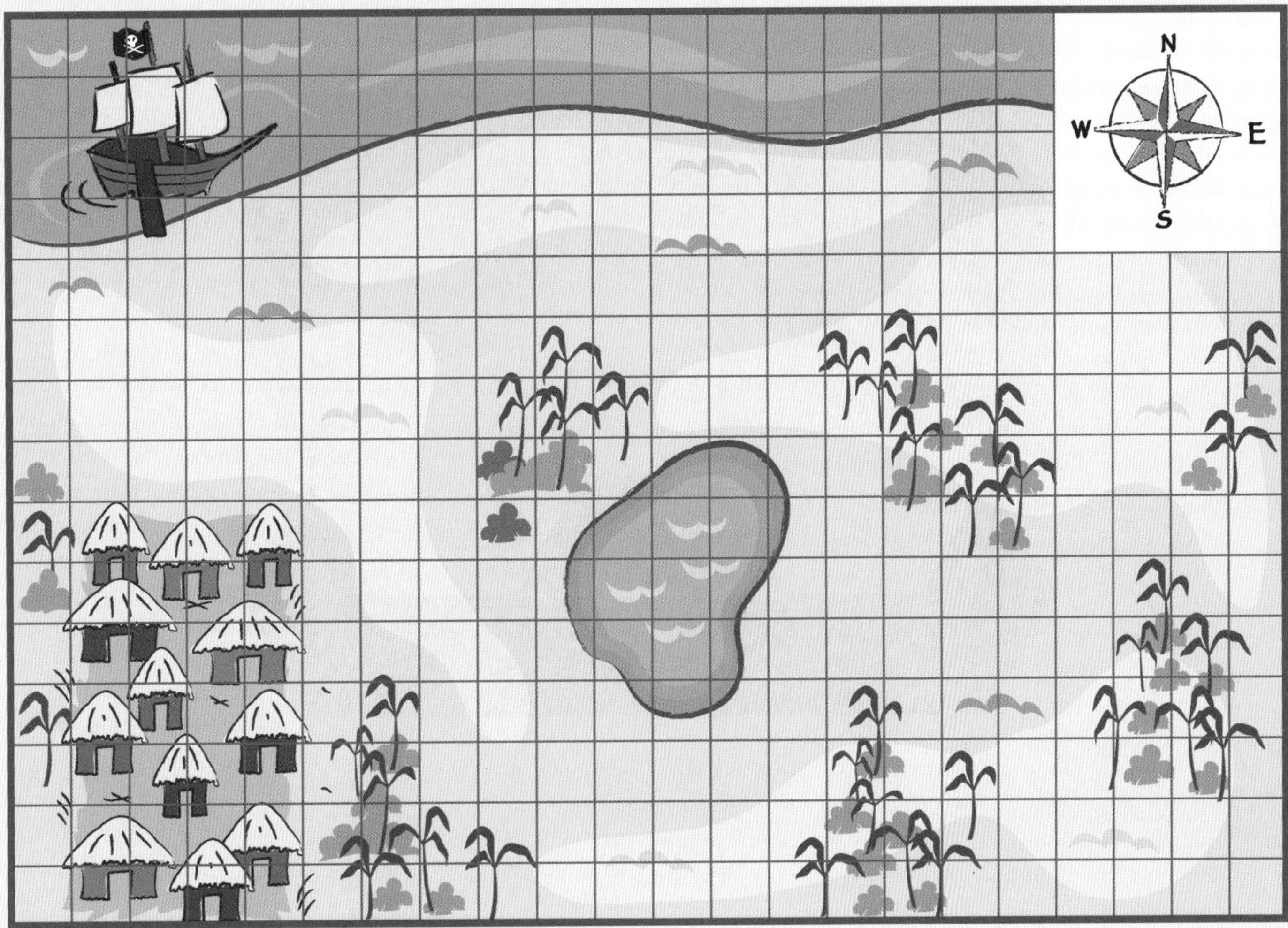

Blackbeard's Treasure

1. From the ship travel 4 squares south. Do not enter the village or the people will be curious.
2. Go 5 squares to the east, and turn to head 5 squares south.
3. Travel 6 squares to the east and 2 squares to the north to get around the lake.
4. Go another 5 squares east and you'll nearly be there.
5. Head 5 squares north. Can the treasure be near?
6. Go 2 squares west and draw an X. That's where the treasure will be!

Shape Shifters

Use the pattern block pieces from page 363, and PLACE the pieces to make the picture symmetrical without overlapping any pieces.

Puzzling Pentominoes

Use the pentomino pieces from page 365, and PLACE the pieces to completely fill each shape without overlapping any pieces.

These shapes all have the same area. WRITE the perimeter, and CIRCLE the shape with the largest perimeter.

1. Perimeter ______ units

2. Perimeter ______ units

3. Perimeter ______ units

These shapes all have the same perimeter. WRITE the area, and CIRCLE the shape with the largest area.

4. Area ______ square units

5. Area ______ square units

6. Area ______ square units

Hamster Hotel

Each hamster is four coins long. MEASURE each hamster with a line of four quarters, dimes, nickels, and pennies. When you find a match, WRITE the coin name.

Sidewalk Slugs

LINE UP dimes and MEASURE each slug. DRAW lines connecting pairs of slugs that are about the same length.

Code Ruler

WRITE the letter that matches each measurement to answer the riddle.

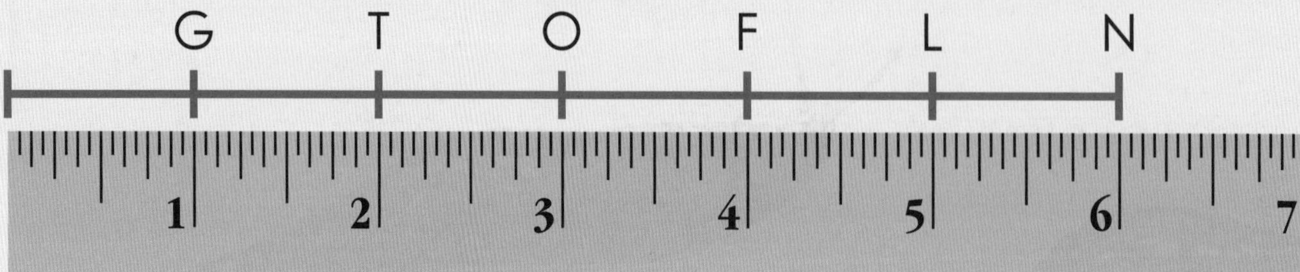

What is a ruler's favorite kind of hot dog?

A ____ ____ ____ ____ ____ ____ ____ ____ .

4 in. 3 in. 3 in. 2 in. 5 in. 3 in. 6 in. 1 in.

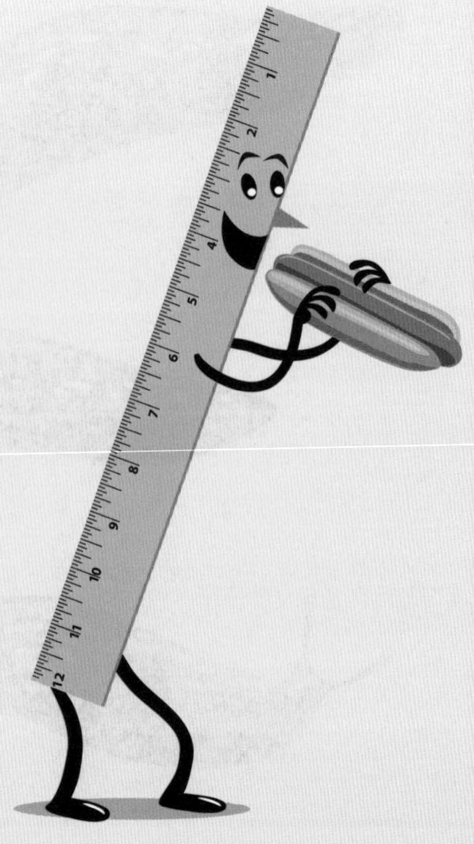

Bowl of Candy

One pack of candy in the bowl is not the same length as the others. MEASURE each pack of candy in inches, and CIRCLE the one that is not the same length.

Code Ruler

WRITE the letter that matches each measurement to answer the riddle.

How do you measure a skunk?

____ ____   ____ ____ ____ ____ ____ ____ -

6 cm 2 cm   12 cm 9 cm 4 cm 2 cm 15 m 6 cm

____ ____ ____ ____ ____ ____ .

1 cm 4 cm 15 cm 4 cm 10 cm 12 cm

Pick a Pencil

One colored pencil is not the same length as the others. MEASURE each pencil in centimeters, and CIRCLE the one that is not the same length.

Minigolf

WRITE the numbers 1 through 6 on the golf balls so that 1 is the ball you think is closest to the hole and 6 is the golf ball you think is farthest away. Then MEASURE in inches to see if you're correct.

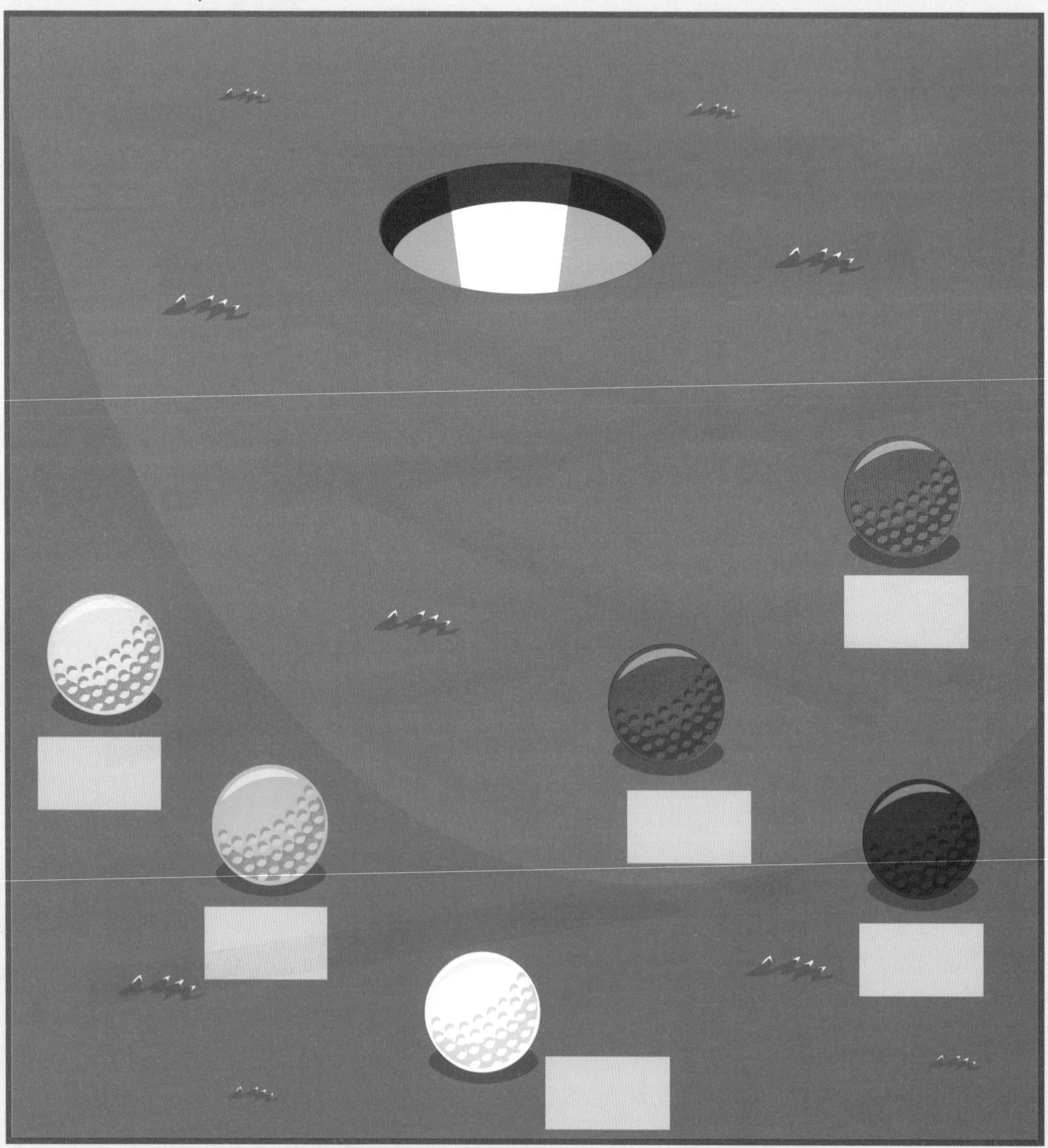

Don't Go Over

GUESS the height of each ice pop and stick in centimeters. Then MEASURE each ice pop. For every centimeter in the difference between the two measurements, COLOR a section in the white ice pop. If you get through the whole page without filling the ice pop, you win!

HINT: To find the difference, subtract the smaller measurement from the larger measurement.

So Far Away

WRITE the numbers 1 through 8 next to the ants so that 1 is the ant you think is closest to the entrance of the anthill and 8 is the ant you think is farthest away. Then MEASURE in centimeters to see if you're correct.

HINT: Use the dots to help you measure.

Don't Go Over

GUESS the distance between each matching pair of marbles in centimeters. Then MEASURE the distance. For every centimeter in the difference between the two measurements, COLOR a section in the white marble. If you get through the whole page without filling the marble, you win!

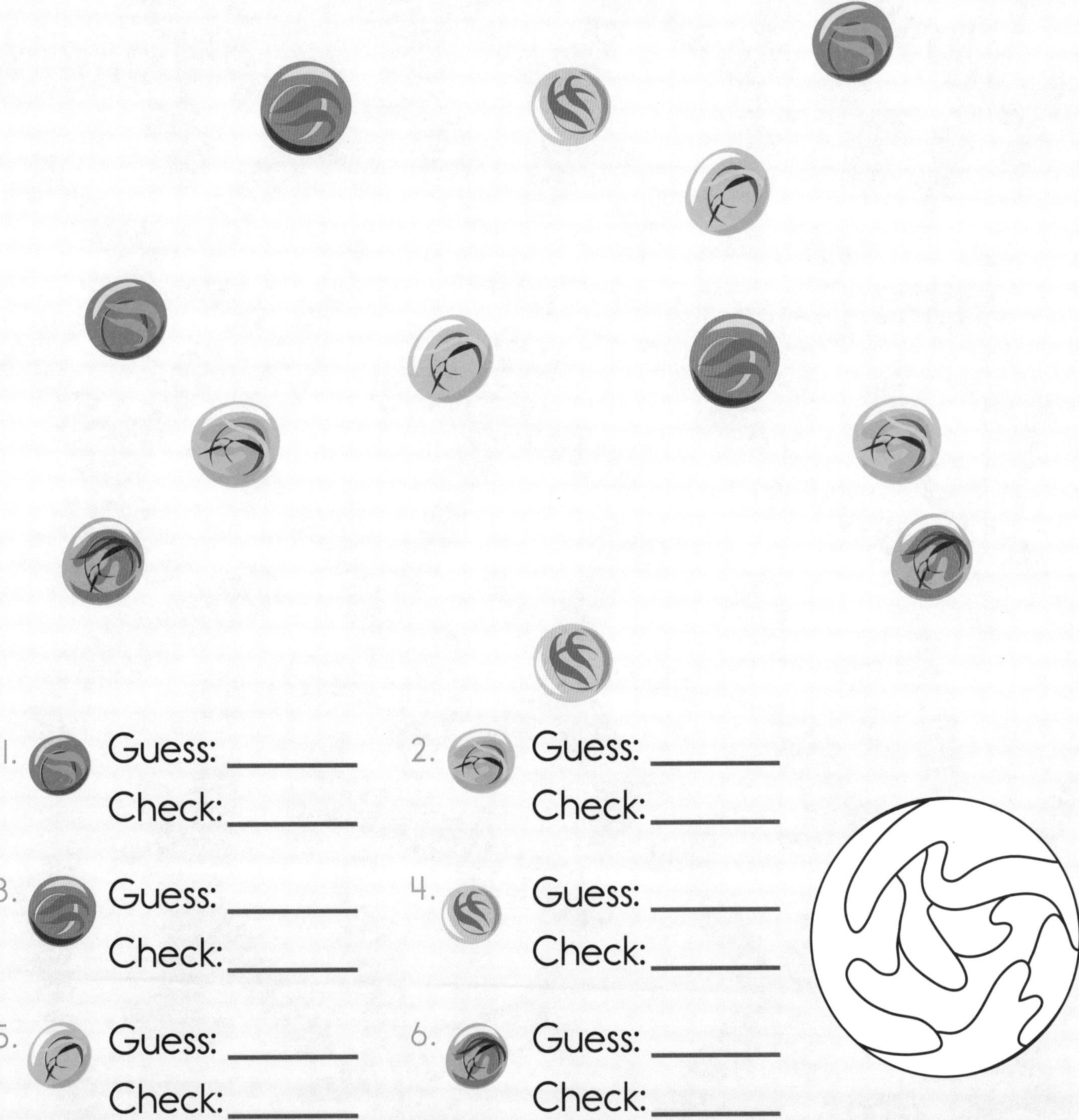

1. Guess: ______
   Check: ______
2. Guess: ______
   Check: ______
3. Guess: ______
   Check: ______
4. Guess: ______
   Check: ______
5. Guess: ______
   Check: ______
6. Guess: ______
   Check: ______

Something's Screwy

One screw is not the same length as the others. MEASURE each screw in centimeters, and CIRCLE the one that is not the same length.

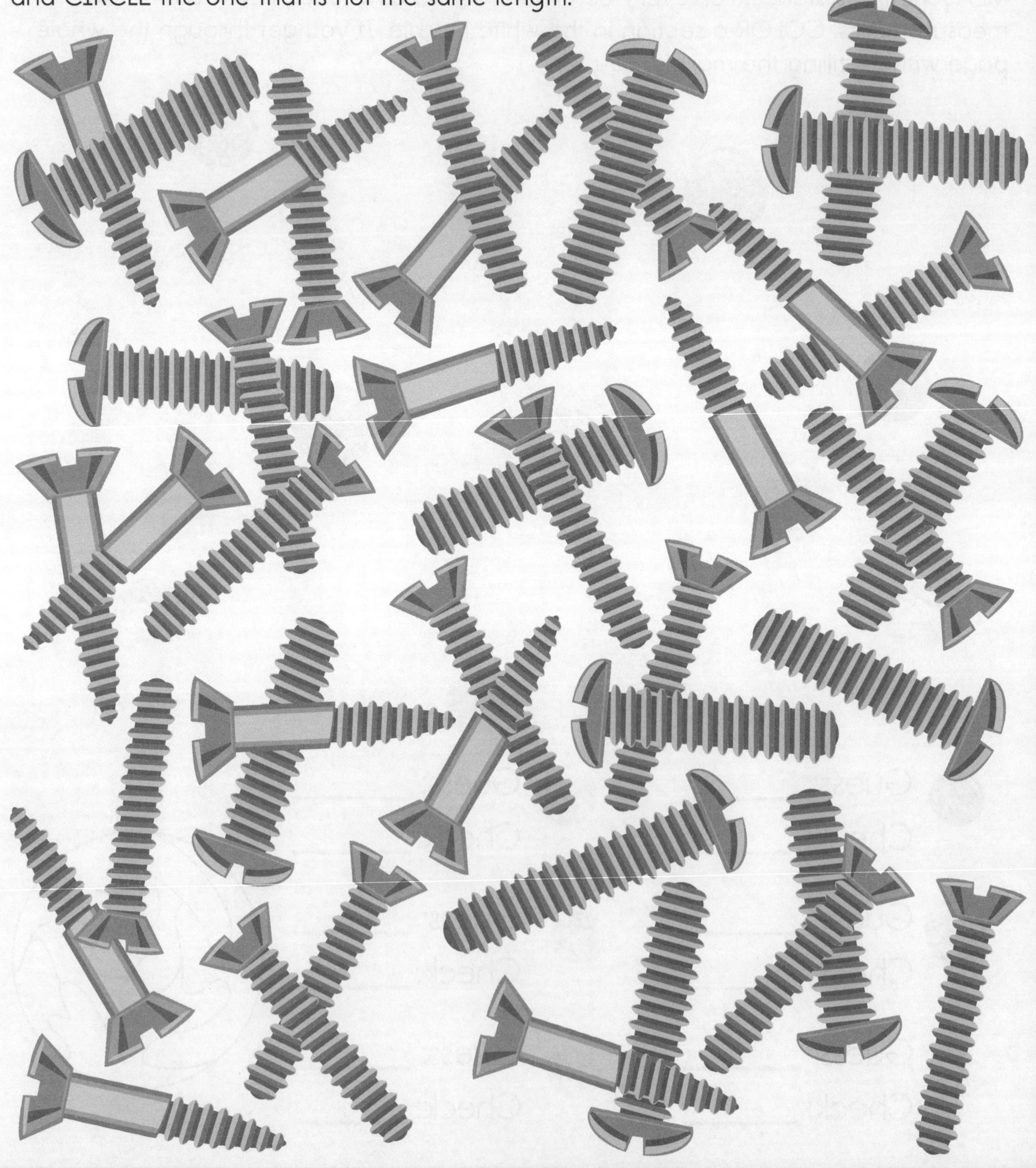

Starry Night

FOLLOW the steps to connect the stars to create the constellation map of Leo the lion. Then GUESS the distance between the star pairs listed, and MEASURE in centimeters to check your guess.

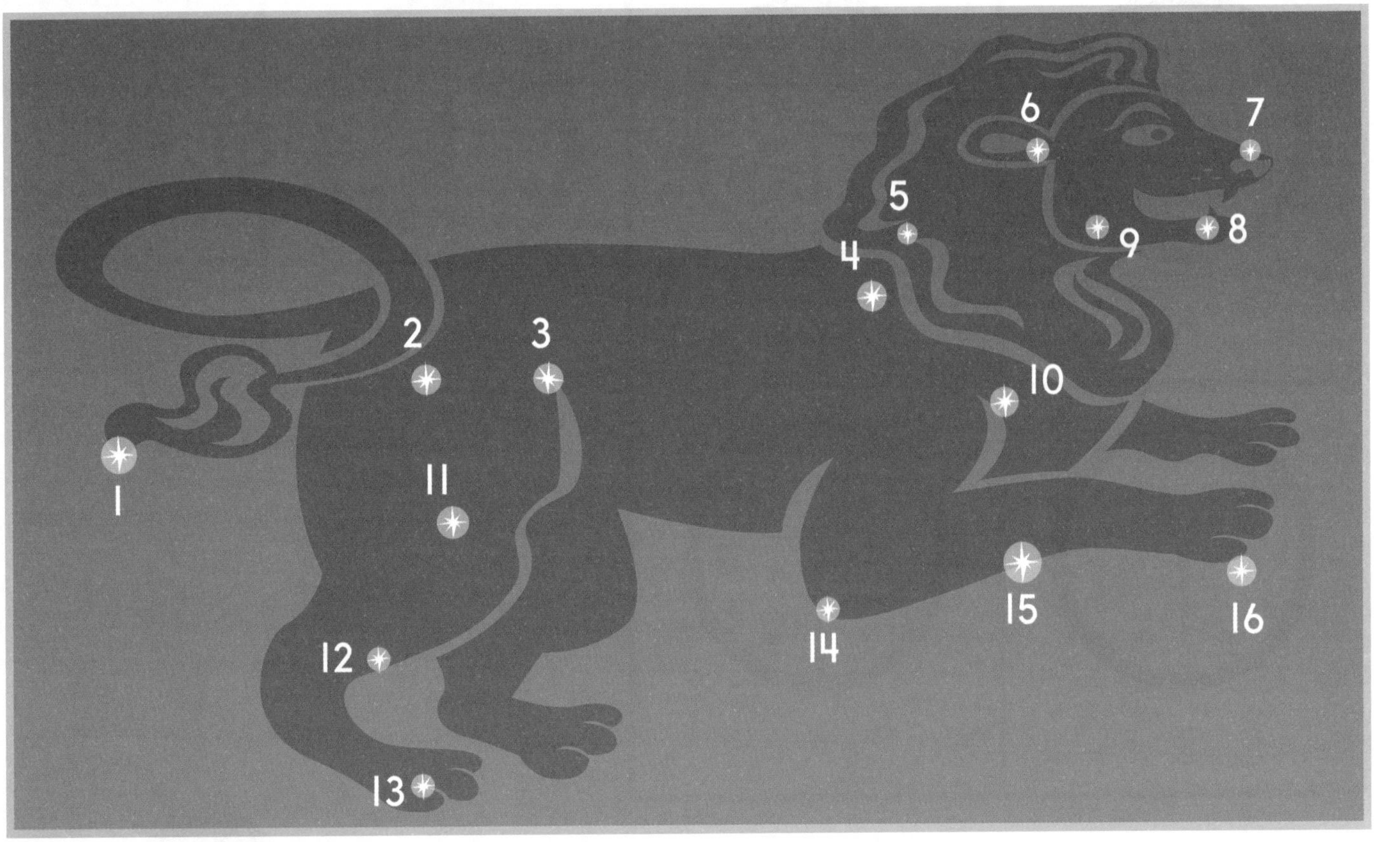

CONNECT stars 1 through 13. Then CONNECT these star pairs:
6 and 9, 4 and 10, 10 and 16, 10 and 15, 2 and 11, 11 and 14.

GUESS the distance between these star pairs, and CHECK your guess.

1. 2 and 11: Guess: _______ cm Check: _______ cm
2. 4 and 6: Guess: _______ cm Check: _______ cm
3. 11 and 15: Guess: _______ cm Check: _______ cm
4. 9 and 16: Guess: _______ cm Check: _______ cm
5. 1 and 14: Guess: _______ cm Check: _______ cm
6. 12 and 15: Guess: _______ cm Check: _______ cm

Code Breaker

WRITE the letter that matches each time to solve the riddle.

What has two hands but can't carry anything?

____ ____ ____ ____ ____ ____.

10:30 6:00 8:30 2:00 6:00 12:30

Mystery Time

COLOR the times in the picture according to the color of the clocks at the top. When you are done coloring, WRITE the mystery time under the picture.

___ : ___

Code Breaker

WRITE the letter that matches each time to solve the riddle.

 E	 T	 L
H	R	

Week Year
Minute

What happens once in a year, twice in a week, and once in a minute?

___ ___ ___

7:45 3:45 10:15

___ ___ ___ ___ ___ ___ ___.

2:15 10:15 7:45 7:45 10:15 8:15 10:15

Mystery Time

COLOR the times in the picture according to the color of the clocks at the top. When you are done coloring, WRITE the mystery time under the picture.

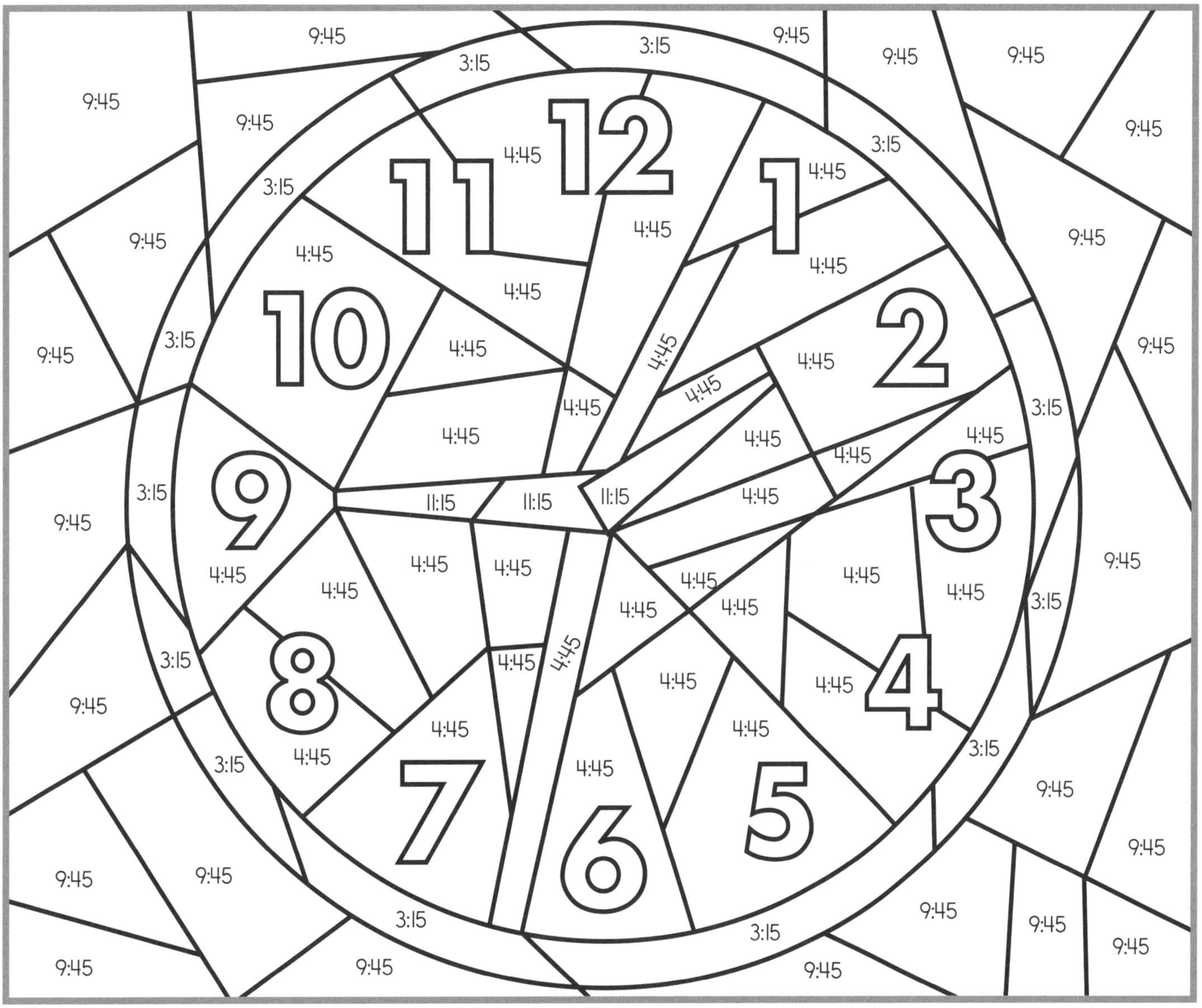

___ : ___

Time Travel

DRAW a line from Start through the clocks to get to the end, traveling 1 hour and 15 minutes ahead as you go from clock to clock.

Start

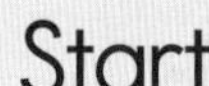

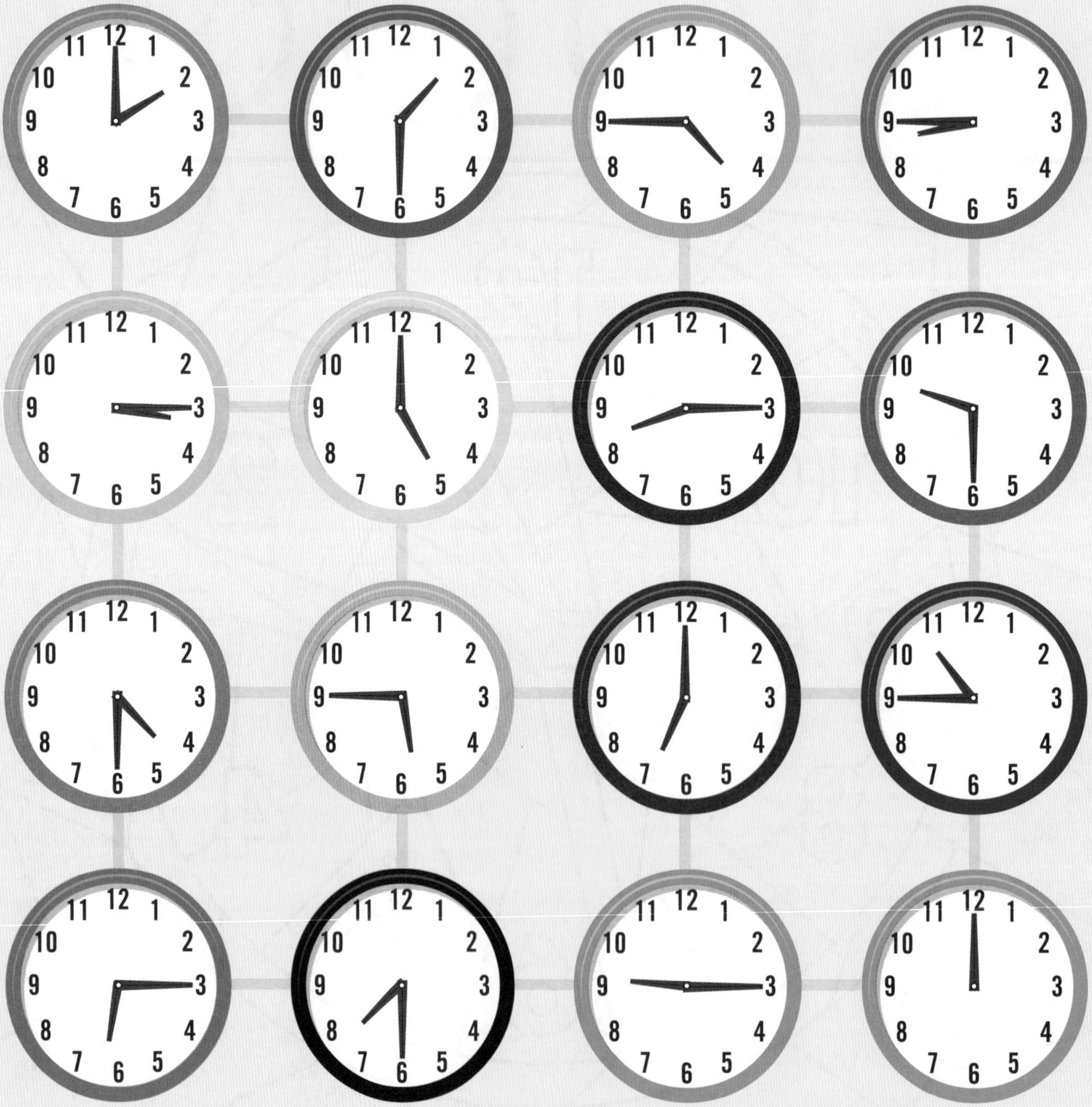

End

Time Travel

DRAW a line from Start through the clocks to get to the end, traveling 1 hour and 45 minutes back as you go from clock to clock.

Start

End

Code Breaker

WRITE the new time for each watch. Then WRITE the letter that matches each new time to solve the riddle.

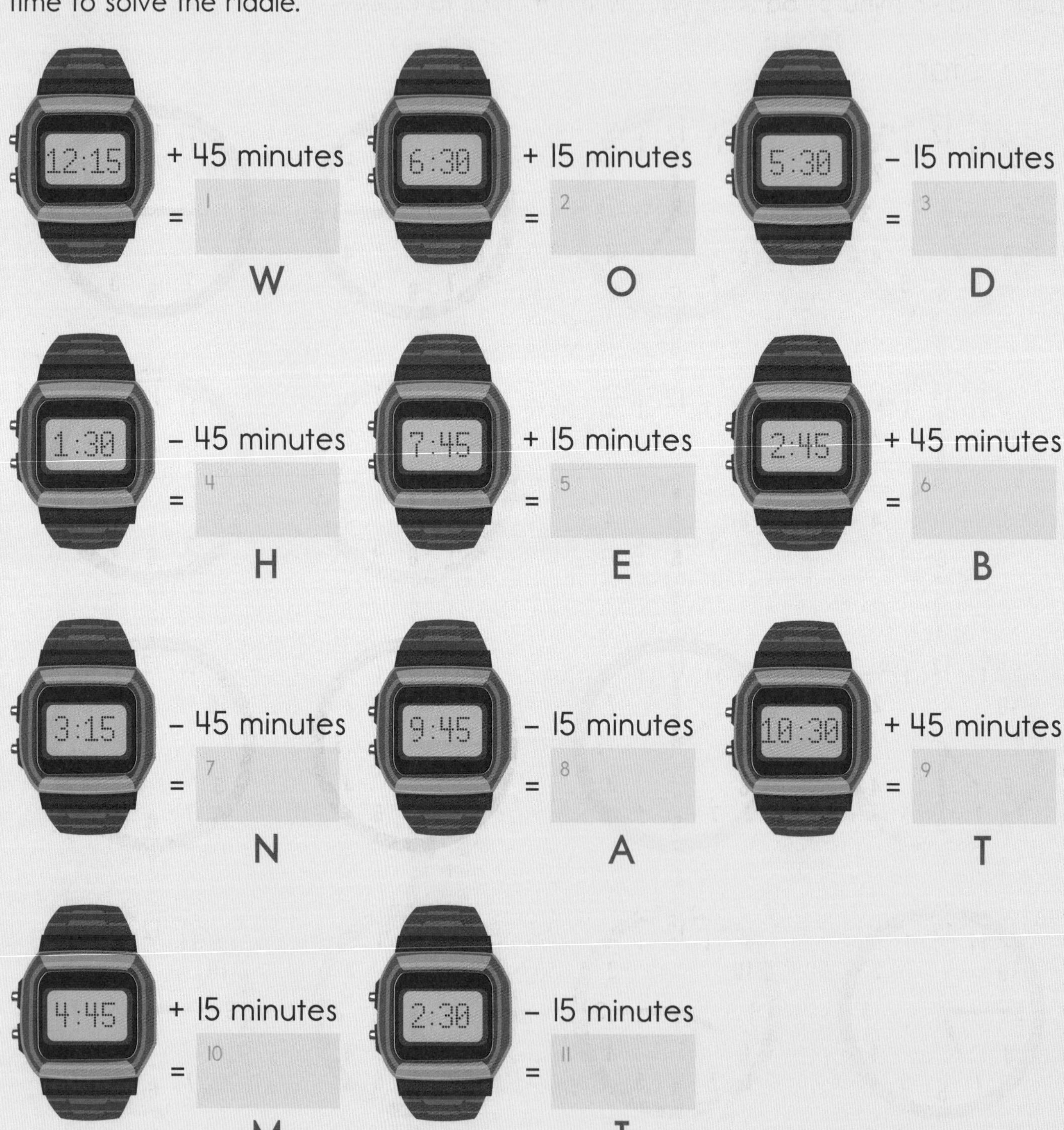

Why did the boy sit on the clock?

____ ____   ____ ____ ____ ____ ____ ____

12:45 8:00   1:00 9:30 2:30 11:15 8:00 5:15

____ ____   ____ ____   ____ ____

11:15 6:45   3:30 8:00   6:45 2:30

____ ____ ____ ____.

11:15 2:15 5:00 8:00

Who Am I?

READ the clues, and CIRCLE the mystery time.

HINT: Cross out any time that does not match the clues.

I am later than 2:00.

I am earlier than 11:00.

I am two hours away from one of the clocks next to me.

In 15 minutes I will be 5:00.

Who am I?

Time Travel

DRAW a line from Start through the clocks to get to the end, traveling 4 hours and 45 minutes back as you go from clock to clock.

Start

End

Code Breaker

WRITE the value of each coin set. Then WRITE the letter that matches each value to solve the riddle.

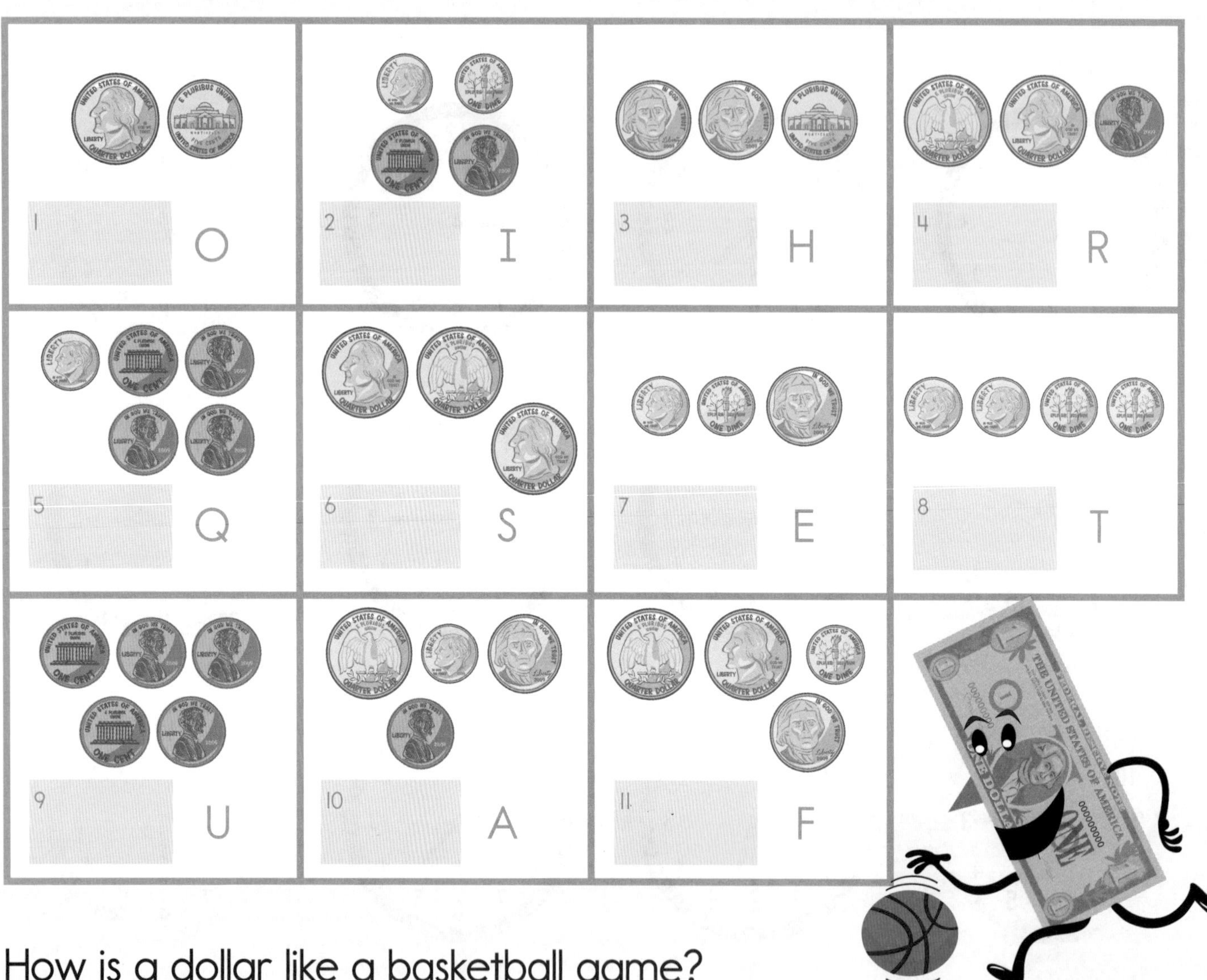

How is a dollar like a basketball game?

___ ___   ___ ___ ___   ___ ___ ___ ___

22¢ 40¢   15¢ 41¢ 75¢   65¢ 30¢ 5¢ 51¢

___ ___ ___ ___ ___ ___ ___ ___.

14¢ 5¢ 41¢ 51¢ 40¢ 25¢ 51¢ 75¢

Slide Sort

CIRCLE the dollar amounts that do **not** match the picture at the bottom of the slide.

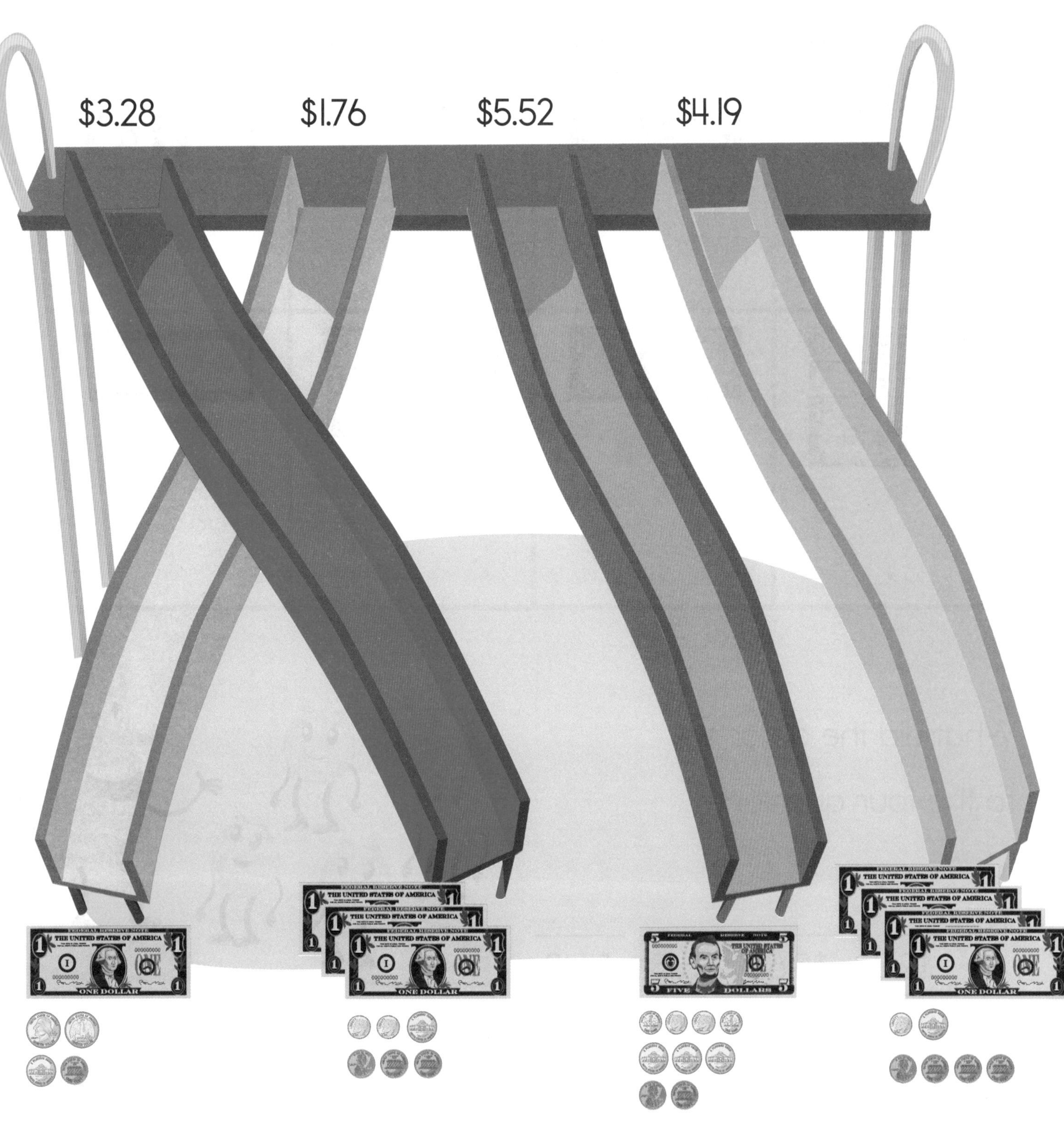

Code Breaker

WRITE the value of each money set. Then WRITE the letter that matches each value to solve the riddle.

 1 ______ N	 2 ______ H	 3 ______ E	 4 ______ V
 5 ______ C	 6 ______ G	 7 ______ D	 8 ______ A

What did the dollar say

to the four quarters?

You ______ ______ ______ ______
$2.02 $5.60 $6.15 $5.10

______ ______ ______ ______ ______ ______ ______.
$3.50 $2.02 $5.60 $1.75 $1.23 $5.10 $2.15

Pocket Change

DRAW two straight lines to create four different money sets of equal value.

Pay the Price

CUT OUT the cards on pages 351 and 352. PLACE cards next to each price tag so that the cards total the same value. How many different ways can you place the cards for each price tag?

HINT: Use as many cards as you want, stacking them next to each price tag.

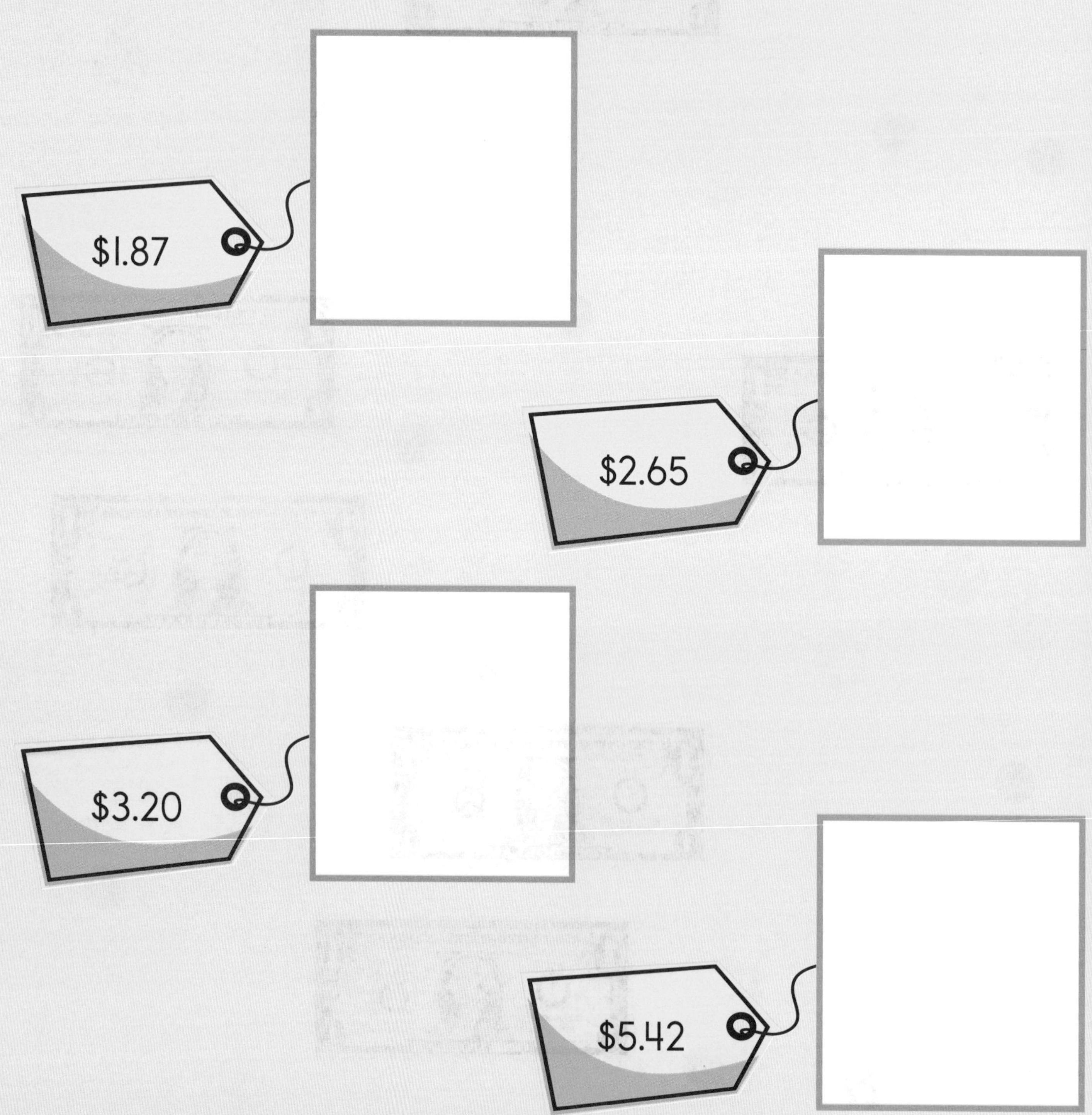

FEDERAL RESERVE NOTE
THE UNITED STATES OF AMERICA
ONE DOLLAR

FEDERAL RESERVE NOTE
THE UNITED STATES OF AMERICA
ONE DOLLAR

FEDERAL RESERVE NOTE
THE UNITED STATES OF AMERICA
ONE DOLLAR

FEDERAL RESERVE NOTE
THE UNITED STATES OF AMERICA
ONE DOLLAR

FEDERAL RESERVE NOTE
THE UNITED STATES OF AMERICA
ONE DOLLAR

FEDERAL RESERVE NOTE
THE UNITED STATES OF AMERICA
ONE DOLLAR

FEDERAL RESERVE NOTE
THE UNITED STATES OF AMERICA
ONE DOLLAR

FEDERAL RESERVE NOTE
THE UNITED STATES OF AMERICA
ONE DOLLAR

FEDERAL RESERVE NOTE
THE UNITED STATES OF AMERICA
ONE DOLLAR

FEDERAL RESERVE NOTE
THE UNITED STATES OF AMERICA
ONE DOLLAR

FEDERAL RESERVE NOTE
THE UNITED STATES OF AMERICA
ONE DOLLAR

FEDERAL RESERVE NOTE
THE UNITED STATES OF AMERICA
ONE DOLLAR

FEDERAL RESERVE NOTE
THE UNITED STATES OF AMERICA
FIVE DOLLARS

FEDERAL RESERVE NOTE
THE UNITED STATES OF AMERICA
FIVE DOLLARS

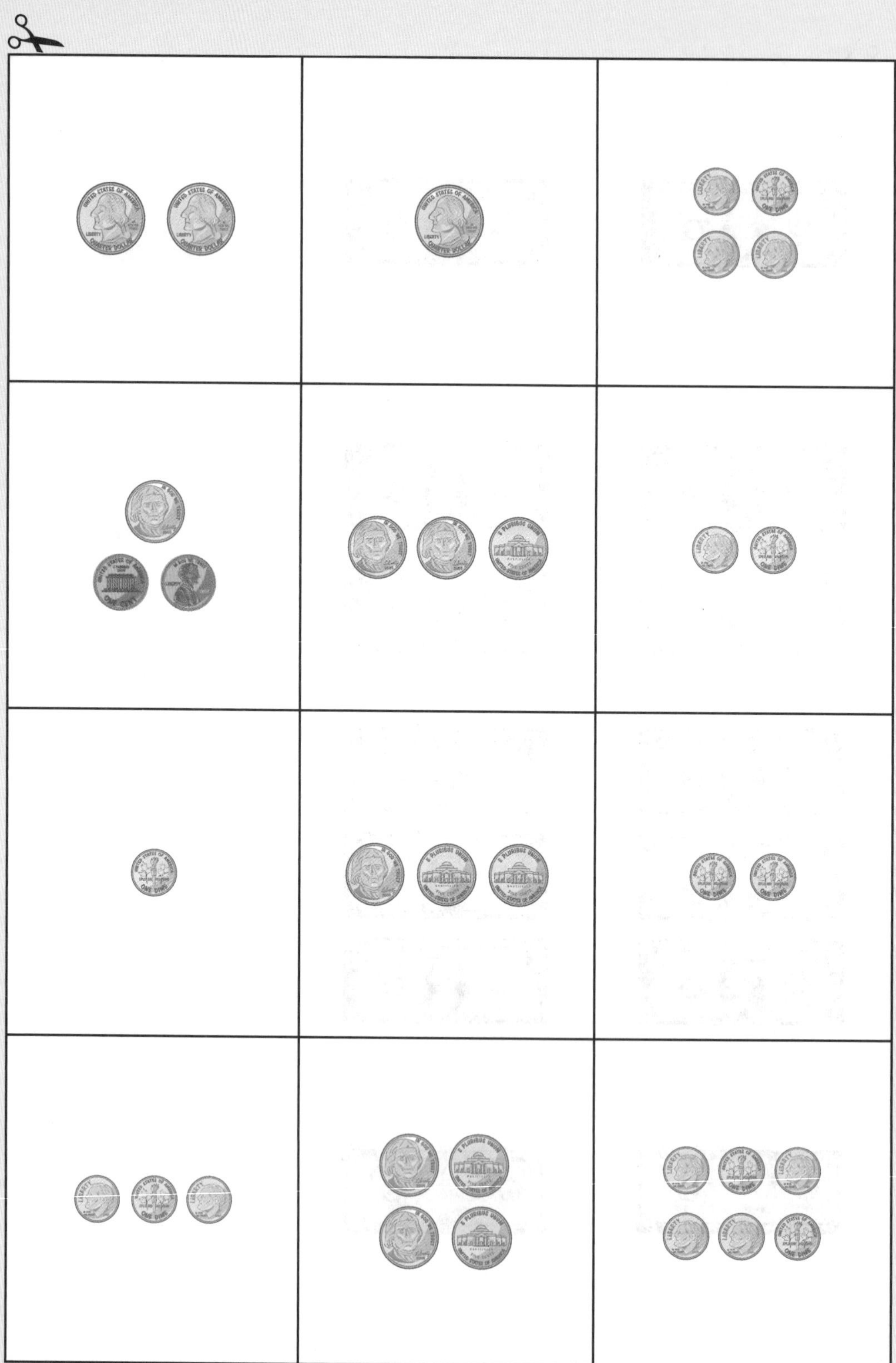

One Left Over

CROSS OUT all of the money that will be used to buy the items to reveal the extra coin.

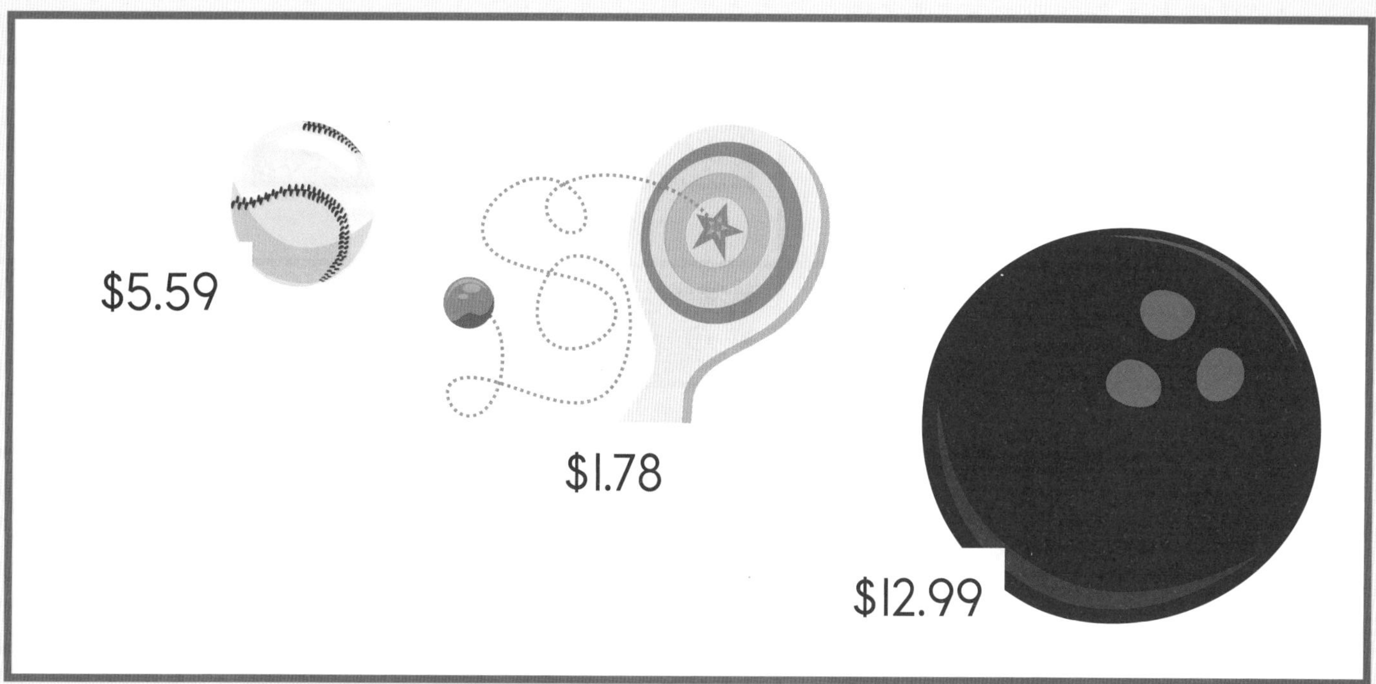

Code Breaker

CIRCLE the picture in each row with less money than the other, and WRITE its value. Then WRITE the letter that matches each value to solve the riddle.

		1 O
		2 A
		3 N
		4 C
		5 I

What has a head and a tail but no body?

____ ____ ____ ____ ____ .

$3.07 $6.19 $1.50 $7.45 $4.98

Just Right

WRITE these dollar amounts so that each one is next to a picture with a smaller value.

HINT: There may be more than one place to put each amount, but you need to use every one.

$2.29 $4.98 $5.14 $1.03 $6.37

1. $ ________

2. $ ________

3. $ ________

4. $ ________

5. $ ________

Code Breaker

WRITE the value of each money set. Then WRITE the letter that matches each value to solve the riddle.

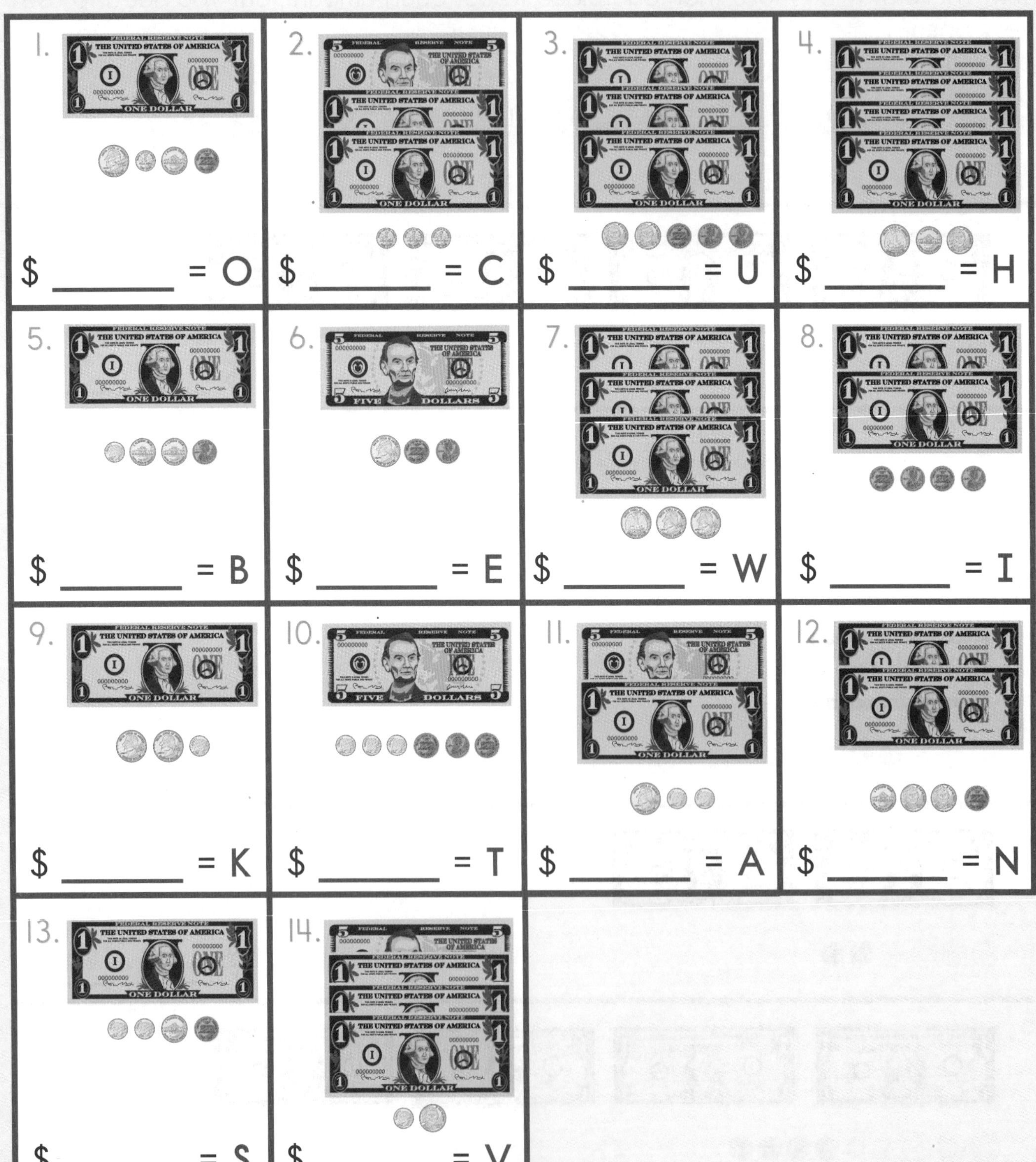

Why did the elephant cross the road?

____ ____ ____ ____ ____ ____ ____

$1.21 $5.27 $7.30 $6.45 $3.13 $1.26 $5.27

____ ____ ____ ____ ____ ____ ____ ____ ____ ____

$5.33 $4.35 $5.27 $7.30 $4.35 $2.04 $7.30 $1.60 $5.27 $2.16

____ ____ ____ ____ ____

$3.75 $6.45 $1.26 $1.41 $2.16

____ ____ ____ ____ ____ ____ ____ ____ .

$8.15 $6.45 $7.30 $6.45 $5.33 $2.04 $1.41 $2.16

Pocket Change

DRAW three straight lines to create six different money sets of equal value.

Beans

CUT OUT the beans.

These beans are for use with pages 288, 290, and 291.

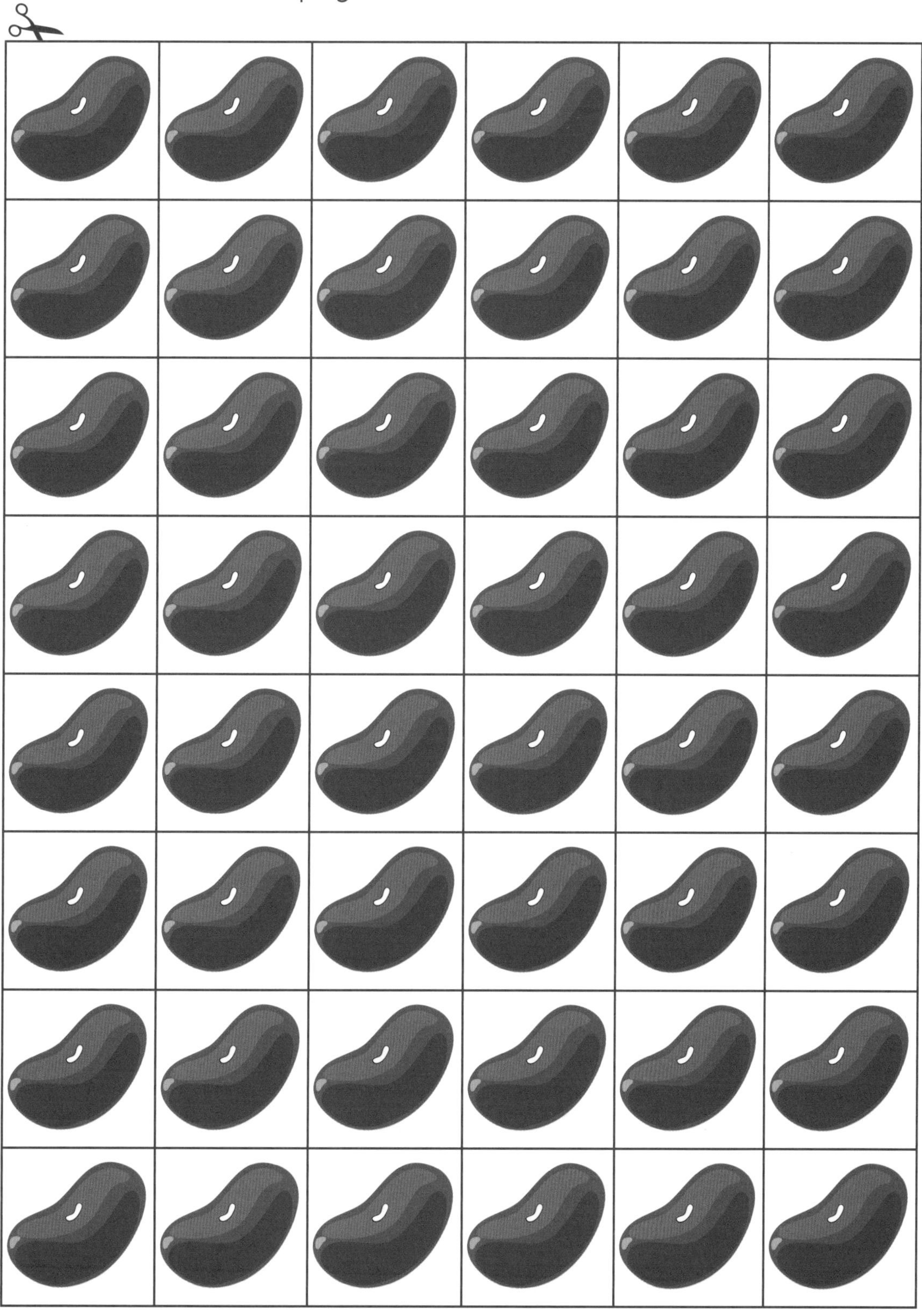

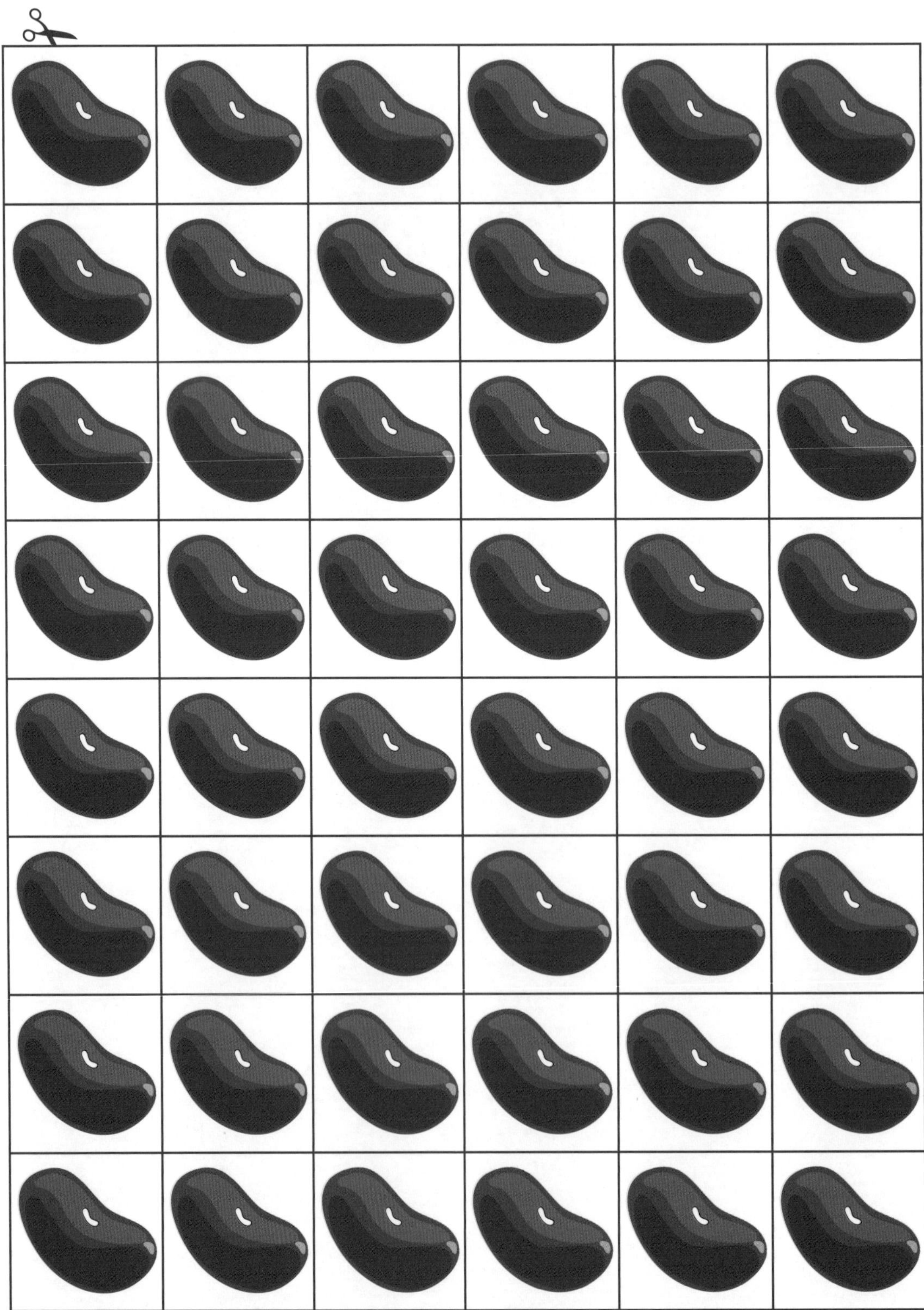

Spinners

CUT OUT the spinner. BEND the outer part of a paper clip so that it points out, and carefully POKE it through the center dot of the spinner. You're ready to spin!

This spinner is for use with page 295, and the reverse side is for use with pages 302 and 303.

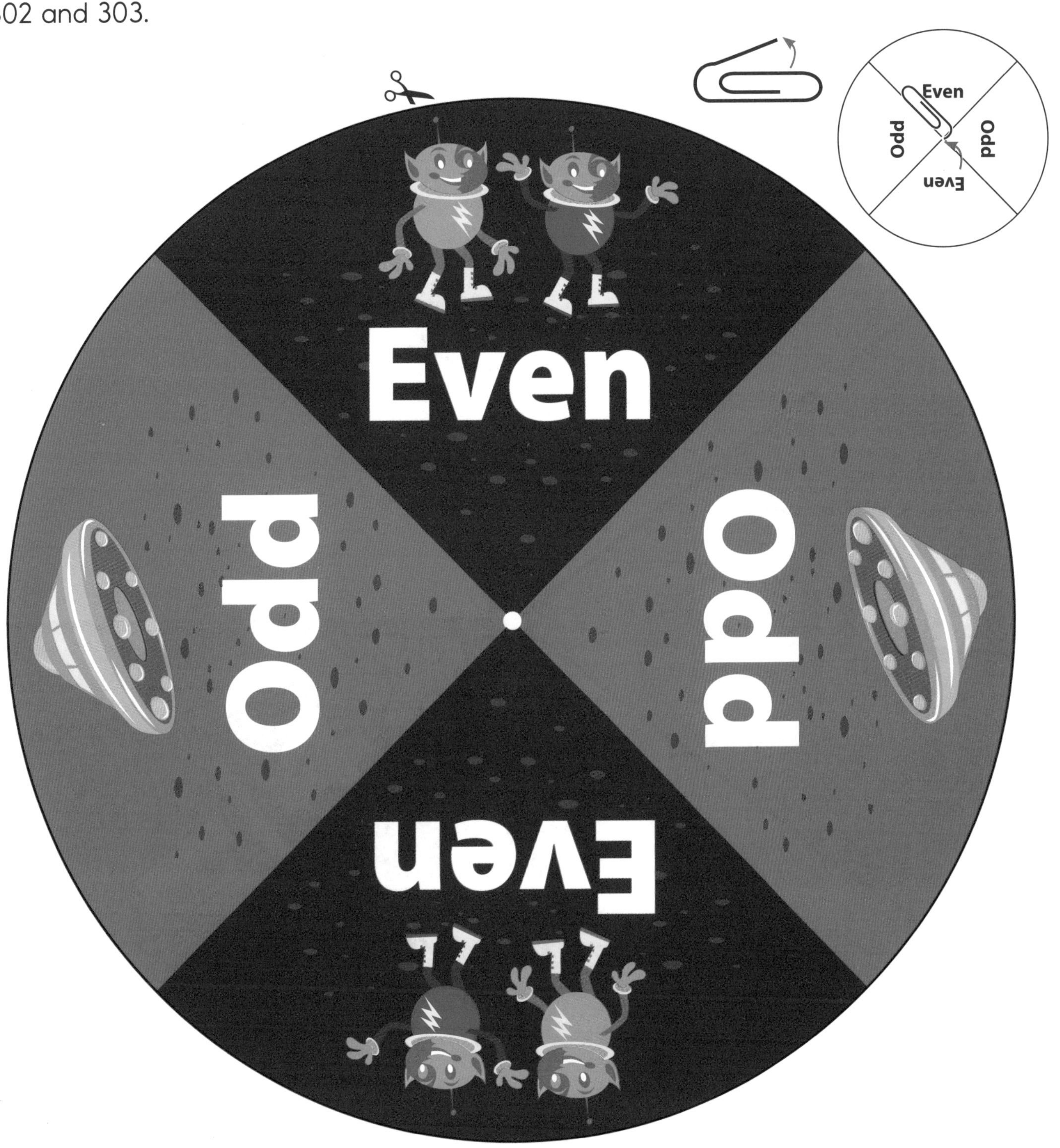

Use the spinner on this side for pages 302 and 303. Pull out the paper clip from the other side, and poke it through the center dot on this side.

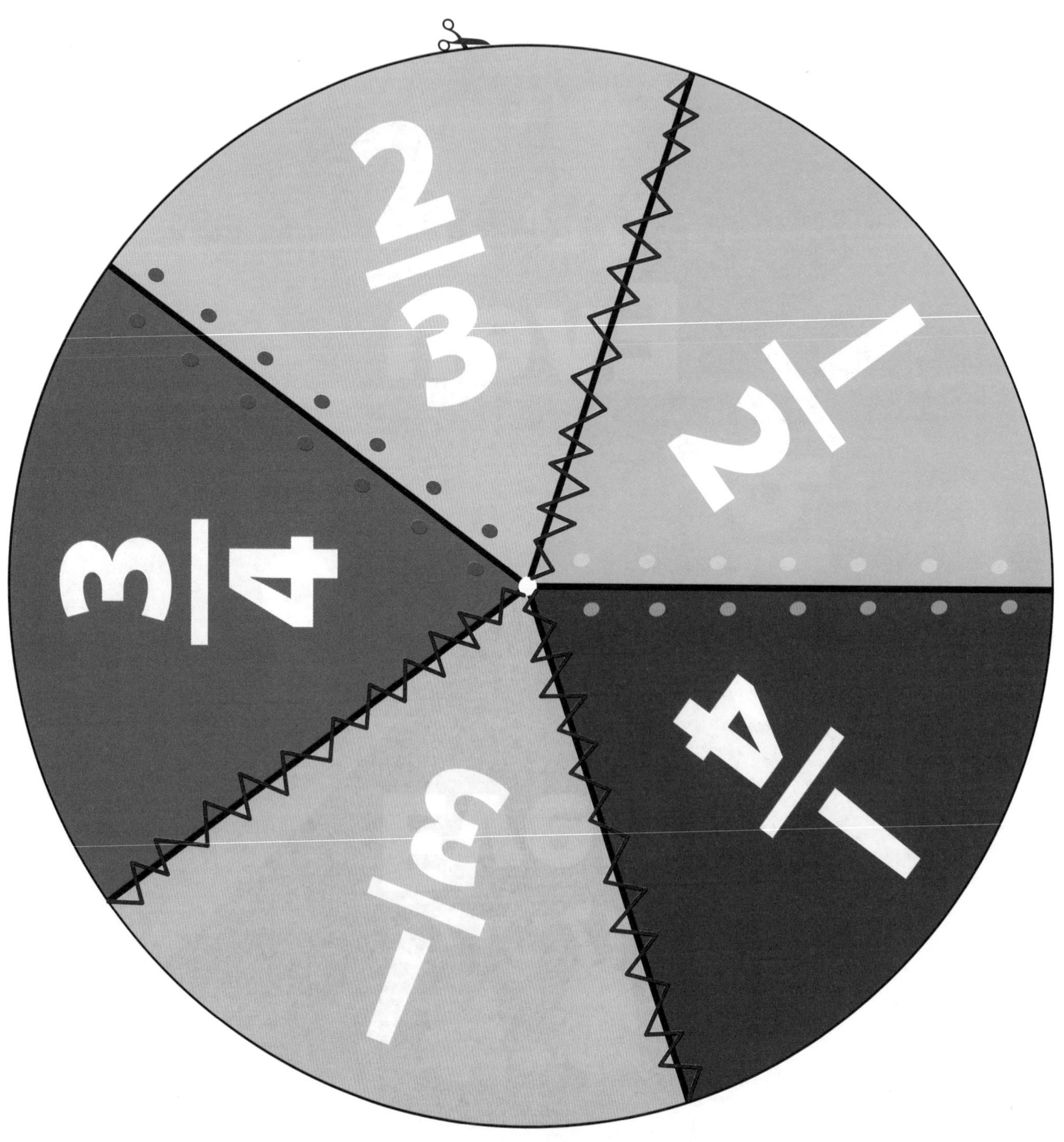

Pattern Blocks

CUT OUT the 31 pattern block pieces.

These pattern block pieces are for use with pages 312, 314, 315, and 322.

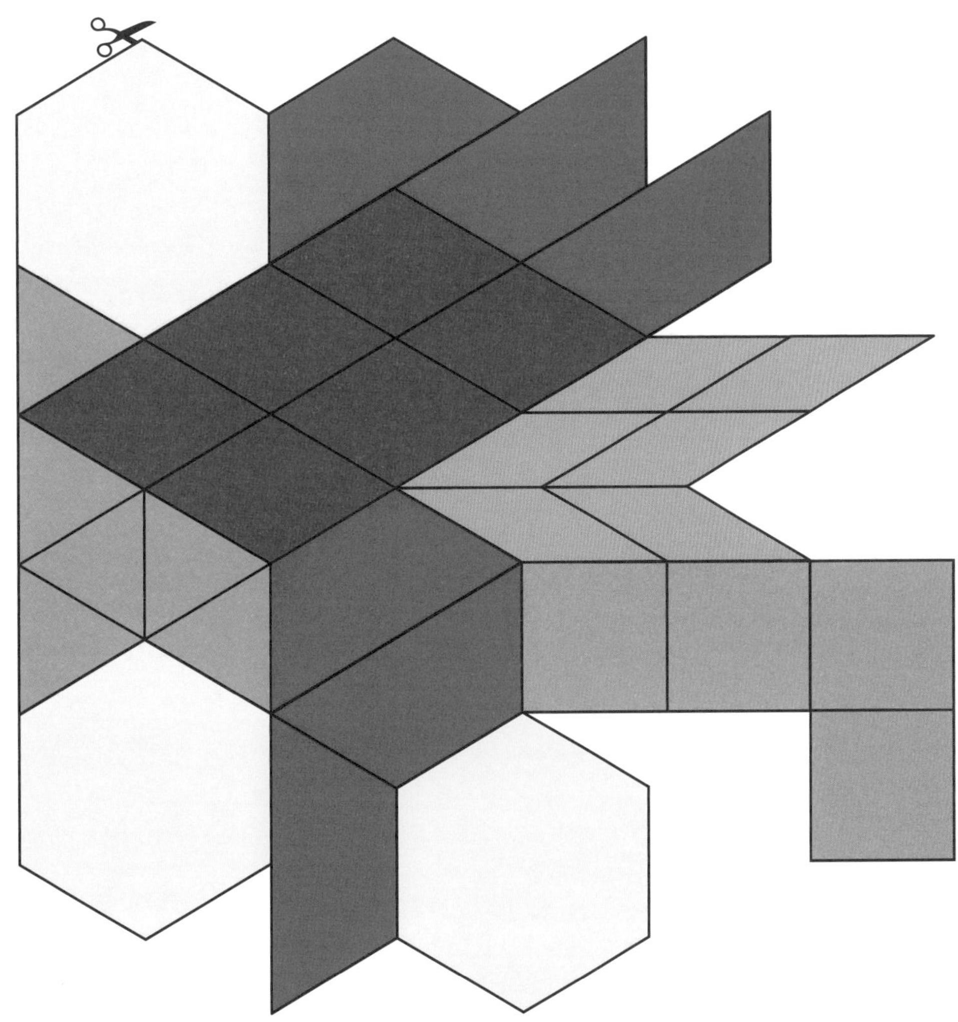

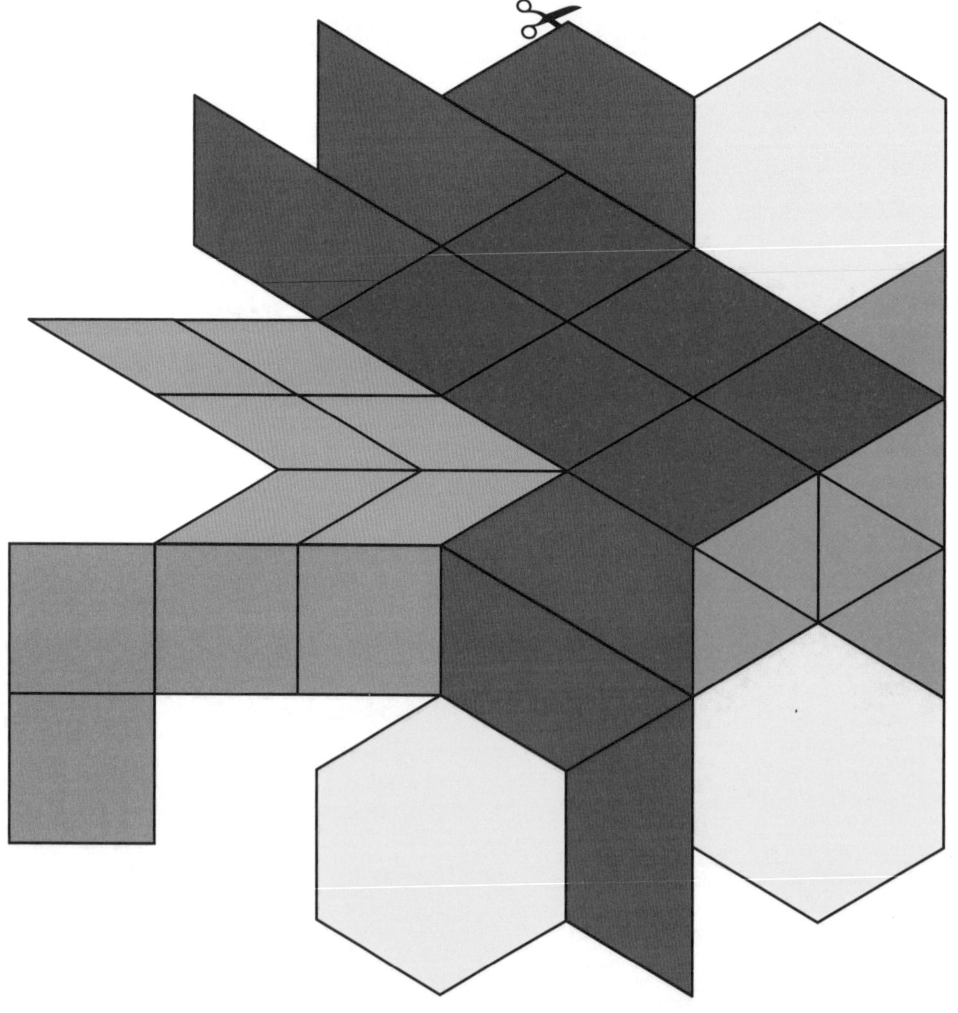

Pentominoes

CUT OUT the 13 pentomino pieces.

These pentomino pieces are for use with pages 316, 318, and 323.

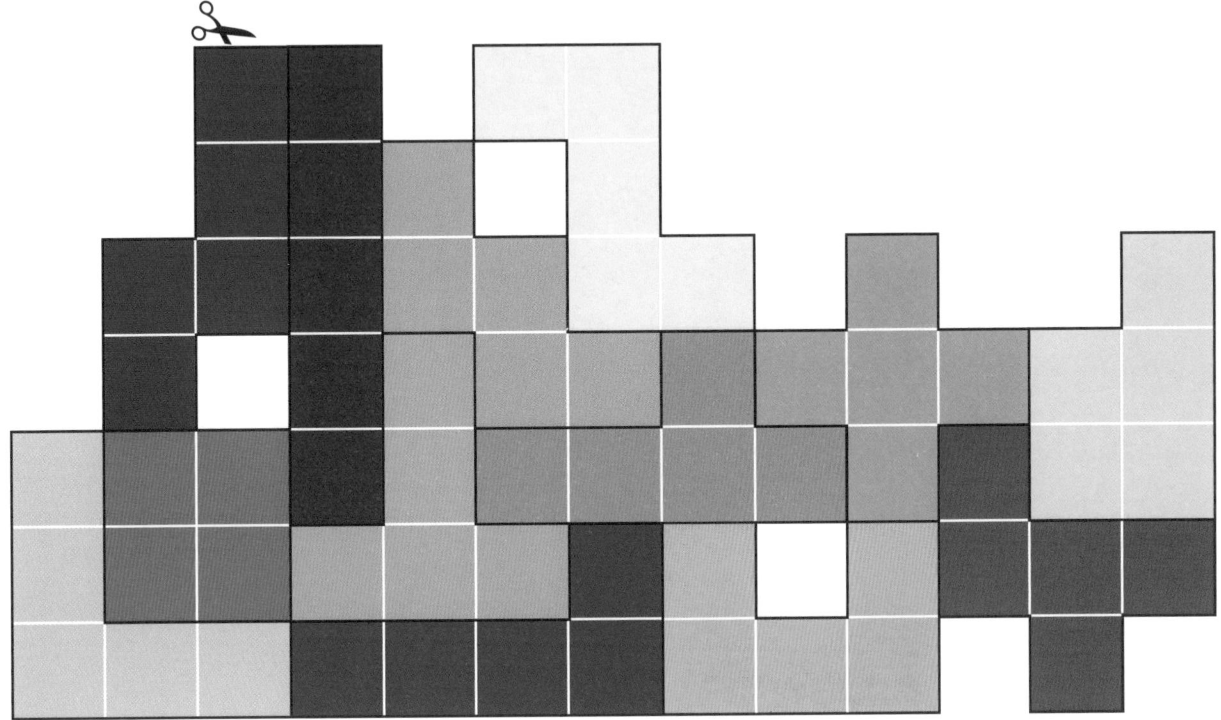

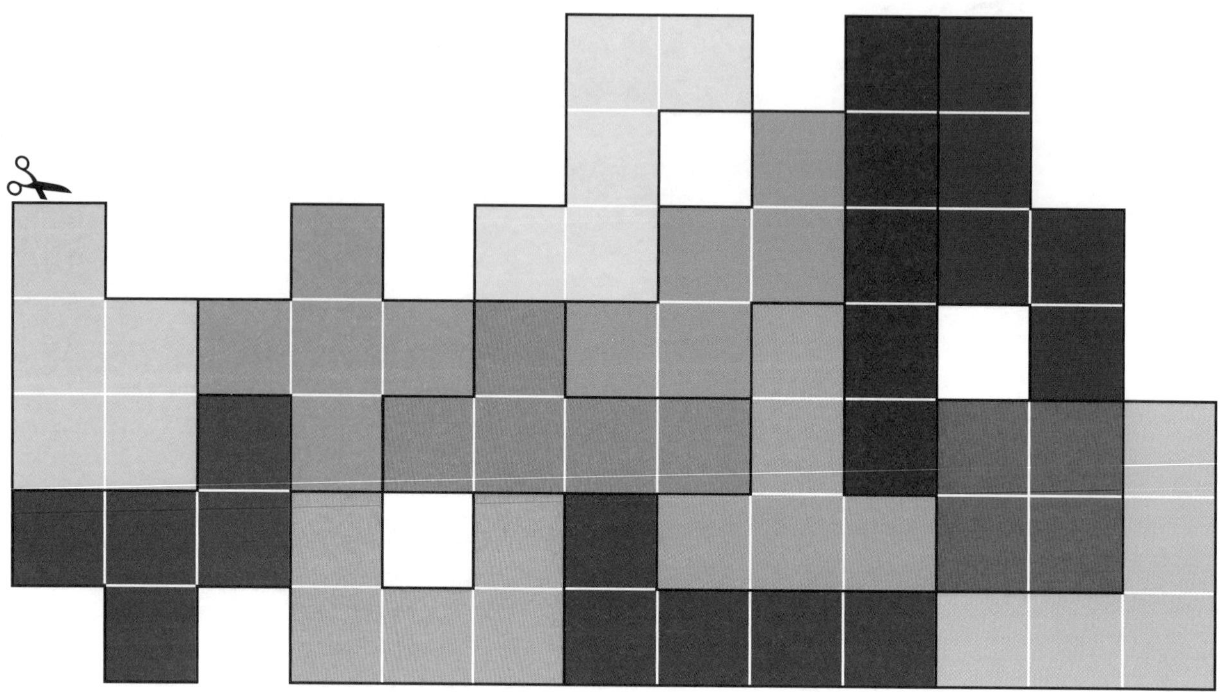

Page 250

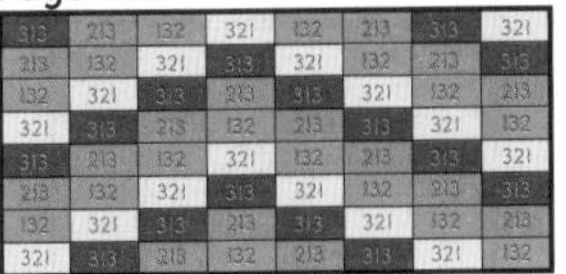

313	213	132	321	132	213	313	321
213	132	321	313	321	132	213	313
132	321	313	213	313	321	132	213
321	313	213	132	213	313	321	132
313	213	132	321	132	213	313	321
213	132	321	313	321	132	213	313
132	321	313	213	313	321	132	213
321	313	213	132	213	313	321	132

Page 251

1. 364 2. 416
3. 195 4. 608
5. 241

Combination 3 4 1 6 2

Page 252

1. 159 2. 344
3. 506 4. 830
5. 718 6. 472

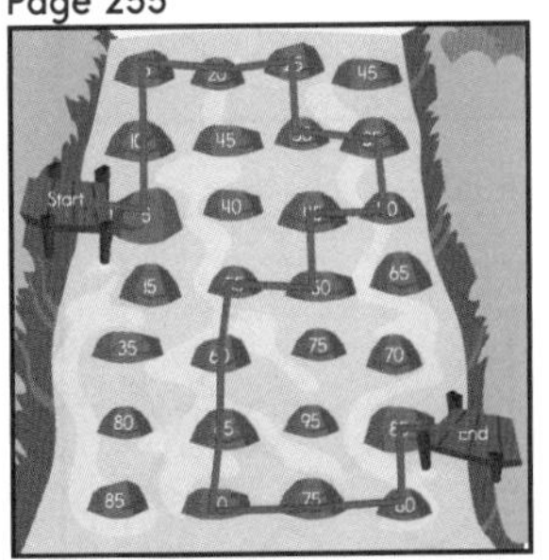

5	8	0	3	1	4
2	1	5	4	7	0
0	5	0	6	8	3
8	9	3	1	3	5
3	3	7	6	0	0
1	5	2	3	4	8
7	1	8	4	2	1
1	9	6	4	7	2

Page 253

Have someone check your answers.

Page 254

1. 97, 100, 103
2. 215, 218, 220
3. 746, 747, 752, 753

I LIKE YOUR BELT!

Page 255

Page 256

1	2	3	4	5	6	7	8	9	10
11	12	13	14	15	16	17	18	19	20
21	22	23	24	25	26	27	28	29	30
31	32	33	34	35	36	37	38	39	40
41	42	43	44	45	46	47	48	49	50
51	52	53	54	55	56	57	58	59	60
61	62	63	64	65	66	67	68	69	70
71	72	73	74	75	76	77	78	79	80
81	82	83	84	85	86	87	88	89	90
91	92	93	94	95	96	97	98	99	100

Page 257

10	4	7		175	116	330
20	8	14		168	112	320
30	12	21		161	108	310
40	16	28		154	104	300
50	20	35		147	100	290
60	24	42		140	96	280
70	28	49		133	92	270
80	32	56		126	88	260
90	36	63		119	84	250
100	40	70		112	80	240
110	44	77		105	76	230
120	48	84	91	98	72	220
130	52	56	60	64	68	210
140	150	160	170	180	190	200

Page 258

1. 677 2. 113
3. 742 4. 556
5. 823 6. 256
7. 981 8. 409
9. 187 10. 399

Page 259

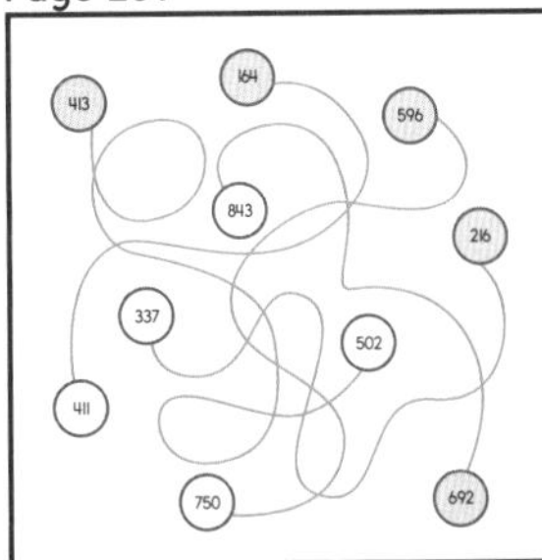

Page 260

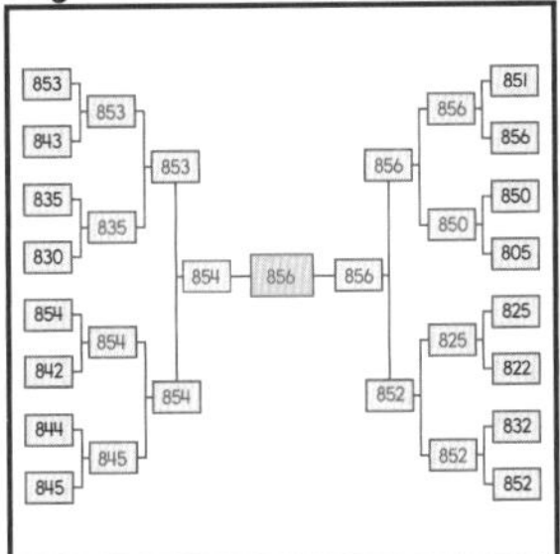

Page 261

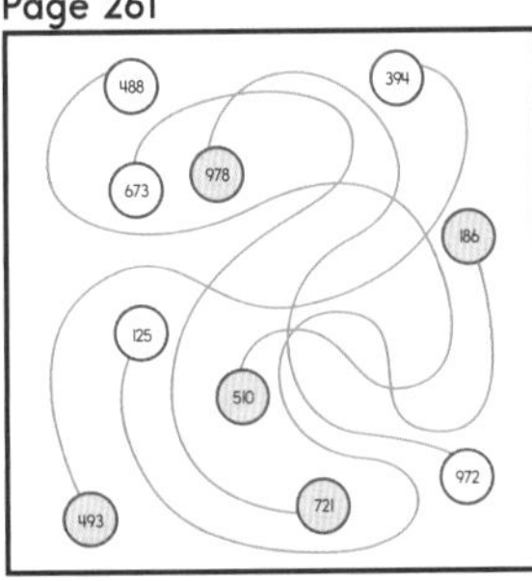

Page 262

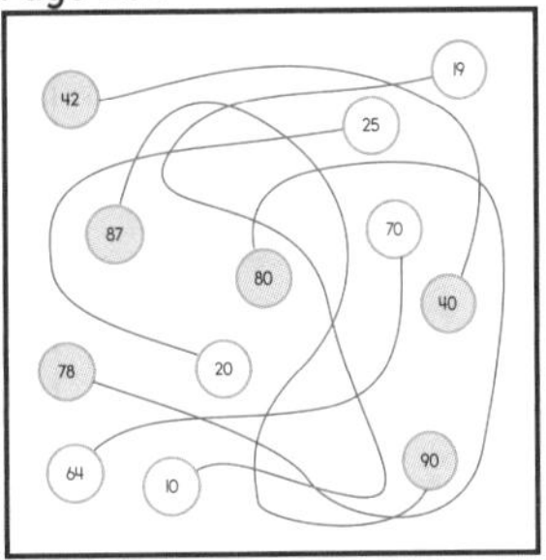

Page 263

Have someone check your answers.

Page 264

1. 285 2. 544
3. 709 4. 952
5. 549 6. 278
7. 932 8. 717
9. 751

Pages 265–266

Check: 117

Page 267

Check: 81

Page 268

6	12	18	24	30	36	42
144	150	156	162	168	174	48
138	240	246	252	258	180	54
132	234	288	294	264	186	60
126	228	282	276	270	192	66
120	222	216	210	204	198	72
114	108	102	96	90	84	78

Page 269

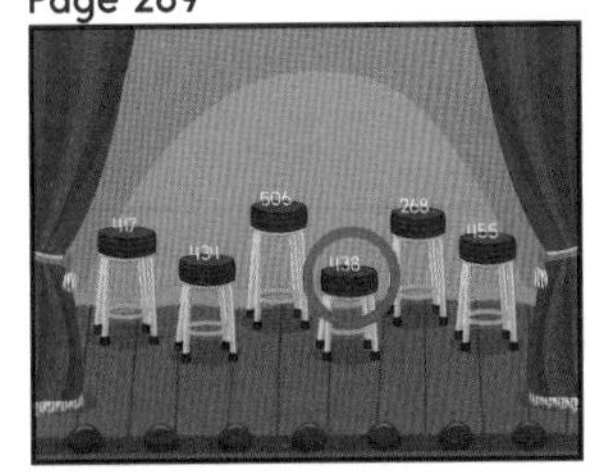

Page 270

1. 21 2. 16
3. 45 4. 37
5. 62 6. 54

Page 271

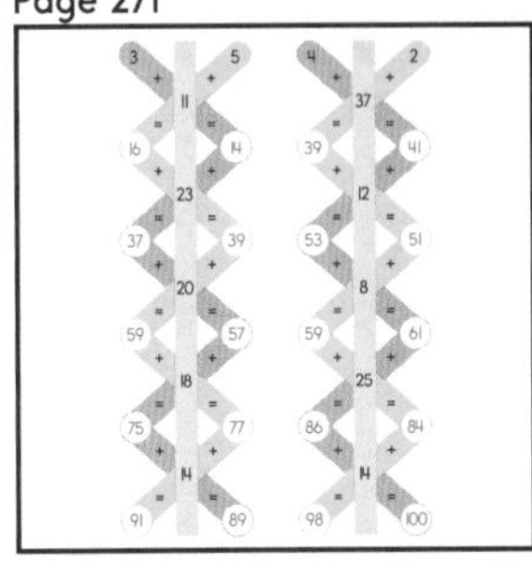

Page 272

3	+	12	=	15
+		+		+
9	+	25	=	34
=		=		=
12	+	37	=	49

Page 273

1. 37 2. 68
3. 59 4. 79
5. 95 6. 48
7. 93 8. 77
9. 63 10. 71
11. 80 12. 91

IT GOES TO PENCILVANIA.

Page 274

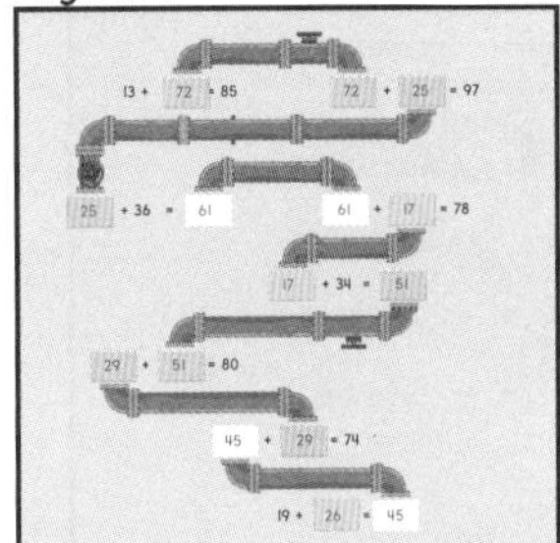

Page 275

Suggestion:

Page 276

1. 12 2. 33
3. 71 4. 48
5. 22 6. 56

Answers

Page 277

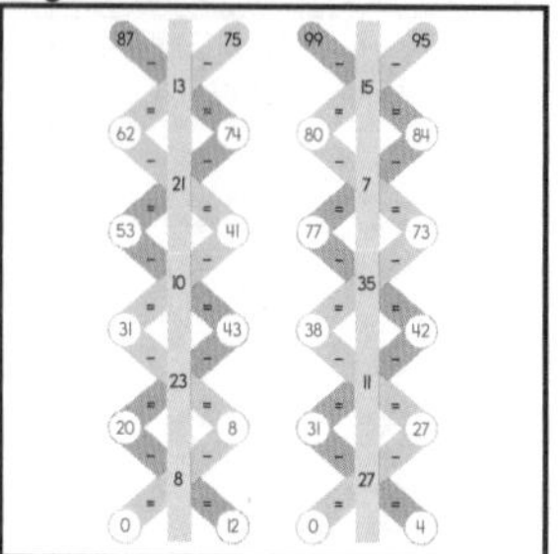

Page 278

95	-	63	=	32
-		-		-
47	-	17	=	30
=		=		=
48	-	46	=	2

Page 279

1. 31 2. 23
3. 2 4. 22
5. 46 6. 49
7. 26 8. 52
9. 13 10. 47
11. 36 12. 16

YOU WOULD HAVE TWO TOYS.

Page 280

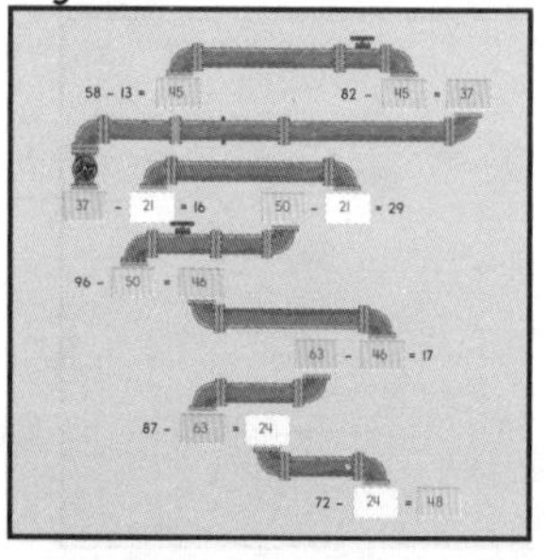

Page 281
Suggestion:

Page 282

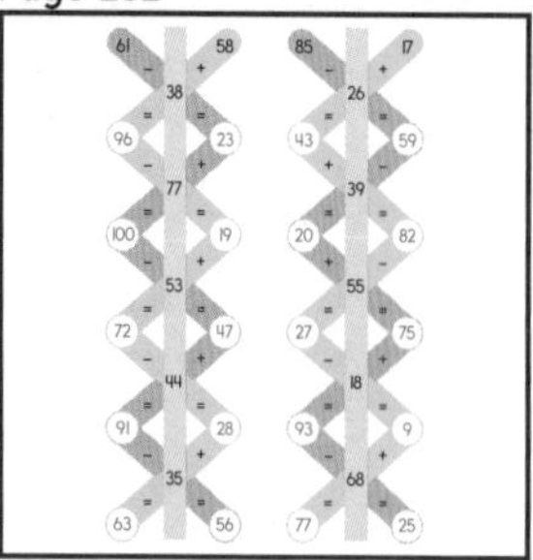

Page 283
Suggestion:

Page 284

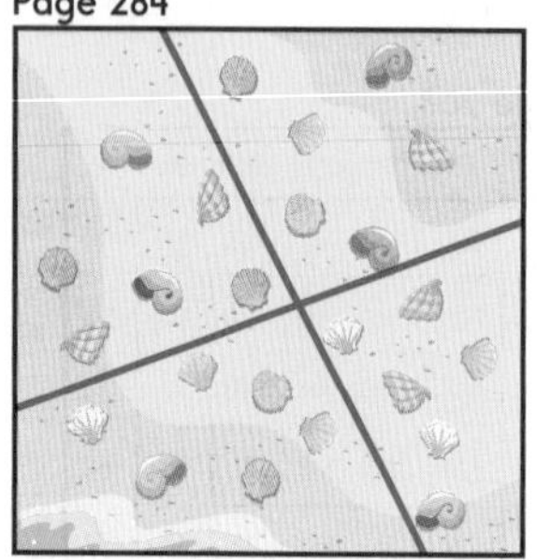

Page 285

1. 3 2. 2
3. 6 4. 2
5. 1 6. 3

Page 286
Suggestion:

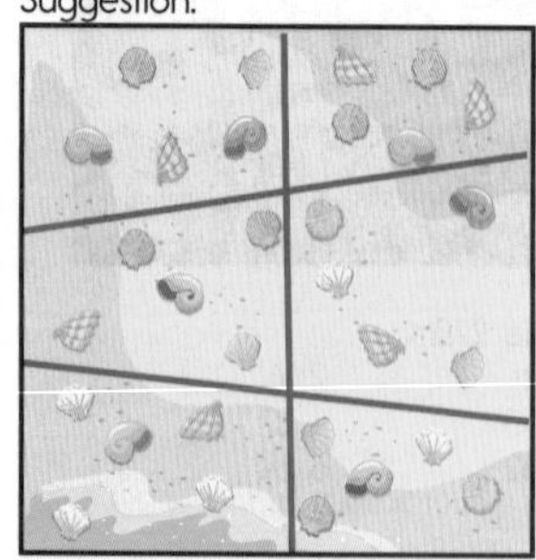

Page 287

1. 2 2. 4
3. 2 4. 5
5. 4 6. 2

Page 288

1. 3 2. 5
3. 2 4. 6
5. 8 6. 4

Page 289
Suggestion:

Page 290

1. 4 2. 8
3. 2 4. 7
5. 5 6. 12

Page 292

1. 3 2. 7
3. 9 4. 1
5. 6 6. 12
7. 8 8. 10

TAKE AWAY THE S.

Page 293

Page 294

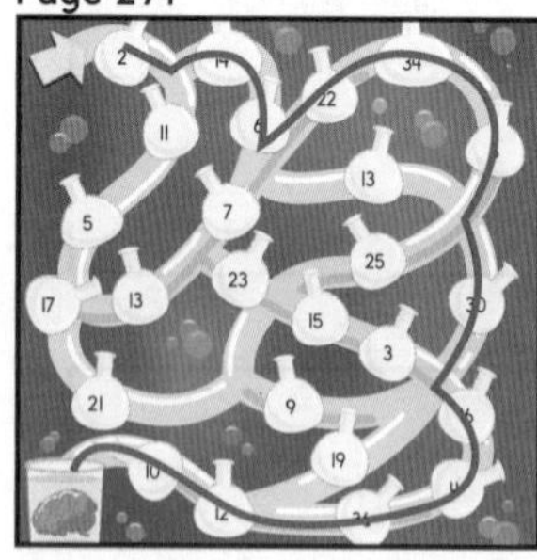

Page 296
Suggestion:

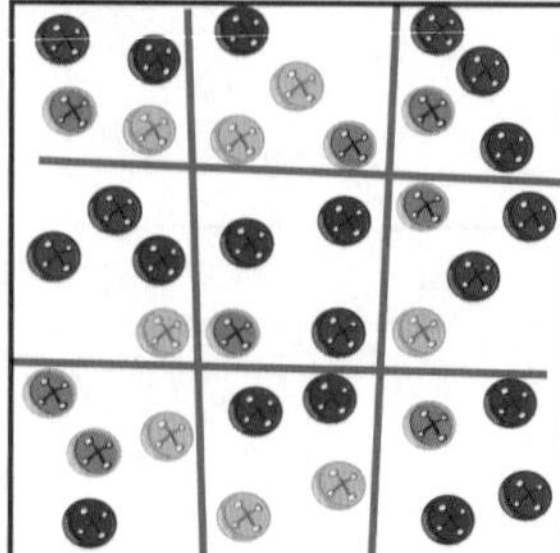

Page 297

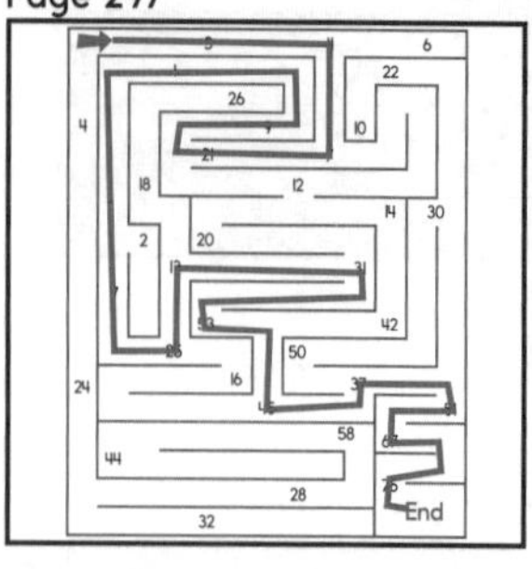

Page 298

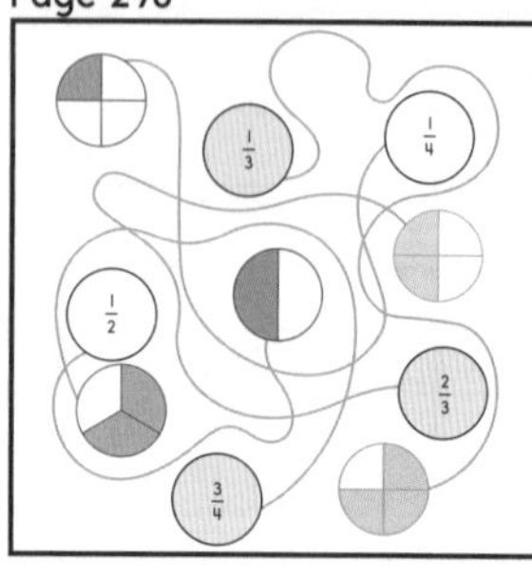

Page 299
Have someone check your answers.

Page 301

Page 304

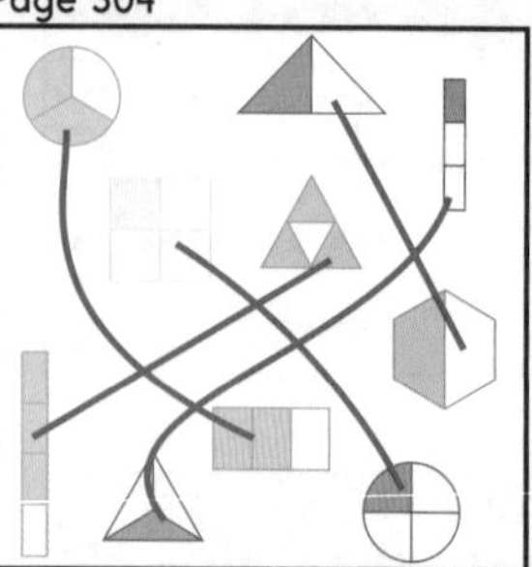

Page 305

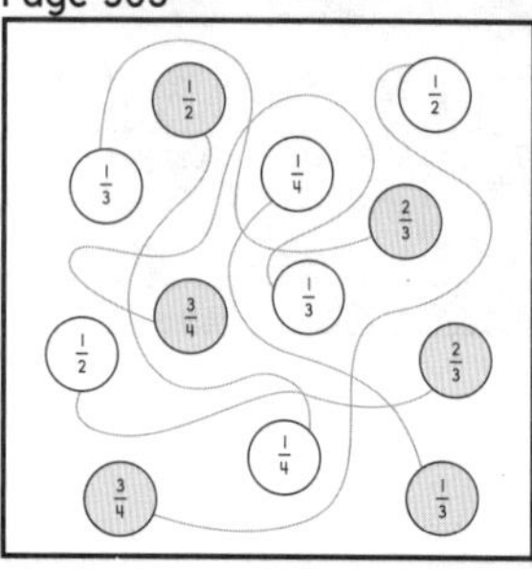

Page 306

1. $\frac{2}{3}$
2. $\frac{1}{3}$
3. $\frac{4}{4}$
4. $\frac{1}{2}$
5. $\frac{3}{4}$

Page 307

1. $\frac{1}{3}$
2. $\frac{3}{4}$
3. $\frac{2}{2}$
4. $\frac{1}{2}$
5. $\frac{2}{4}$
6. $\frac{3}{3}$
7. $\frac{2}{3}$
8. $\frac{4}{4}$

There was a WHOLE IN IT.

Page 308

1. PE
2. N
3. C
4. IL
5. E
6. R
7. AS
8. ER

PENCIL ERASER

Page 309

Page 310

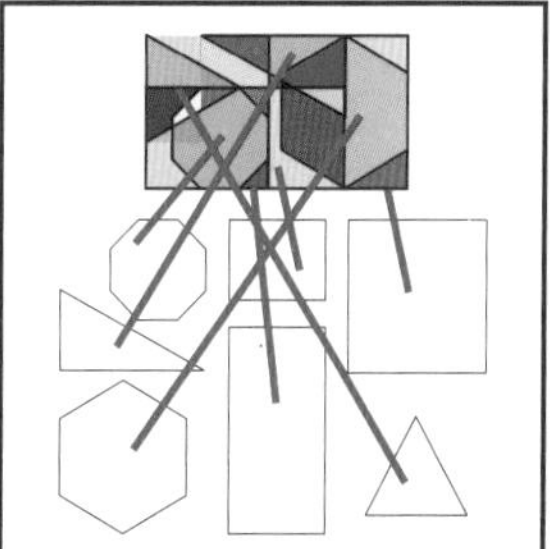

Page 312
Suggestion:

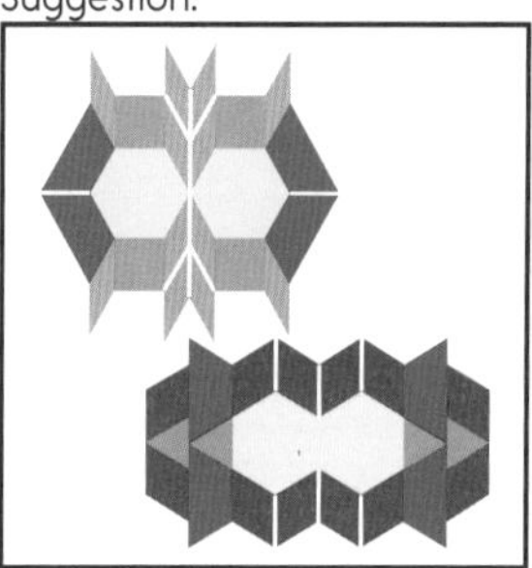

Page 313

Page 314
Suggestion:

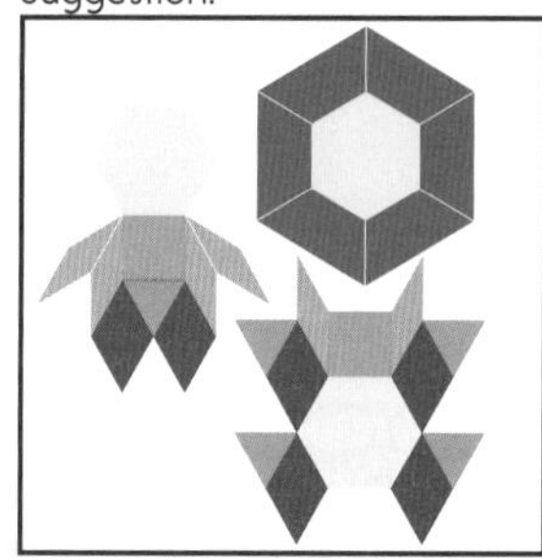

Page 315
Suggestion:

Page 316
Suggestion:

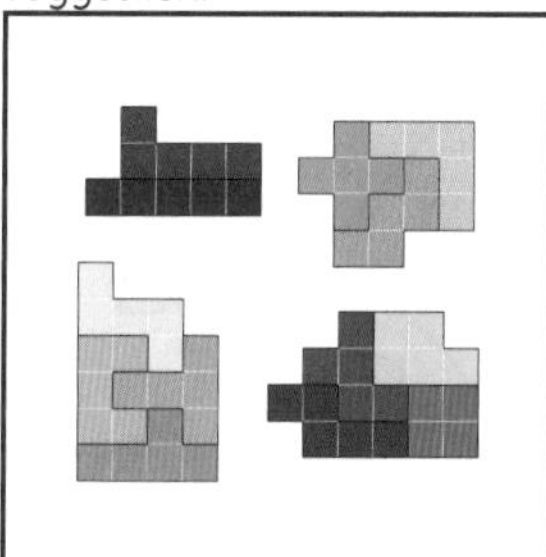

1. 16
2. 18
3. 20
4. 20

Page 317
Have someone check your answers.

Page 318
Suggestion:

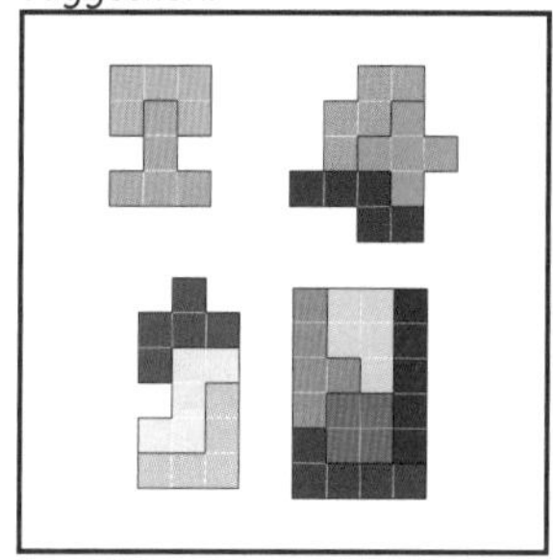

1. 10
2. 15
3. 15
4. 24

Page 319
Have someone check your answers.

Page 320

1. Monkeys
2. Penguins
3. Polar Bears
4. Elephants
5. Camels
6. Reptiles
7. Lions
8. Sea Lions
9. Zebras
10. Giraffes

Page 321

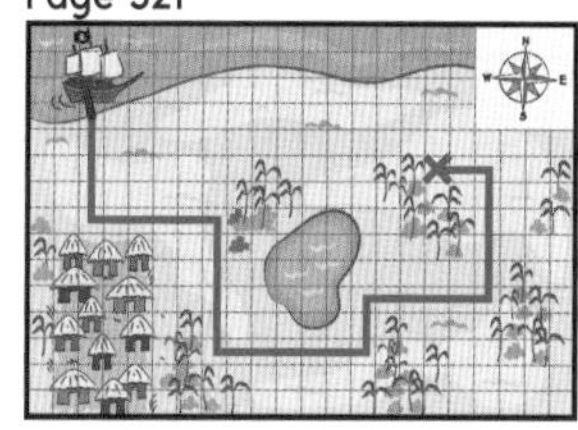

Page 322
Suggestion:

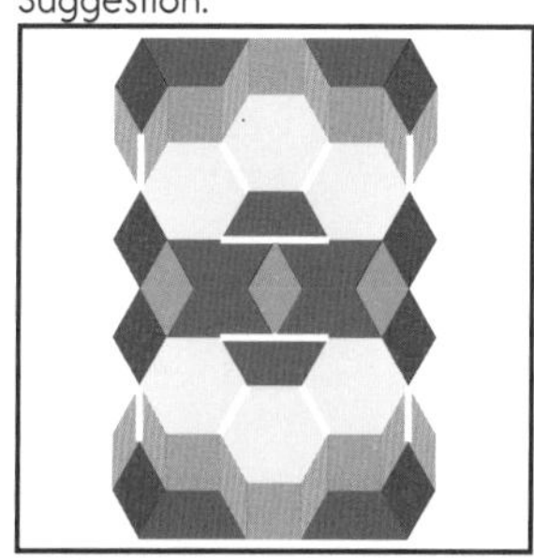

Page 323
Suggestion:

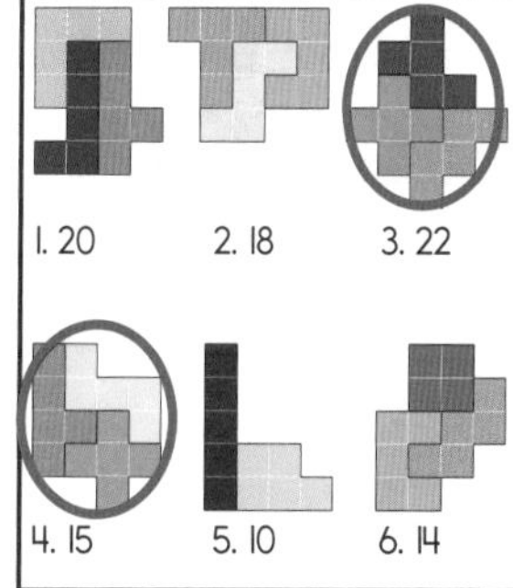

Page 324

1. quarter
2. nickel
3. dime
4. penny

Page 325

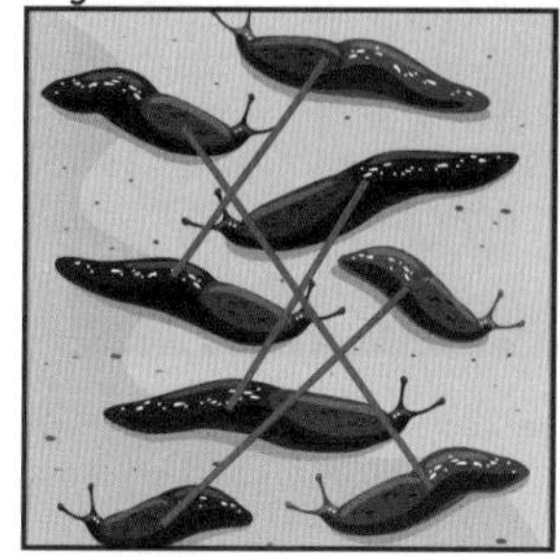

Page 326
A FOOTLONG.

Page 327

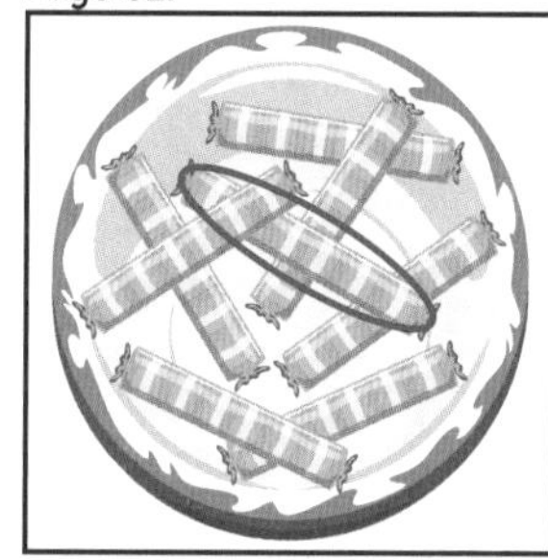

Page 328
IN SCENTIMETERS.

Page 329

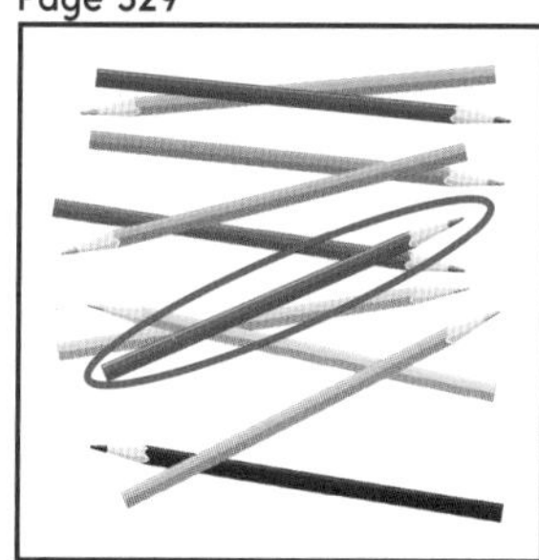

Page 330

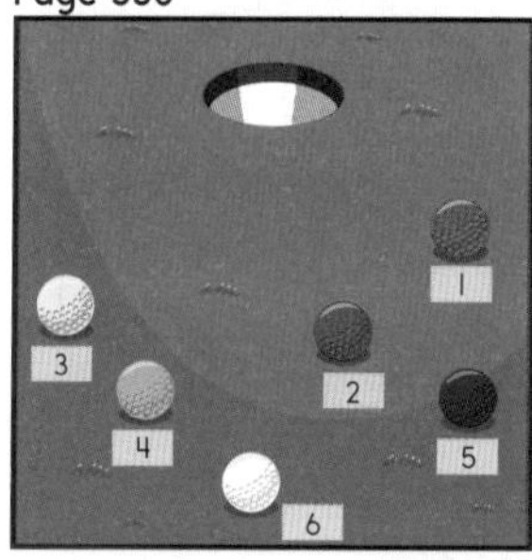

Page 331
Check:

1. 10
2. 12
3. 16
4. 13

Answers

Page 332

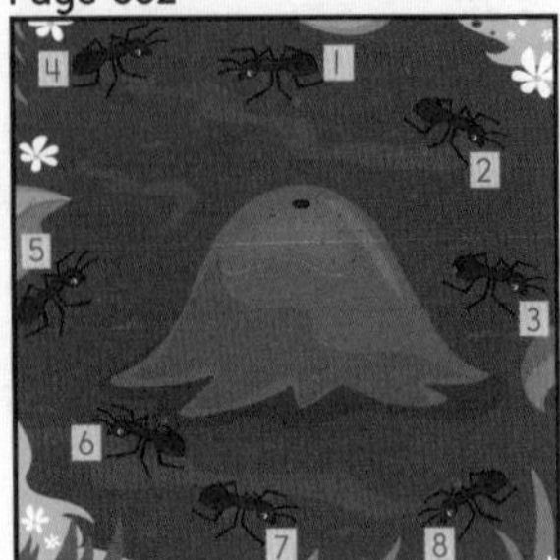

Page 333
Check:

1. 12
2. 10
3. 7
4. 8
5. 4
6. 13

Page 334

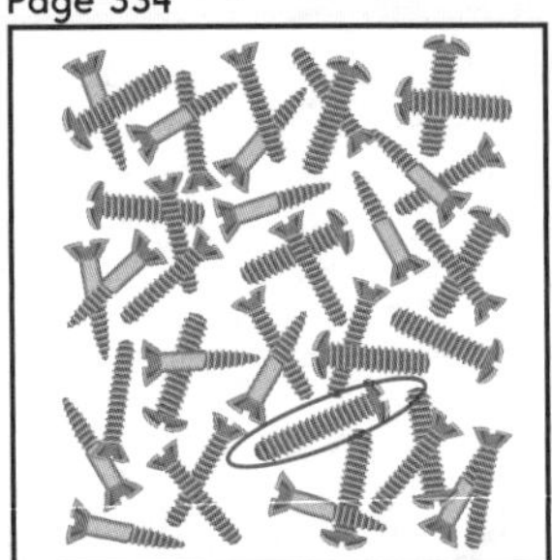

Page 335

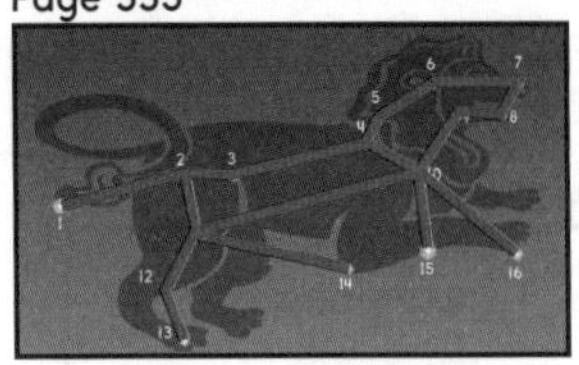

Check:

1. 2
2. 3
3. 8
4. 5
5. 10
6. 9

Page 336
A CLOCK.

Page 337

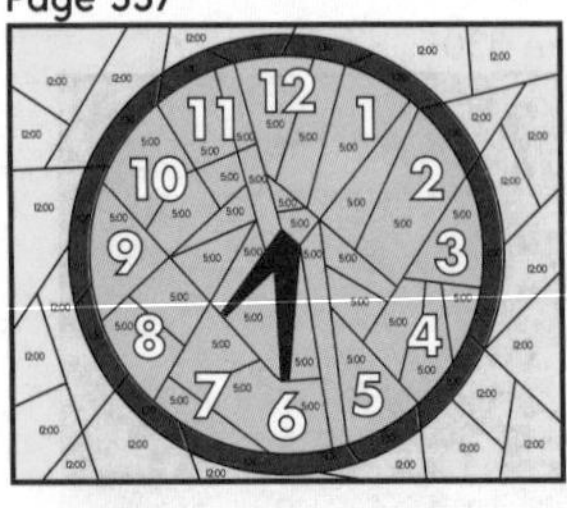

7:30

Page 338
THE LETTER E.

Page 339

1:45

Page 340

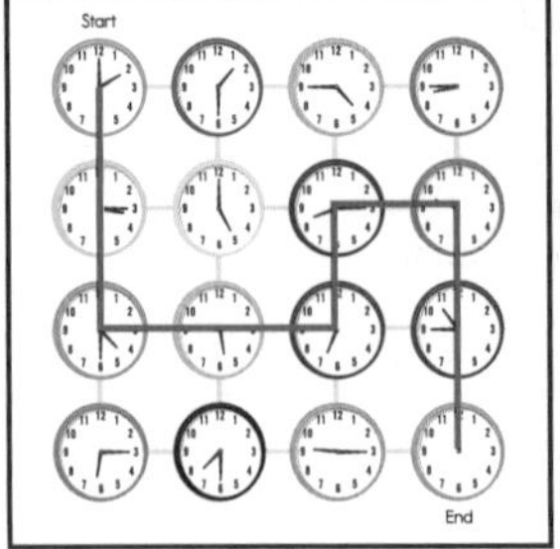

Page 341

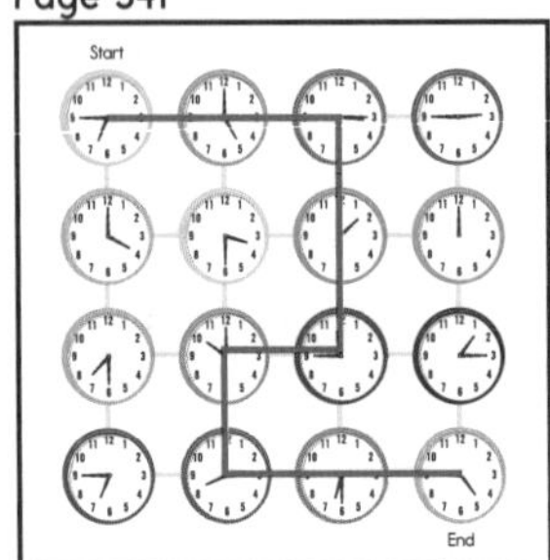

Pages 342–343

1. 1:00
2. 6:45
3. 5:15
4. 12:45
5. 8:00
6. 3:30
7. 2:30
8. 9:30
9. 11:15
10. 5:00
11. 2:15

HE WANTED TO BE ON TIME.

Page 344

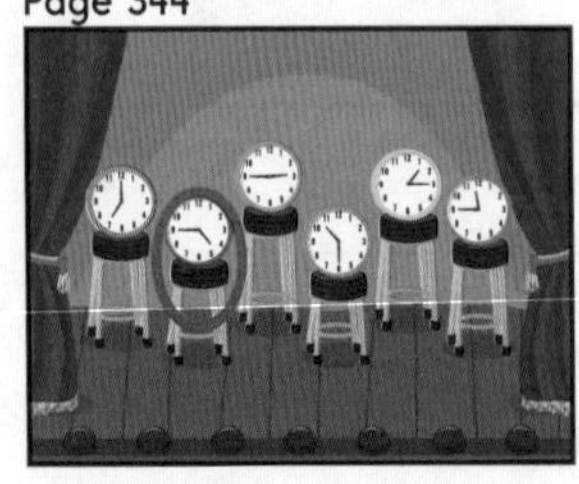

Page 345

Page 346

1. 30¢
2. 22¢
3. 15¢
4. 51¢
5. 14¢
6. 75¢
7. 25¢
8. 40¢
9. 5¢
10. 41¢
11. 65¢

IT HAS FOUR QUARTERS.

Page 347

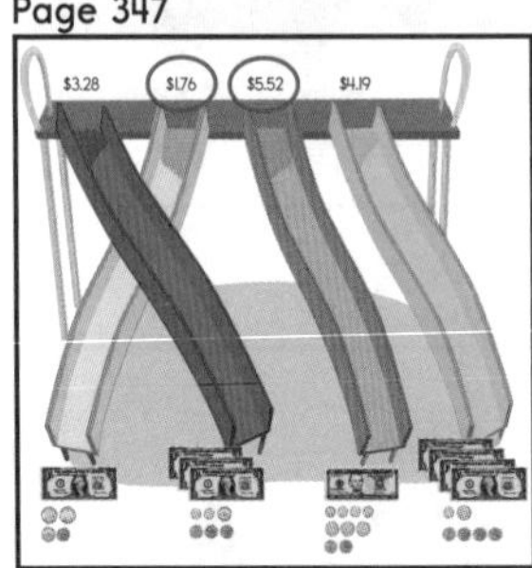

Page 348

1. $1.75
2. $2.02
3. $5.10
4. $6.15
5. $3.50
6. $1.23
7. $2.15
8. $5.60

You HAVE CHANGED.

Page 349

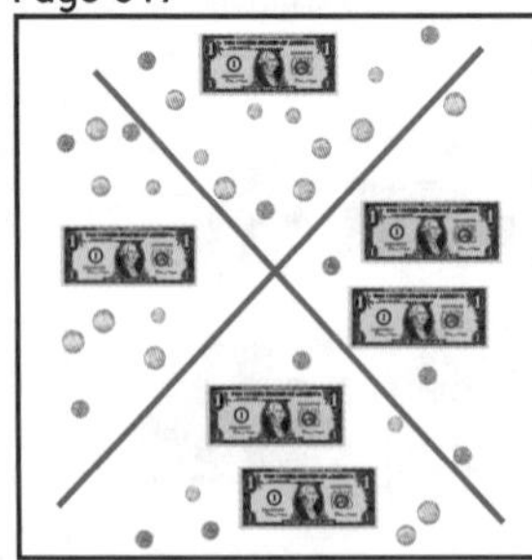

Page 350
Have someone check your answers.

Page 353
Extra: 

Page 354

1. $1.50
2. $3.07
3. $4.98
4. $6.19
5. $7.45

A COIN.

Page 355

1. 4.98
2. 1.03
3. 6.37
4. 2.29
5. 5.14

Pages 356–357

1. 1.41
2. 7.30
3. 3.13
4. 4.35
5. 1.21
6. 5.27
7. 3.75
8. 2.04
9. 1.60
10. 5.33
11. 6.45
12. 2.16
13. 1.26
14. 8.15

BECAUSE THE CHICKEN WAS ON VACATION.

Page 358

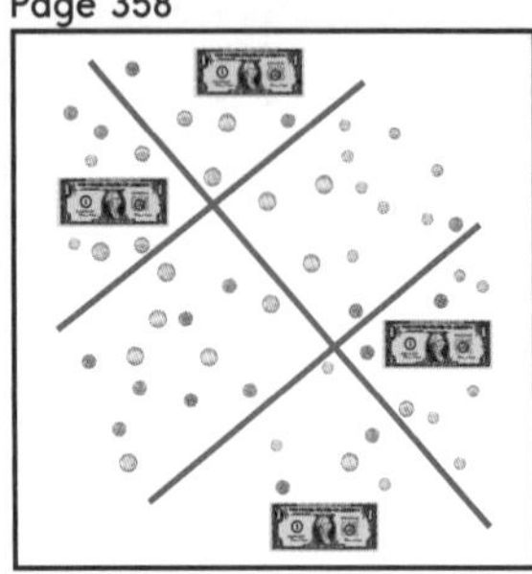